For DKJ

accountant, mentor, and friend

Contents

Preface

I would like to thank the U.S. Department of Education Center for International Education (Fulbright-Hays), the Chiang Ching-Kuo Foundation for International Scholarly Exchange, and the Pacific Cultural Foundation for funding various stages of this project. I am also indebted to Drs. Chang Ying-hwa and Lin Mei-rong for generously providing me with affiliation at the Institute of Ethnology, Academia Sinica, during my fieldwork and for providing me with good advice over the years. My gratitude is also owed to Teacher Lin and Ms. Xu for patiently agreeing to be interviewed, perhaps a few too many times, by the anthropologist who just wouldn't go away, and to Johnson Lin for consistently going out of his way to make me feel at home at Dragon Lake Temple and for being a good friend. Thanks also to Chen Chen-yun, Liu Mengyi, and Tung Yenying for patiently helping me with my Chinese-language questions. Chen Liyuan and Hsu Yaopeng were exceptionally helpful both in teaching me Chinese over the years and in their assistance in finding and/or arranging interviews for me.

I am also beholden to several people who gave various stages of this project very careful readings and without whom this book would be far weaker. They are Jonathan Brookfield, Barbara Folsom, Tim Naughton, Gary Seaman, and Robert Weller. Paul Katz made extremely detailed comments both on the manuscript and on my translation of Dragon Lake Temple's red contract (Appendix). My students at Lake Forest College showed great patience when I inflicted an earlier version of my manuscript on them, and they gave me excellent feedback.

Chapters 4 and 5 are revised versions of an article published in the *Bulletin of the Institute of Ethnology, Academia Sinica* (Moskowitz 1998).

This book is based on my Ph.D. dissertation at the University of California, San Diego. I could not have completed this project without the help of my dissertation committee; F. G. Bailey, Joseph Esherick, David K. Jordan (chair), Richard Madsen, and Michael Meeker. I was blessed with an extraordinarily supportive and insightful committee, and for this I am grateful. David Jordan and F. G. Bailey, in particular, were so detailed and prompt in their feedback on every stage of this project that I was the envy of my peers. The unwavering support and good advice of all of my committee members throughout my graduate career have given me the strength to carry through this project. Each of them has served as an inspiration in his own way, both as a teacher and as a scholar.

Thanks also to the staff in the UCSD anthropology department; especially to Marian Payne and Kae Knight for their help with bureaucratic and financial matters, and to J. C. Krause, whose infinite patience and impressive efficiency allowed me the luxury of staying in Taiwan to write my dissertation. My family has been wonderful, both in their unflagging emotional support and in their patience with my prolonged time abroad. Thanks, especially, to my father, who allowed me to use his painting as the cover design for this book.

Of course, none of this would have been possible without the help of my editor, Patricia Crosby, who believed in my project and who has consistently been both amazingly efficient and extremely helpful, single-handedly eliminating many a stereotype I might have held about the nature of publishing.

Many of the strongest points of this work are the result of the insights the above-mentioned people have provided. Its weaknesses are not only my own, but often the result of a stubborn tendency on my part to ignore good advice.

1

Introduction

W HEN I was a child my mother showed me a picture of one of her college friend's sculptures: a life-sized work of a woman in a long evening gown crafted in the medium of snow. It has been over twenty-five years since I saw that picture, yet the image and elegance of the work, rendered all the more beautiful by its ephemerality, still remain vivid in my imagination. This book holds a bit of the same meaning for me as a fixed record of a transitory moment in time. And it is with some apprehension that I relate the story of these temples, for in presenting them I fear that I can only describe a brief period of experience, whereas the events I speak of are part of a larger continuum. Even as I conducted my research and wrote this book, certain temples' popularity ebbed and waned. One temple stopped appeasing fetus ghosts altogether, whereas another that had annually appeased a little over a thousand fetus ghosts in the years previous to my investigation is dealing with over five thousand fetus ghosts a year at the time of this writing.

Yet, if particular aspects of certain temples are shifting, the basic elements of the belief remain the same, in that the meanings attributed to abortion and fetus spirits form a continuous link from the past to the future which crosses religious, generational, and economic boundaries. Thus, while particular details about certain temples are likely to become outdated, the concerns that I raise here should continue in importance for some time to come.

I had already lived in Taiwan for a year and a half before I first heard of the Taiwanese belief in the haunting fetus. In February 1995 I was studying Chinese in Taibei and discussing what was at that time my proposed dissertation topic on family planning in Taiwan. My

1

teacher mentioned fetus ghosts in passing, assuming that I knew all about them. At first I did not really register her words, and it was only after a few minutes that I stopped and said, "Back to what you said about fetuses that return to haunt their mothers. . . ." After that discussion I began to question others as to whether or not they knew about fetus spirits. To my surprise, every person I asked had heard of fetus ghosts and most said that they believed in the spirit's existence. A good friend of mine took the haunting fetus as such a natural part of the world that she incredulously asked me, "Don't you have them in the United States?"

My understanding of Chinese and Taiwanese[1] culture draws upon the year I lived in mainland China (July 1988–June 1989) as well as the years that I have lived in Taiwan: a total of one year in the south of Taiwan in the late eighties and early nineties, and five years in Taibei, the nation's capital in the north, from September 1994 to September 1999.

The majority of interviews for this topic were conducted between April 1996 and August 1998, with a handful of subsequent interviews. Examination of written documents preceded this by approximately one year. I interviewed forty-three women and twelve men who had direct experiences with fetus ghosts and/or who were appeasing fetus ghosts, and ninety-three people with friends or relatives who had had such experiences. I also had informal conversations with countless others who had heard of the phenomenon and held opinions about it, even if they had had no direct contact with the spirits. Those interviewed were primarily Taibei residents, but I also conducted interviews in Miaoli, Taizhong, Tainan, Gaoxiong, and in several smaller cities on the western coast. I also interviewed Buddhist and Daoist masters who dealt with fetus ghosts.[2] These included interviews in Taibei at two loosely affiliated Buddhist temples and with a Daoist master who worked out of his home, a Daoist temple just outside of Miaoli (in northwest Taiwan), a Daoist temple in the city of Douliu (in mid-west Taiwan), a Buddhist temple and three Daoist temples in Gaoxiong (in southwest Taiwan). I have also been witness to hundreds of people appeasing fetus ghosts at Dragon Lake Temple in Miaoli County.

Many people I have spoken with, both American and Taiwanese, assume that those who appease fetus ghosts are uneducated and therefore superstitious and gullible. The fact that Taiwanese newspapers are full of academics being taken in by one deception or another did not seem to enter into their opinions on the subject. Although I knew some appeasers who were illiterate, I also met believers who were educated at the best universities in Taiwan, and a few who had earned undergraduate and graduate degrees in the United States. A brief list of some of the people I interviewed who had appeased fetus ghosts includes a company president, a farmer, several housewives, saleswomen and -men, a scuba instructor, secretaries, laborers, a prostitute, university students, teachers in both lower education and technical colleges, and many others.

I should emphasize that, though this belief is thought to be a bit bizarre by many, for the most part the people whom I interviewed were well-adjusted members of society, holding jobs and fulfilling their roles within their families. Many of the Americans whom I knew in Taiwan thought the idea of fetus ghosts was the stuff crazy people's dreams were made of. What they did not know is that many of them were close friends with people who had told me of their experiences with fetus ghosts.[3]

Belief in fetus ghosts is best known in Japan, where it is quite prevalent; but it has also been documented in Korea (Tadesco 1999) and in a Buddhist congregation in Hawai'i (Hughes 1999). I have also spoken with people from Hong Kong, Spain, and Russia who told me that their countries have this belief.[4] I also met one woman who, in the early 1990s, went to a private Catholic high school for Colombian immigrants in the United States. She told me that the nun who was teaching them warned her class that if they had abortions, the spirits of the fetuses would come back to haunt them.[5]

The most informative interviews tended to depend on *guanxi*[6] in that they depended on my friendship with that person or with her or his friends. Failed attempts to arrange interviews were usually the result of the unlikelihood of future relations, which meant that the people in question had less reason to spend the time and energy telling me about their experiences.

One example of a failed interview occurred in August 1998 when I went to a Buddhist temple in Muzha in the suburb of Taibei city. I had guessed from the advertisement that the religious master might be reluctant to meet with me, so I went directly to the temple. The temple was really just an apartment with, I am told, an area for prayer set up on the second floor. When I got there, the Buddhist master's wife was not going to let me in. We were talking through the intercom at the entranceway when one of their clients arrived and she had to open the door. When I had explained my project, she said, "We don't deal with fetus ghosts." Somewhat surprised, I responded, "Um, but I have this advertisement." I showed her the advertisement with her husband's picture prominently displayed above a list of things he was able to do, one of which was to help appease fetus ghosts. She paused for a long moment and then said, "Well . . . he used to let the magazine that made the advertisement use his picture, but he never dealt with fetus ghosts himself."

Another example is a temple in Taizhong. I had a friend call to obtain its address. When she called, the temple representatives refused to give her its location, insisting that they pick her up at the train station. Because she did not have a chance to tell them why she was calling, one can presume that they used this approach for every caller. Thus, my interviews tended to be with temples that had less to hide. In general, the more exploitative Daoist and Buddhist masters were less likely to be willing to be interviewed unless I had connections with one of their better-paying customers. Judging from the costs of other Daoist and Buddhist services that contacts have told me they paid, it is probable that many people are charged more than the average amounts I will cite here.

To protect the identity of those I interviewed, I use fictional names for everyone except people who have published religious tracts or short stories about fetus ghosts—namely, Cai Wen, Lin Jianyi, Xu Qiongyue, and Zhong Xing. In two cases I have also changed identities further by altering their occupations and the cities where they lived. Even in these cases, however, I preserved the information, such as their religious backgrounds, that I thought was relevant to the belief itself.

Another preliminary point to mention is that of language. In three of my interviews I had assistants translate from Hokkien (Taiwanese) to Mandarin Chinese. I conducted all of the other interviews in Chinese and without assistants. Also, I taped two of the Taiwanese interviews so that I could have them transcribed into Chinese. On the whole, however, I found that the tape recorder made the people being interviewed uncomfortable, and it was only when the interviews were supposedly over and I had stopped taping that they began to give me more interesting information. After this, I did not use a tape recorder but took notes either during or immediately after the interviews. Because of the sensitive nature of this research, I tried to let the person being interviewed direct the course of conversation. While I might ask questions to clarify a point they had made, I relied on a casual conversational model of interviewing. In many cases interviewees raised issues I would not have thought to ask about, and I believe this style of interviewing made them more comfortable and candid about their personal lives. My interviews with religious masters were more formal, and I asked more specific questions. I was, however, careful to let them speak their minds about issues I had not raised.

Being faced with women talking to me about their abortions was a moving experience, the emotional impact of which I cannot begin to convey. Many people have asked me why I chose such a morbid topic. In fact this is fairly easy to explain. Here was a subject that had not been addressed before for Chinese or Taiwanese religion, an issue so fundamental to my country of origin that some have compared it to a modern civil war. In addition, it is a perfect junction for religious and gender studies, and it is integrally connected to economic change and modernization.

One woman in her seventies who was visiting Dragon Lake Temple with her children and grandchildren had a more interesting explanation, however. When she asked me why I had chosen this topic, I gave her the rather innocuous response that because we did not hold this belief in the United States I thought it was interesting. She looked at me for a moment, then shrugged her shoulders and said: "Yes, but why you and not someone else? Maybe you were aborted in your last life. That would make sense. Perhaps this was your fate."

Abortion and the Spirit World

Faye Ginsburg has outlined the American antiabortion movement's use of fetal images beginning in the 1970s, pointing out that those images became an important and effective part of the pro-life campaign in the United States (Ginsburg 1989: 104). Imagine if this movement could not only use images of infants to represent aborted fetuses, but could portray them as speaking directly to the parents of their sadness and suffering in a way that would be taken seriously by those who have had or are thinking of having abortions. Stories of fetus ghosts do just this.

The maladies that the haunting fetus spirits (*yingling*) cause are similar to those brought about by other kinds of discontented ghosts that inflict sickness, injury, or death. Yet *yingling* are distinctive in a number of unusual ways. In exploring the significance of the haunting fetus we can learn how women and men come to grips with abortion and how this affects their relationships with their spouses, lovers, children, and other family members. The appeasement can be financially exploitative, yet it provides important psychological comfort to those involved in the choices that lead to abortions as well as a much needed means to project personal and familial feelings of transgression onto a safely displaced object, thereby bringing underlying tensions to the surface and providing a means of working out those problems.

The appearance of fetus-ghost appeasement in the mid-seventies seems to have been inspired by the Japanese practice. Its substantial growth in the mid-1980s seems to have reflected the legalization of abortion in 1984, which in turn led to a great deal of discussion in the press of abortion and related issues concerning morality. Therefore, a study of this belief also provides us with a means of monitoring the ways in which religious conceptions, as well as traditional concerns with sexuality and self-restraint, family structure, and morality, are shifting to meet the new demands of a modernizing Asian society.

The belief in fetus ghosts provides a perfect focal point to examine both religious and gender theory, and to investigate the ways in which the two overlap. An examination of who is held responsible for abortion, and of who is affected by the *yingling*, provides a view of conceptions of parenthood, morality, and the heavens. In examining Chinese perceptions of the spirit world we not only further our understanding of gods and ghosts but also explore the cultural belief systems that lie behind everyday interactions of the living.

In conducting my fieldwork I discovered that there are in fact two different kinds of fetus spirits in Taiwan, neither of which has been systematically studied. The first, which I call fetus ghosts (*yingling*), is the primary focus of this work. The second, a literal translation of which would be "little ghosts" (*xiaogui*), I call fetus demons because they are associated with evil. Although both are fetus spirits, the issues surrounding the two are so different that they are quite clearly two separate ghosts. Fetus ghosts exemplify a concern with guilt and redemption, and are highly personal because people pray on behalf of a ghost of their own flesh and blood. Fetus demons are concerned with what might be called more traditional black magic and arise when sorcerers use evil spells using the spirits of other people's dead fetuses. While those appeasing fetus ghosts are primarily female, those dealing with fetus demons are male; whereas those appeasing fetus ghosts are interested in healing the wounds of both their families and their ghosts, fetus demon worship allows for the expression of greed, loathing, and revenge.

Belief in fetus ghosts and fetus demons provides an excellent point of comparison for contrasting images associated with abortion and the very different ways in which people react to these issues. With fetus-demon sorcery, there is a pronounced lack of emotional attachment to the spirit, and the images of abortion and death as evils that can be manipulated for one's own benefit serve to highlight people's fears and hopes in a way that highly contrasts with most fetus-ghost appeasement. This is useful not only in exploring other aspects of conceptions of fetus spirits, but also as a point of comparison helping us to better understand the belief in fetus ghosts.

A Historical Overview of Taiwan

It is hard to fathom the extent of change that has occurred in Taiwan in the last century. The Dutch occupation of Taiwan from 1624 to 1662 was perhaps too long ago to have a lasting effect, but the Japanese occupation from 1895 to 1945, the huge influx of mainlanders fleeing the communists in 1949, and the American military presence from 1947 to 1975 have all had a profound influence on contemporary culture in Taiwan. Also, American aid and foreign political pressure, as well as exposure to foreign music, movies, and travel, have influenced Taiwan dramatically. I will not attempt to explain why these changes came about—that would be a book, or several books, in and of itself. But just to outline some of the differences that have taken place in Taiwan in the last century: Taiwan's population rose from a little over three million in the early 1900s to seven times that number in the late 1990s. Many people currently in their mid-fifties had arranged marriages, and I have talked with people in their thirties who told me that their mothers were "sold" into marriage against their will. Although matchmaking continues to be strong today, to marry a woman against her will is now illegal. At the beginning of the century it was common for families to consist of five to ten children, whereas now couples usually have only one or two offspring. In the 1950s the majority of the population lived in rural areas, whereas most Taiwanese today live in urban areas. The average life expectancy has more than doubled in this century. In the early 1900s many people did not attend high school, and a very small percentage attended college—women were not allowed to attend university at all. By the late 1980s, a little over 30 percent of all high school graduates attended college or university, and almost half of them were women. A generation ago, most women worked in the home and most men worked on the family farm. Now, the majority of unmarried women and men work outside of the home and to some degree have their own income, with a corresponding greater autonomy from parental control. Twenty years ago it was universally expected, if not always the case, that a woman would remain a virgin until her marriage. Whereas once a woman was expected to marry her first boyfriend, dating is now common, and, especially in urban areas, this often includes sexual activity, although this is still contested ground.

Abortion was legalized in 1985 and, while it is hard to know the degree to which this actually changed abortion rates, it gave state legitimization to the practice and brought the issue to the forefront of public discussion. The press, though still censored behind the scenes, has far greater freedom than ever before. Martial law was lifted in 1989, free presidential elections were implemented in 1996, and people who had once been imprisoned for their ideas are now writing popular fiction or running for government office. It is in this setting that belief in fetus ghosts emerges as a serious religious force.

The Religious Setting

Steven Harrell (1974) suggests that religious doubt is more prevalent in Taiwan than one might expect. While I do not debate this point, a good deal of this argument depends on where one draws one's lines. For instance, Harrell repeatedly cites the Chinese saying "half belief and half doubt" (*ban xin ban yi*), emphasizing the nonbelief in this phrase (Harrell 1974). It is true that this is a common phrase and expresses doubt, but the people who use the term more often than not shape their actions around religious beliefs. Indeed, Harrell acknowledges that *ban xin ban yi* includes the fear that "there are enough examples pointing to [religious and superstitious practice] working that one ignores them at one's peril" (Harrell 1974: 86).

I maintain that when people shape their actions around the possibility that a belief might be true, it is for all intents and purposes belief, albeit a qualified one. Accepting this definition, the vast majority of people in Taiwan believe in ghosts. The few who say that they do not think that ghosts exist quickly add a qualifier, often fearfully waving their hands back and forth for emphasis, "But I'm not saying that ghosts do not exist!" lest they anger a spirit with their statements. In other words, there are those who doubt but few who do not believe. Belief in fetus ghosts is less universal than belief in ghosts in general, although it is still quite common. Fetus-demon sorcery, as an offshoot of a fairly heterodox belief, is indeed small—yet it exists.

Sometimes people agree on the broader prescribed beliefs of ghosts and gods while disagreeing on the details. Much of Taiwanese religion is very flexible in beliefs, so no two temples, or indeed people, share the exact same conceptions of their religious participation (Jordan 1972: 28; Jordan and Overmyer 1986: 212). Thus it often happens that certain practices, or sometimes entire belief systems, are questioned. In the cases of fetus-ghost appeasement and fetus-demon sorcery there are some agreed-upon outlines, but on the whole the ways in which one appeases such spirits, and the true nature of the ghosts, are often left to the interpretation of the particular religious master appeasing them. This contestation can be seen in the images of fetus ghosts, the fees, and the wide array of gods and goddesses that are appealed to for appeasement.

Of course, such contested interpretations are not limited to the belief in fetus ghosts and fetus demons. Religious practices in Taiwan are very open to interpretation and diversity, and as a result there is often a fine line between whether or not an individual's religious interpretations or actions will be deemed to be true by others. Jordan and Overmyer (1986) give a wonderful example of the ways in which support within a sect can be given and withdrawn. After a spirit medium delivered a divine revelation that other temple members should contribute money for him to buy a truck (with divine instruction on where to get the best deal, no less) the spirit medium lost credibility and was dismissed from the temple (Jordan and Overmyer 1986: 169–171). Margery Wolf provides an account of a woman who was diagnosed as having mental problems rather than being a shaman, as she claimed (M. Wolf 1990).

I once witnessed a similar example of contested religious interpretation at Dragon Lake Temple, a fetus-ghost temple in Miaoli. A pregnant woman in her mid-twenties fainted because of the heat and her husband looked like he was about to panic. A short stocky man in his mid-forties started to shout at her as if she were possessed by a fetus ghost. The first time he shouted she didn't wake up. The second time he addressed the fetus ghost that he assumed was causing this problem, screaming in a high-pitched shriek, "Go back to the temple, you don't belong in this woman!" and she looked up at him groggily. By this time, of course, there was a crowd of gawkers. The woman was clearly displeased and embarrassed that this man had drawn so much attention to her. After a while the crowd wandered off. So as not to lose his moment of glory the man shouted, "It's OK, you can go now," for the most part to people's backs as they were walking away.

Now does this count as possession or not? Clearly the man thought so, but the onlookers were openly laughing at him. Certainly, most of the people at this temple believed in fetus ghosts or they would not have been there. What they did not support was the stranger's claim to having the power to exorcise the spirit, though one might guess that had the master of the temple done the same thing it would have been taken as a legitimate exorcism.

On a larger scale, one can find many people who believe in ghosts and gods but reject the idea that aborted fetuses can become ghosts. As I will discuss in the following chapters, the images of fetus ghosts vary tremendously among believers, and the practice of appeasing these spirits is enmeshed in an ongoing debate concerning religious orthodoxy, morality, and modernization.

Gendered Realities of Religious Belief

Abortion is so prevalent in Taiwan that one scholar has asserted that Taiwanese people "regard abortion as a natural part of life" (J. Wang 1981). This statement, while accurately portraying the frequency of abortion in Taiwan, misleadingly suggests that there is no emotional investment in the process. Women in Taiwan have abortions, not because it is an easy choice, but because they are placed in a structural position that within their culture makes bearing that particular pregnancy difficult. Reasons might include being a single mother, the pressure to bear a male heir (combined with the fact that the fetus is female), economic difficulties, and many others. When faced with these dilemmas, a woman, her husband, or her husband's parents might decide that she should have an abortion. There is a wide range of societal and psychological pressures involved, however, and it would be a mistake to think of abortion in Taiwan as a routine matter. Confucian filial responsibility to continue the family line, the Buddhist belief that it is sinful to kill any form of life, and prevalent Taiwanese conceptions of women as nurturers all lead to personal anxiety and familial disharmony when an abortion occurs.

This study is in a sense a continuation of Shahar and Weller's (1996) attempt to examine gods and ghosts that do not fit in with the far more studied bureaucracy of the spirit world. Not surprisingly, in leaving the world of bureaucratic hell one also leaves a hypermasculinized image of the hereafter in favor of establishing women's domain in conceptions of the spirit world.

As Brigette Baptandier has suggested in speaking of the symbolic meaning of religious washing, both of newborns to welcome them to the world of the living and of the dead to ease their passage to the next world, the presentation of femaleness in Taiwanese religion can be seen as a "commentary on femininity and on the social role of women, which appears between the lines" (Baptandier 1996: 117). Traditional associations with women, death, and pollution are fundamentally linked to sickness and decay (Ahern 1975a, 1988; Sangren 1996; Seaman 1981). As Steven Sangren has suggested, religious belief has differing emotional meaning according to one's gender—both by virtue of women's and men's differentiated gendered life experiences and because of their different structural positions within their patrilines (Sangren 1996: 152–153).

We see this with women and fetus ghosts, as for the most part women take the blame for the spirits of aborted fetuses. Yet, in an important way, fetus-ghost appeasement gives women the opportunity to right these perceived wrongs and to reinforce more life-affirming images of women's religious roles. If women are blamed for the infant spirits, so are they credited with restoring order and supernaturally based familial harmony.

Along the same lines, Emily Ahern asks the important question,

"Are the ideology and practice of death in Chinese society different, depending on one's gender?" (Ahern 1988: 164). She goes on to ask: "Could it be that buried within these practices and symbols of birth, marriage, and death is another view of how these experiences inter-relate, one that is derived from women's own quite different experience of life and that is stamped with a quite different message?" (Ahern 1988: 164). Approximately 70 percent of those appeasing fetus ghosts are female, and because the meaning and experience of abortion are ultimately experienced and perceived of differently according to one's gender, the above-mentioned questions form a founding basis for this book. Although I do not want to discount male participation in this practice, there are many cultural factors in Taiwan which place abortion and fetus-ghost appeasement in women's domain.

It is rare for a religious belief in Taiwan to cater specifically to women. As Huang and Weller have noted, although women have tra-ditionally been in charge of day-to-day prayers for the ancestors, the fact that these forefathers are their husbands' ancestors means that such religious practice "offers little more to women than housework does" (Huang and Weller 1998: 387). Huang and Weller go on to explore a fascinating women's religious movement, the religious group Ciji, and the ways in which women participating in this orga-nization strengthen their status as women by working toward social good in an urban environment that is increasingly evincing a "market-oriented morality" (Huang and Weller 1998: 392). Appeasing fetus ghosts has many of the same resonances, but on a more private level in that many of the women appeasing fetus ghosts believe themselves to have become a part of what they see as a greater social moral decay. In appeasing their aborted fetuses, they strive to redefine themselves as moral beings by making up for their perceived sins. Because women now have greater access to their own financial resources than they once did, an increasing number of temples are willing to perform such duties to meet this new demand.

Yet an equally important question in this study is how men feel about abortions and belief in fetus ghosts, both of which are com-monly thought to be in a woman's sphere of influence. Men often have a large say in the decision to have abortions, and the negative connotations of the act in both religious and social spheres certainly influence them in profound ways as well.

The Haunting Fetus

In the following chapters I will examine this "new" ghost in Taiwan. As we trace the reintroduction of the belief from Japan to Taiwan in the mid-1970s and 1980s, we witness an intriguing story of greed, healing, religious adaptation, and modernization. In the late 1980s and early 1990s, newspapers in Taiwan began to react to this new trend, voicing the assertion that practitioners of fetus-ghost appeasement used images of the *yingling* to frighten women or exploit their guilt to make money, a criticism that has been echoed by Helen Hardacre (1997) in her work on the practice in Japan. This is in many cases a valid criticism, but such an approach often overlooks the full complexities of this new religious practice.

Instead of focusing on women's structural or symbolic weaknesses as an end point for analysis of gender relations in Chinese culture, several scholars have examined areas in which women have traditionally been seen to be marginalized or even victimized, and have explored the ways in which these same women have used such structural conditions to their advantage. This has been shown in the familial and community setting (Ahern 1975a; M. Wolf 1968, 1972, 1974) and in religious belief and taboo imagery (Ahern 1988; Furth 1994). It is true that images of fetus ghosts are sometimes used to convince women to pay large sums of money.[7] Yet I argue that fetus-ghost appeasement also provides important services. This belief gives psychological comfort to women who have had abortions. It also creates an outlet that can be used to vent unspoken resentment toward one's family members, allowing for the expression of grievances ranging from the abortion itself, to intergenerational conflicts and marital tensions.

I should conclude this introduction by emphasizing that this is a record of some of the strongest emotions of the human race. While researching the belief in fetus ghosts it was impossible for me to remain a detached observer at all times. If I am successful in the following pages, while including things that might be bizarre or even humorous to an American reader, I hope that I have also conveyed the beauty, the sorrow, and the hope that I have witnessed in relation to this belief.

2
Beyond the Percentages
Abortion and Meaning in Taiwan

C HINA's population, which was approximately 65 million at the beginning of the fifteenth century, more than doubled to 150 million
in 1600, reached 583 million in 1953 (Ho 1959: 277–278), and has
nearly doubled again to 1.2 billion today. In traditional China, the
desire to have fewer children was less one of preference than of sur-
vival. Pierre-Etienne Will speaks of the massive population growth in
the eighteenth and nineteenth centuries, which contributed to food
shortages caused by floods and droughts (1990: 1) when most had a
bare subsistence even before the natural disasters struck (1990: 303).
He portrays the hardships of traditional China: disease and mass star-
vation (Will 1990: 27, 36–37), people forced to eat dirt and sell children (1990: 54). Bernice Lee uses the 1929 famine, when more than
three million are said to have died, to emphasize that the challenge
of feeding their families was a very real concern for those who practiced infanticide (Lee 1981: 173).

Infanticide has a long history in China, written mention of it dating
back to the period between 800 and 600 B.C. and extending up to
modern times (Lee 1981). Records of ingesting substances to induce
abortion date back at least as far as the early eleventh century, though
it is likely to have preceded this date by hundreds of years (Ebrey
1993: 181).

In modern Taiwan, economic pressures are hardly so dramatic,
yet crowding has reached all-time highs. The population rose from
a little over three million in 1906 (Sun and Chang 1990: 15) to 21.63
million in 1996 (Anonymous 1997: 4). One large factor in the population pressure is that people are living longer. In 1906 the average
life expectancy in Taiwan was approximately thirty years old (Her-

malin et al. 1994: 54). By the late 1980s, the average man could expect to live to the age of seventy-one, and the average woman until seventy-six (Sun and Chang 1990: 9).

Another important factor in Taiwan's population growth is the reduction of infant mortality. This changed age-old reproductive habits in that high death rates for children had traditionally kept family size down, whereas in recent years the number of surviving children has been too large to maintain (Freedman and Takeshita 1969: 5).

Taiwan has quickly changed from a rural society into an urban one. In 1949, almost 25 percent of the population lived in cities with a population of 50,000 or more; in 1988 this rose to 72.9 percent (Hermalin et al. 1994: 56). This shift from a rural to an urban setting, combined with extremely expensive property values, has resulted in cramped housing. This also means that, in the majority of families, the help that children once provided on farms is no longer needed.

Another factor in this examination is the increasing investment in children. A great many families send their children to night school, usually beginning at the elementary school level and continuing until the student has passed, or given up on, the college entrance exam. In 1952, 1.5 percent of the population between the ages of eighteen and twenty-one attended college; by 1988 this had risen to over 30 percent for the same age group (Hermalin et al. 1994: 68). While university is relatively inexpensive, the fact that such a high percentage of high school graduates now extend their schooling means that they continue to be a financial drain on their parents, without contributing significant labor or outside income to the family, well into their early twenties and beyond.

People in Taiwan are marrying later, and a greater number of them are having premarital sex. In 1905, a little over 25 percent of all women from the ages of twenty to twenty-four had already married at least once; 68 percent had done so by the age of twenty-five to twenty-nine (H. S. Lin et al. 1994: 204). In 1990 these percentages had dropped to 8.6 percent for twenty- to twenty-four-year-olds, and 43.7 percent for twenty-five- to twenty-nine-year-olds (H. S. Lin et al. 1994: 204). One study noted that between the early 1960s and early 1980s, the number of respondents reporting premarital sexual activity increased from 9 to 40 percent (Thornton et. al. 1994: 196). Another study reported that in 1980, of the thirty-five- to thirty-nine-year-old female respondents, 13.5 percent responded that they had had premarital sex, as compared to 49.9 percent of twenty- to twenty-four-year-olds (H. Lin 1990: 256). In short, on average people in Taiwan are marrying later, and more women are engaging in premarital sex. These factors, in combination with cultural mores that strongly condemn having children out of wedlock,[1] are some of the most significant elements of the abortion issue.

A changing value system associated with more individualistic and hedonistic principles is also an important factor. Though still the norm, fewer adult children are living with their parents, and children are becoming less reliable retirement plans than they once were. Thus, having fewer offspring fulfills a desire for less work and more free time, while the benefits of having children are decreasing.

Family Planning in Taiwan

Unlike mainland China, which faces more drastic population pressures, Taiwan has never had punitive laws for having too many children. However, over the years it has promoted the idea that a certain number of children was optimal, and the populace has responded with a surprising amount of compliance. The government outlined ideals for families to follow in regard to family size:

> Before the announcement of the [family planning] policy, the emphasis was on the health of mother and children. A slogan of "five 3" was created in 1967, meaning to have the first child 3 years after marriage, have a baby every 3 years, stop at 3 children before age 33. The ideal family size was 4 at that time. In 1969, the slogan was "Fewer children bring more happiness." The slogan introduced in 1971 was "3321," indicating: have the first child 3 years after marriage, have the second one 3 years later, stop at 2, boys and girls are the same (1). Today, the emphasis is on the social responsibility of an individual for increasing population problems. (Sun and Chang 1990: 14)

The Taiwan Family Planning Center, and by extension the government that created and funded it, was not only seen to provide a service but also to outline the rules by which its citizens should live. To borrow Judith Stacey's analogy comparing mainland China's authoritarian stance to that of a patriarch (Stacey 1983), family planning literature takes the tone of a guiding father, if a comparatively benevolent one. Citizens are asked to think not only of their own welfare but of the effects of their actions on others and the strength of the nation as a whole. Thus, the government not only provides information about contraceptives but also promotes its view on how many children to have and when to have them. Ideas about citizens' actions ranging from marital happiness to childcare and sexual behavior were and are unabashedly seen as the domain of the state.

In the 1990s an unexpected problem arose. It turned out that people really *preferred* to have fewer children. So much so that the government is now worried about negative growth and the effect that the reverse-age pyramid, in which the elderly outnumber the young who have to support them, will have on the economy and society as a whole. For this reason, the government is restrategizing and trying to encourage families to have children but not too many (Sun and Chang 1990: 34–36).

As an example of the government's family planning propaganda, movie houses in Taiwan used to be required to play the national anthem before each film while the audience stood respectfully. When I first came to Taiwan in 1989 this music was accompanied by scenes of a prospering Taiwan with images of farming, industry, and happy workers. In 1996–1997 the previews had switched to scenes of a young daughter and the happiness she brought to her parents and grandfather, which was accompanied by the soundtrack of children singing the national anthem. Having one child, and significantly one daughter, was now presented not only as the foundation for familial harmony and happiness, but as the basis of national strength.

In spite of the government's efforts, however, current family planning education has had many failures. Statistics suggest that there is an increasing use of contraceptives in Taiwan. Yet to say that more people are using contraceptives is not to say that the contraceptives work—after all, Taiwan is not famous for its quality control. Nor is it to say that the contraceptives are being properly used. Although sex education and family planning classes are given to all middle-school students, the classes more often than not fail to include instruction on the practical application of what is taught, if they are taught at all. Most people in Taiwan do not learn about sex or proper contraceptive usage because they are embarrassed to ask, and because others are unwilling to tell. Many teachers of sex education simply skip over the more embarrassing pages of textbooks.

Taiwan's Provincial Family Planning Center is aware of the limitation of its success in middle-school education. One study reported that 16.8 percent of its respondents said they had not been taught about family planning in middle school, 4.7 percent were told to read the contents on their own, 55.5 percent said they had been taught briefly, and 22.7 percent said they had been taught carefully (H. Lin 1990: 266). The same study laments that only 25.3 percent of secondary school students in their survey were able to answer simple questions on a quiz concerning reproduction and contraception (H. Lin 1990: 265). In spite of acknowledging that the students are not receiving proper education in family planning, there is little mention of what in fact they are being taught. For example, according to my interviews and informal conversations, family planning classes often place a greater emphasis on avoiding sexuality than on more practical applications such as teaching birth control methods.

A number of newspaper articles (K. Li 1997: 3; W. Lin 1997: 3; J. Lu 1992: 15; Luo 1997: 5; Qi 1997: 3) share a common critique of inadequate sex education. The following Taiwanese newspaper editorial is one example of this:

> In the first day of our first year college class on hygienics and health, the teacher carefully told us, "Whatever you do, don't get pregnant before you get married." Then, she almost threatened us, frightening us with a story: "There was a young woman. Before her boyfriend went off to serve in the military she offered herself to him for the first time in her room. Several months later the landlord discovered she had fainted in bed and her entire body emitted a terrible stench. When the landlord took her to the hospital, her whole uterus had rotted. When she first discovered she was pregnant she went to a private clinic and had an abortion. The abortion operation was unsanitary and she got an infection, but she didn't dare to tell anyone else about it. In this way she lay on her bed until she was discovered and taken to the hospital. Afterwards she was brought back to health from near death."
>
> I don't remember the rest of the story. I only listened to the teacher go on and on about the terrible things that could happen if you got an abortion at private clinics. My classmates listened to these dramatic stories and exclaimed in terror every time the teacher made a point, but I had already become numb.
>
> The teacher violently opposed premarital sexual activity, or maybe she thought that inspiring terror was the best way to scare us from doing anything. But what help could this be for a class of university stu-

dents? Did she think that after we were married none of us would need abortions? I was confused, starting in high school when the health education teacher used the same methods and told the same stories, using the same threats. She just showed us a movie and made us memorize the names of all the contraceptives, but never taught us to understand the need for contraceptives or the ways to really use them. Why didn't the teachers help us to really understand how to use contraceptives and protect ourselves? Where could we go for help when we were in trouble? Where could we find qualified doctors and safe and sanitary hospitals? What is the abortion process and how does it work? Instead we learned wrong information that was passed through gossip. [The teachers'] threats might have made even more female students lie on their beds crying, but it did not help them. Besides the physical harm, they were also covered with the shadows of their sad hearts. Shouldn't the hygienic and health class teach accurate knowledge? In teaching the class in the way they did, even after marriage we would still have a fear of abortion.

I once went with a friend while she had an abortion. There she was lying on the abortion operation table; flustered, confused, and weak, not knowing how to endure the operation, and guilt [*zuiegan*] was eating away at her. I had no way to help her. I was also afraid that one day I would be in the same position as she. Couldn't our teachers and our hygienics and health teacher give us any help? Instead, they only prepared our hearts to see the worst that might come and focused the blame of all problems on premarital sexual behavior. (J. Lu 1992: 15)

Such gaps in sex education are highlighted by people's opinions about pornography, though not in the ways one might have anticipated. I taught English in Taiwan for a number of years. One of the discussion topics I used in class was "Should pornography be legal?" To my surprise the majority of women in these classes felt that it should be legal because they felt that pornography served as means of educating oneself about sex. Half to two-thirds of the women in each class told me that, because sex education in junior high school and high school was inadequate, they had learned about sex from watching Japanese pornographic movies. Because Japanese pornographic movies usually involve scenes with bondage, rape, and sex with minors,[2] one can only wonder what these women's images of sexuality are.

The level of ignorance about sexuality and reproduction that one frequently encounters in Taiwan is indeed astounding. I talked to women who laughingly related how in high school they thought they could get pregnant from kissing. One woman in her forties told me that as a junior high school student she thought that women gave birth out of their armpits. Although many will protest that this has changed in the last two decades, in the early nineties I met an eighteen-year-old woman who thought she could get AIDS from holding hands with a boy. Another college-educated woman told me that she could not get AIDS because she had a "strong body." As evidence of this she said: "Other women need to go to the doctor to get pain killers when they are having their periods. I don't have to do this because I am strong, therefore I don't need to use condoms because I'm too healthy to get AIDS." The misinformation about sexuality, venereal diseases, and contraception is surely a large factor in the prevalence of unwanted pregnancy and abortion. Also, although the use of contraceptives is rising, many, if not most, of the people I have spoken with on the matter do not use them.

Issues of privacy also come into play. Taiwanese parents almost universally expect their daughters to remain virgins until they marry, even if this is not until their late twenties or early thirties.[3] Because many people in Taiwan live with their parents until they get married, and because there is little privacy among family members, it is difficult for young women to keep contraceptives in their homes or in their purses.

Abortion Rates

Statistics imply that abortion rates have risen since its legalization in 1985. It is likely, however, that rather than indicating a dramatic shift in the actual number of abortions, the rise in abortion rates reflects the growing tendency to have legal abortions at government-sponsored hospitals instead of at private clinics. Even before its legalization, abortion was easily obtainable throughout Taiwan (Tietze and Henshaw 1986: 26). Freedman and Takeshita's 1969 study states that approximately 10 to 20 percent of their respondents reported that they had had abortions (1969: 94). In a later study, Freedman and others provided 1980s statistics in which 34 percent of the female respondents between the ages of thirty-five and thirty-nine reported that they had had at least one abortion in their lifetime (Freedman et al. 1994: 290). Another research project estimated that approximately 130,000 illegal abortions were performed in 1984, the year before the abortion law was implemented, pointing out that this would mean there was one abortion for every three live births (Sun and Chang 1990: 13).

Since the implementation of The Eugenics and Health Protection Law (Yousheng baojian fa) in 1985 (EL 1984),[4] abortion has been legal in the case of a deformed fetus or to protect the physical or mental health of the mother, provided she has the consent of her guardian or spouse (EL 1984: Article 9) and that the fetus is within the first twenty-four weeks of pregnancy (EL Bylaws: Article 15). In practice, government-run hospitals are fairly loose in their interpretation of the risk of physical or mental health and will essentially perform abortions on request, provided that the woman has the consent of her spouse or guardian. In the two public hospitals where I interviewed, the husband's consent was the only stipulation mentioned. When I asked about the other restrictions, the staff at both hospitals assured me that anyone with her husband's consent could get an abortion regardless of the other stipulations in the law.[5]

Surprisingly, almost no one I interviewed had a strong sense of what the law contained. Many were surprised to find out that they needed the agreement of their husbands to have abortions, further support for the idea that consent stipulations might be overlooked at many clinics.

In the last few years, married women have had approximately 120,000–150,000 reported abortions a year (W. Lin 1993: 4; Sheng 1993: 11, 1994: 8; Wei 1998: 43). In the mid- and late 1990s, approximately 30 percent of all pregnancies in Taiwan ended in abortion (W. Lin 1994: 1; Wei 1998: 43; Wu 1993: 9), with reported teen abortions slightly above this (H. Huang 1994: 14).

True abortion rates are likely to be far higher than the statistics suggest. As was the case before The Eugenics and Health Protection Law was instated, private clinics are notorious for conducting illicit abortions regardless of legality. One woman, for example, told me of a private clinic which recorded that a patient went for treatment for a headache when in fact she had gotten an abortion.

The vast majority of women go to private clinics to obtain abortions, and they do so precisely because private clinics will conduct illegal abortions and maintain anonymity (H. Huang 1990: 5; S. Lin 1989b: 13). Because the majority of abortions go unreported, the statistics on reported abortions can be seen to reflect only a small fraction of the actual numbers (Lai 1990: 5; Zhou 1989: 5).

What we can see with precision, however, are birth rates. In the early to mid-1900s, women on average had six to seven children; by the mid-1980s, this had dropped to an average of approximately two children (Hermalin et al. 1994: 53). It has been estimated that nearly half of all adult women in Taiwan have had at least one abortion in their lifetime (J. Wang 1985), but considering the failures of contraceptive use and the sharp drop in the birth rate, one could conclude that the percentage of women who have had abortions is in reality even higher.

To be sure, abortion is never absolutely safe. Private clinics in Taiwan exacerbate this risk, however, for they are notoriously unsanitary and often staffed by unskilled practitioners. For example, I met one woman who continued to have irregular bleeding for a year after her abortion, and I have talked with several women who attributed their having frequent miscarriages or becoming sterile to earlier abortions.[6] One newspaper article outlined the dangers of having abortions in Taiwan:

> [The] most commonly seen problems [caused by abortion] are for women's wombs to be scraped, for pincers to rip the uterus lining, for the medical tools to be unsanitary and spread germs after which the uterus becomes infected or the menstrual cycle becomes irregular. Women's menstrual flows can also go the wrong direction, causing serious stomach cramps. (Sheng 1990: 6)

Thus, although abortions are easily accessible in modern Taiwan, for the majority of women abortion is fraught with the danger of serious physical side effects. Such maladies can easily be interpreted as spiritually polluting. An example of this in the mainland is that it is believed that after a woman goes through a sterilization operation she will lose a great deal of her *qi*, or life energy, which is remedied by ritual gift giving (Yan 1996: 230–231). In Taiwan, the interpretation of loss of life energy is associated with the presence of fetus ghosts, which are excessively *yin*.

Divorce, Structural Inequality, and Abortion

I find myself in the awkward position of acknowledging that divorce rates in modern Taiwan are rising while stressing that the divorce law strongly discourages women from seeking divorce. This becomes important for the topic at hand, because women's justifiable fear of divorce often results in their seeking abortions they might not choose were the decision theirs alone.

Factors leading to divorce include a combination of loosening family ties, an increase in expectations of individual happiness, and a greater percentage of women in the work force who therefore have independent incomes. Also, as some scholars have pointed out, increased life expectancy means that divorce is replacing death as a way out of marriage (M. L. Lee et al. 1994: 258).[7]

Yet despite the rising divorce rate, in general both women and men in Taiwan are extremely reluctant to divorce. In addition to the trauma of ending long-standing emotional attachments, many feel that they would be disgraced by divorce. To acknowledge divorce is to admit failure and weakness in perseverance, and perhaps in one's moral character as well—a shame that extends to one's parents and the family unit as a whole. Thus, divorce is enmeshed in a complicated web of considerations in which public opinion and family unity would seem to take precedence over individual happiness. Many marriages are continued purely for appearances, while husbands and wives pursue other romantic or physical relationships with the knowledge of their spouses, with whom they reside but no longer have physical contact.

For women, the choice to divorce is especially fraught with emotional burdens and real economic dangers. Taiwan's divorce law protects the husband's rights far more than the wife's—no doubt a reflection of traditional beliefs in which marriage was less a union of equals than a woman joining her husband's family. After a divorce, the man keeps the children and all property and money once belonging to the couple, *including* all that was owned by the woman at the time of the marriage. A good example of this is Mr. Chen, a businessman in his late thirties. Mr. Chen had married and divorced twice in a period of a few years. After divorcing his wives, he kept the houses and other assets that his wives had owned before marriage. He now rents out the houses and collects a nice income from them. He also walks around with a baseball bat in case he is attacked by one of his ex-wives' associates—but that is another issue.

Although this is an extreme example, countless tragedies ensue from this law. Women are often refused any visiting rights whatsoever with their children, and because legally this is left to the father's discretion, there is little the woman can do to appeal.[8] Women's structurally weak positions within their marriages often result in their accepting otherwise unacceptable situations in their relationships within their affinal families. Thus, if a woman's husband or his parents pressure her into having an abortion, she is confronted, not only with traditional expectations that a woman should obey the orders of her husband and his parents, but with the threat of potentially being cast out into the cold if she refuses. This, in combination with extremely strong pressures from the husband and his family to produce male heirs to continue the patriline, means that a woman may be forced into an abortion she does not want. She may also be forced into giving birth, if her husband or his family is anxious for heirs. Thus, with the exception of those who have illegal abortions without informing their husbands, many women may in fact have very little power over their own bodies in the choice either to have, or not to have, an abortion.

In many cases a woman has an abortion because she hopes to secure her position in her household by producing a male heir. In other instances she may do so to maintain her physical attractiveness. One example of this emerged in an interview I conducted with Ms. Li, a high school graduate who, as a housewife, relies on her husband for financial support. When Ms. Li became pregnant for the third time, she decided to have an abortion. This is the reason she gave:

> I don't know about Americans, but in Taiwan the only thing a man cares about is how beautiful his wife is—smart, funny, gentle [*wenrou*], sure he will say this is important. But what makes him proud, and what keeps him at home, is this [making a hand gesture at her body]. You men don't realize how hard we women have to work to look like this. If I had another child I'd be finished [*wo wandanle*].

Li's statement "I'd be finished" suggests not only that she was afraid she would not be able to keep her husband at home, but that she also believed her position as wife to be precarious. This anxiety is a common one among women without sons, and a worry that is justified considering the continuing preference for male progeny.

Women Killing Women: Aborting Female Fetuses

It is a truth universally acknowledged that Chinese daughters are the byproducts of attempts to produce Chinese sons. (Gates 1996: 121)

Modern technology has provided a means of determining the sex of a fetus. As a result, in both Taiwan and mainland China, abortion is far more likely to take place if the fetus is female.[9] Perhaps surprisingly, it is often women who decide to abort female fetuses. There are a number of reasons for this. The first is pressure from their husbands and husbands' parents to produce a male heir to carry on the family name.

A second reason is for their own security as well as their husbands', because of the expectation that the oldest male will live with and take care of his parents. This is changing somewhat in that women are taking a larger role in supporting their biological parents and men a smaller one. Yet the majority of Taiwanese still stress patrilineal links and bearing sons. As Margery Wolf points out, by having male children a woman achieves more status, more protection for herself within the family, and greater power in making family decisions through her sons (M. Wolf 1968: 127, 136; 1972: 160–161). Also, there is a particularly strong mother–son bond in Taiwan that often surpasses any other emotional relationship either of them has in their lives (Ebrey 1993: 187; M. Wolf 1968: 42, 127).

Unexpectedly, Taiwanese women do not seem to perceive the issue of women killing women as a factor in the guilt associated with abortion. Most women seemed genuinely surprised when I asked about this, asking in turn why I thought they would feel any less guilty for aborting a male fetus.

Religious Beliefs

Abortion seems to be remarkably unpoliticized in Taiwan. Those I have interviewed in Taiwan look at the events surrounding abortion in the United States, for example, with surprise, and they are puzzled at the violent controversy over what most Taiwanese consider to be a private issue. Yet if abortion in Taiwan is not as politically charged as it is in other regions of the world, there is still a wide range of religious, societal, and psychological pressures involved; it would be a mistake to think of abortion in Taiwan as a routine matter.

One example of this is the strong Confucian obligation to produce heirs for the patriline and to avoid harming one's own flesh. Traditional and current Confucian thought stresses that to injure oneself is to harm the property of one's parents and ancestors. This responsibility to protect one's body extends to a fetus. Thus, in killing a fetus, one is perceived to sever familial ties, to fail in one's duty to procreate, and to mutilate familial flesh, which is an unfilial act.

An equally important condemning factor is the fundamental Buddhist belief that one should not harm any living being. Buddhists maintain that in having an abortion one kills a human with the soul already in place. The concept of reincarnation emphasizes this guilt, because in obtaining an abortion one has killed the soul of a person whose fate (*yuanfen*) is intrinsically linked to one's own. From this perspective, a spirit chooses to occupy a particular fetus because it has interacted with one or both of its parents in past lives. Therefore, it is believed that in having an abortion one not only kills one's own child but possibly a spouse, friend, or parent from another life.

The Buddhist proscription against killing any life form introduced an element of religious transgression into attitudes toward abortion very early on. Considering the range of possible violations in popular Buddhism, and the extremity of punishment at each level of Buddhist hell, it is unclear to me whether in strict logic abortion would bring significantly more punishment than, say, eating meat or being unfilial. For instance, van Gulik cites a Yüan dynasty Confucian text that had a "Table of Merits and Demerits," used to keep track of one's sins and moral deeds (van Gulik 1961: 249–250).[10] In this text, "Abortion" earned 300 demerits, "Abortion—If done to conceal an illicit relation" 600 demerits, and "Infanticide" 1,000 demerits (van Gulik 1961: 249–250). Note that the penalty for abortion and infanticide was not equal. Also note that the demerits for abortion were doubled according to how the woman had been impregnated, suggesting a moral framework that reached beyond the act of killing a fetus.

Clearly the above transgressions were considered to deserve serious demerits as opposed to categories such as "Keeping books or inscribed fans in one's bed," which cost only 3 demerits, or "Failure to marry off maidservants" 200 demerits (van Gulik 1961: 249–250). However, abortion was significantly lower than "Producing [or publishing] erotic books, songs, or pictures" which cost 1,000 demerits, or "Offending against one's parents or ancestors," also 1,000 demerits (van Gulik 1961: 249–250). Thus, the idea that abortion was a moral offense was present but did not significantly stand out beyond a range of other actions, many of which strike the modern reader, Chinese or Western, as less pernicious.

As a third point, growing permissiveness toward nonmarital sexuality has led to a strong backlash from more conservative Taiwanese who criticize nonmarital sex, and to increasing criticism of sexuality within the bounds of marriage if it is for pleasure rather than for procreative purposes. People in Taiwan are less tolerant of abortion if a woman is married but has no children than if a woman is unmarried or already has children (Lin Fangmei 1996: 17). Those who oppose abortion in Taiwan are really objecting to nonmarital sexuality, asserting that this is perceived as giving such women an opportunity to "escape the consequences of what these activists saw as sexual license" (C. Chang 1996: 19). Accordingly, in addition to the natural grief of having an abortion, a couple must also face the societal intimation that in pursuing sexual pleasure for nonreproductive purposes they have been highly individualistic, decadent, and irresponsible toward others.

The Traditional Role of Women as Care Givers

Although Rosaldo's universalistic model of separate spheres for women and men (Rosaldo 1974) has many weaknesses, some of which she later addressed herself (Rosaldo 1980), the public/private dichotomy is in fact a familiar Chinese and Taiwanese concept. Good examples of this can be found in the traditional Chinese phrases "Men rule outside, women rule inside" (*nan zhu wai, nü zhu nei*) and "Men till, women sew" (*nan geng nü zhi*). As these terms suggest, women in Taiwan are perceived, and many perceive themselves, primarily as care givers, while men are expected both to work hard to provide financial support and to set good examples for their children. While this division is increasingly breaking down in recent times, it still holds true today. Women feed, clothe, and discipline their children, and they take primary responsibility for their studies and emotional support. As Patricia Ebrey has noted for traditional China, the "association of women with the inner [sphere] both limited and empowered: it kept women out of the public sphere but legitimated their authority in the domestic sphere" (Ebrey 1993: 44).

In contrast, traditional Chinese views stress that fathers should be both distant and strict authority figures, which often made enemies of their own children (Stacey 1975: 69). The expected distance between fathers and sons can be found in the Confucian Analects: "Tzuch'in came away delighted, saying, I asked about one point, but got information about three. I learnt about the Songs, about the rituals, and also learnt that a gentleman keeps his son at a distance" (Waley 1938: Book XVI, no. 13). Waley also notes that this separation extended to ritual acts: "There is a definite ritual severance between father and son. A father may not carry his son in his arms. A son may not, when sacrifice is being made to his deceased father, act as the 'medium' into whom the spirit of the deceased passes" (Waley 1938: 208, n. 2).

As Margery Wolf has pointed out, in modern Taiwan fathers are often physically and emotionally distant from their children, separated from them because of their responsibilities outside of their home and by their expected role as patriarchs (M. Wolf 1968: 42, 127; 1975: 132). The film *Red Persimmons* (T. Wang 1997) further exemplifies the distance between fathers and their children. This movie portrays a Chinese family that moves to Taiwan to flee the communists. The story centers around the mother, who raises her children with the help of her mother-in-law while her husband is away most of the time in the military. Each time he returns home, his children line up to greet him and he tries to guess each child's identity, often guessing wrong.

In the average Taiwanese household, "Ask your mother" is the usual response to a child's question, while "You wait till your father gets home" is a foreign concept. When I tell Taiwanese people of this maxim, mothers and children alike laugh. "Why," they ask, "would a mother wait to punish her child?"

Abortion and Guilt

Many of the women and men I interviewed spoke of the guilt they felt in relation to abortion.[11] Although I never introduced the subject of guilt into my interviews about fetus spirits, the majority of women with whom I talked who had had abortions told me that they felt bad, felt guilty, or regretted their actions. This is not to say that they would not have had the abortions if they had to make the choice again, but it does emphasize the fact that the experience was not one they took lightly.

One area of interest related to this study is the often mentioned paradox that Asian cultures, which place such a high value on family, have such surprisingly high abortion rates. In these pages I have outlined a wide array of important reasons that might lead to abortions in Taiwan. Yet the high rate of abortion should not be thought to reflect a lack of emotions associated with the act. This study has set out in opposition to such a viewpoint by examining the case of Taiwan—the reasons why abortions take place there, and the personal, social, and religious disequilibrium they can cause. Ms. Wang, a Taiwanese woman in her early thirties who has a master's degree in English literature sums this issue up far more eloquently than I could:

> I think that maybe you Americans don't understand that we Chinese have a three-thousand-year history of emphasizing morality. We grow up on the teachings of Confucius and others. These teachings tell us that the difference between animals and people is in our morality; the way we treat our parents and other family members, our obligations to our country, and our responsibilities toward our children. So of course we feel guilty when we know that we have done something wrong. How could we not?

Behind the Mask: Men, Abortion, and Guilt

In light of the information I have outlined here, it is hard not to portray Taiwanese men as completely removed from the emotions associated with abortion. But men are very much a part of the decision to have abortions, a fact that is highlighted by the consent regulations of the abortion law itself. I have discussed the fact that in Taiwan the responsibility for abortion is considered to be the woman's domain. In doing so, however, I run the risk of wrongly suggesting that men do not care about abortion. Though I have already pointed out the distant role of fathers in Chinese culture, no one can argue against a father's sense of the importance of progeny. In any park in Taiwan or mainland China one can see fathers lovingly playing with their daughters and sons, and fatherhood is a role that brings many men their greatest pleasure. Also, to infer that men do not care about abortion is to ignore the fact that males also inherit the religious moral training of the Confucian, Buddhist, Daoist, and Christian traditions.

Part of the misperception that men are completely removed from abortion involves communication. In Taiwan, men are taught that they must be strong, and that to show an excess of emotion is by its very nature a loss of face. Robert Silin's discussion of the Confucian tradition lucidly outlines the conceptions of personhood and morality that set the background for this discussion.

> In the Confucian conceptual system society exists within the universe. There is no concept of man as separate from other men. Man's supremely human element is his ability to act morally. [. . .] The man who fails to observe "morality" threatens to remove himself from humanity. Fear of regression into egocentricity—the failure of the individual to uphold his commitments to himself and society—remains a focal concern of interpersonal relations. The individual who understands and acts on universal principle is the ideal man. (Silin 1976: 35–36)

First, applying Silin's analysis, I suggest that in a culture that emphasizes family so strongly, abortion violates perceived moral actions as well as potentially being seen as a supremely egocentric action—that of ending another's life for one's own benefit. Second, Silin's emphasis on the integral connection between morality and conformity is an essential component discouraging open displays of emotion. This gives an insight into the controlling forces that keep emotions hidden behind a mask of male strength.

The following newspaper editorial gives a vivid account of male emotions that contrasts with more reserved day-to-day conversations or interviews.[12]

> At the hospital a nurse and my wife came out of the delivery room and went in the direction of the recovery room. My wife said to me in a weak voice, "Giving birth is very painful! But at least you were by my side." For a moment tears came to my eyes. The nurse lightly patted my wife's shoulder, "You really are lucky to be married to a husband who loves you so much."
>
> That evening I stayed with my wife in the hospital. I sat back in a reclining chair by my wife, but I couldn't sleep. I just tossed and turned so I got up and went by myself to the room where the newborn infants are kept to look at my baby. As I looked at my baby crying, my heart suddenly had a spasm of emotional pain. Before my eyes slowly appeared the image of my girlfriend of ten years before whom I had given no thought to. Tears trickled down her face. . . .
>
> I thought about a girlfriend I had in university. One day she suddenly told me she was pregnant. When I heard this news, I was young and selfish. In my heart I wanted to run away from this responsibility and then fear turned to anger: "Get an abortion."
>
> "I don't want to," she said with an expression of sorrow in her eyes.

I firmly said: "You're crazy. After graduation I have to serve in the military. When I'm done with that I still want to go abroad to study. If you have that child then my whole life's prospects will be destroyed, won't they?" I was intentionally looking for trouble being so angry with her.

"I can look for work and I will raise the child and wait for you to finish your military service. Then we can go abroad together. You can continue your studies and I'll look for something to do. . . ."

"Get an abortion. I don't want to hear you say any more unreasonable ideas."

"We've been together for four years and only now do I realize that you are so selfish. You only think of your own future prospects but you never think about my health. I couldn't bear to abort a child *again*" [original emphasis]. She shivered and cried as she said this, after which she left.

At that time I didn't have any regrets. My head was only full of my ambitions and ideals. Afterwards I never saw her again. Later, I heard that she had very bad morning sickness and in order not to let too many people know about "this matter" she dropped out of school.

After I finished my military service I didn't want to ask others about what had happened in my ex-girlfriend's life because I really didn't want to know. If I thought about it at all I only hoped she wouldn't want to look for me to "accept the responsibility." After I finished military service I could do whatever my heart desired, so I went abroad to study. So I really did achieve my dreams and ideals.

More than ten years quickly passed and I never heard any news about her. Every day I missed her more and more, and my sense of guilt and regret [*kuijiu*] grew stronger and stronger. When I came back to Taiwan to be with my wife when she had her child, I saw my wife giving birth and screaming loudly to the heavens and my "girlfriend's" image inexplicably slowly appeared in my mind. [The girlfriend] was giving birth, and not only had to endure the pain of giving birth but also had to endure the harm I had inflicted on her heart and spirit.

Suddenly I felt like I had been stabbed in the heart. Many years had gone by and my heart's feeling of guilt and regret toward her, which I had tried to suppress, could no longer be controlled. Therefore my tears came rolling down and the nurse, who did not know why I was really crying, still believed my tears were because I loved my wife so much. This only added to my regret and guilt.

To my girlfriend, I can only silently say "I'm sorry" deep in my heart. I don't know whether or not I will have the chance to make up for what I've done. (Si 1996: 32)

The man in this account in many ways typifies the image of men in this system; he is self-serving, career-oriented, and quite callous at the moment when his lover needs his support the most. Yet the article also exemplifies the fact that, while some men might act callously, it is possible that in many cases they later regret their actions.

Another example of men's hidden emotions about abortion came up in two conversations I had with a man I will call Mr. Zhou. Mr. Zhou is a white-collar worker in his mid-forties and is the father of two daughters. When I first interviewed him in March 1997 he told me the following:

> Some families have more than two children already. Unfortunately, they get pregnant again. People get confused. Should the baby come into this world or should we get an abortion? Sometimes a family has no ability to feed its baby, but if they choose to have an abortion they are afraid that a fetus ghost will take its revenge. Another example; if a doctor used an ultrasound check and discovered that a baby would be abnormal, should the couple still keep the baby and be prepared to feed this child for their whole lives? I personally think that this is unfair to both the family and the child.
>
> As a last point, I would like to say, try to keep the situation from happening altogether. If it still happens, I still have two choices. I will have the baby if he or she is normal, no matter if I am rich or poor. If the doctor tells me the baby is abnormal, I will give up the baby.

This interview was a troubling one. The way in which Mr. Zhou switched from third-person to first-person hinted at the fact that he was relating his own story but did not want to admit it.

A month later I was having dinner with Mr. Zhou and some other friends. This was one of many social situations in which I would just as soon have put my fieldwork aside for the evening, but Mr. Zhou wanted to talk more about the issue. He began by saying that he knew a couple who decided to have an abortion because they were not married yet. Years later, long after they had married, he told me, a spirit medium informed them that their aborted fetus had become a fetus ghost. A few minutes later he said, "Actually, it was me."

> I feel a little bit guilty about the abortion, but my wife feels especially bad. We weren't married then, and at that time you couldn't just have a baby if you weren't married yet. Also, we were very poor so we didn't really have a choice. Years later we went to a spirit medium who told us that our aborted fetus

had become a fetus ghost, so we paid a temple money for three months but we were really angry. We felt that the temple just took our money and didn't do anything. I wanted to give the money to an orphanage so that it would do some good. But my wife, she felt bad about the abortion and wanted to do this. I still might donate money to an orphanage. I'd like to make up for what I've done.

Although Mr. Zhou stated that his wife felt worse about the abortion than he did, it is clear that he also had difficulty in coming to terms with the action.

In Taiwan women are closer to abortion experiences than men, both physically and emotionally. But there is a tendency to simplify such settings to make them more amenable to academic analysis; thus women are represented in oppositional terms to men as competitors for economic, political, and social rights, and nothing more. In discussing these issues, one runs the risk, in pursuit of a logical and concise argument, of oversimplification and misrepresentation. In the cases I have described, for example, male distance could easily be interpreted as a lack of investment, and cultural mores discouraging emotional display could be misconstrued as a lack of emotions altogether. Such misinterpretation is both wrong and dangerous, for it plays into the very same stereotypes about gender and race that academic endeavor sets out to overcome.

This is the setting in which fetus-ghost appeasement has developed, and as such the information here presented should give us a better feel for the emotions that come into play with belief in the haunting fetus.

3

Made in Japan?
The First Stages of the Adoption and Adaptation of a Japanese Religious Practice in Taiwan

A LMOST everyone I have spoken with in Taiwan, including those appeasing fetus ghosts, agrees that fetus-ghost appeasement is a modern import that arrived from Japan in the mid-1970s and grew substantially in the mid-1980s. Those who condemn the practice assert that religious entrepreneurs adopted the Japanese practice in order to exploit women who feel guilty about their abortions. Most of those who are sympathetic to the practice also acknowledge that it came from Japan during the same time period. In the following pages I will outline the emergence of this belief in Taiwan and briefly compare and contrast it to the practice in Japan.

I will not delve too deeply into the practice of fetus-ghost appeasement in Japan, as William LaFleur (1993) and Helen Hardacre (1997) have already written extremely thorough and compelling books on this topic. Emiko Ohnuki-Tierney (1984) and Laury Oaks (1994) have also discussed fetus ghosts in modern Japan. But as it is likely that the Taiwanese practice of fetus-ghost appeasement can for the most part be considered a direct import from Japan, I will now give a quick overview of the Japanese belief to provide a point of comparison.

The Japanese god Jizō originated as the Chinese god Dizangwang Pusa, a somewhat androgynous god who is an overlord in the court system of the underworld. In Japan this is also the god in charge of children and fetus ghosts. There was a slow transformation of the god, who was already thought to be particularly compassionate as he protected people in the underworld (LaFleur 1993: 47). Sculptures of Jizō imitated Chinese prototypes in the ninth and tenth centuries (LaFleur 1993: 49), and in the middle ages, when there were festivals focusing on children and the image of Jizō, there was a gradual infantilization of the god (LaFleur 1993: 51). William LaFleur suggests that this transformation of the god during the sixteenth century, and probably before, came about as a reflection of increasing anxiety about abortion and infanticide in Japan during that time period (LaFleur 1993: 51).

In December 1995 I visited the Hase-dera temple just outside of Tokyo. The temple is devoted to fetus ghosts and has become something of a tourist attraction. The Hase-dera temple is part of a complex of approximately seventy temples and shrines in the area. Many make a devotional trek from one temple to another. The atmosphere is part devotional, part circus. People can pray to the fetus ghosts, then traipse off to a teashop on the temple grounds, where they can snack on the outdoor patio while dropping a coin in one of the telescopes that have been set up to better see the ocean view. After this they can wander off to the money-washing temple or one of the many other temples in a two- or three-mile radius.

Because of the setting it might be tempting to suggest that this religious belief has been diluted, coopted, and assimilated to the point that it has lost its meaning. Mixed in with the tourists, pilgrims, and occasional anthropologists, however, are women who are close to tears with grief. In the midst of this crowd of gawkers they light incense, pray, and hang up chains of one thousand origami birds in tribute to their dead.[1] While visiting there I saw a mother instructing her son to pray for his "older brother," and one cannot miss the hundreds of small statues, each representing a departed fetus or child. Some worshipers had placed miniature baseball mitts, an ultra man, and other toys beside the statues, while others had placed small knitted scarves on the statues' shoulders.

The Move to Taiwan

One factor in the timing of the Taiwanese adoption of the belief in fetus ghosts could be the loosening of Taiwan's government control over religious practices. Until recent years many religious practices, such as participation in the religious organization Yiguandao, for example, were illegal.

One might think that the fact that Japan occupied Taiwan from 1895 to 1945 would be a decisive factor, but the belief did not spread to Taiwan until some twenty to thirty years later. Nevertheless, Japan's former presence in Taiwan and its present economic power have kept it in Taiwanese eyes in a way it might not have done otherwise. Many Taiwanese who grew up in the Japanese era, for example, learned Japanese. The older generation in Taiwan has continued to be interested in Japan, and it may be that some people in this age group read Japanese religious tracts concerning fetus ghosts. Also, frequent commercial interaction between Japan and Taiwan provide ample opportunities for business people to be exposed to new ideas. For example, a trip to Tokyo with a side trip to the Hase-dera temple as a tourist seems a likely experience for many Taiwanese who visit Tokyo.

More important, many Taiwanese look to Japan as a model—an Asian symbol of financial and political power that has successfully overcome many of the problems currently facing Taiwan, such as a growing crime rate and environmental problems. Partly because of this, Japan has had a great influence on Taiwan's fashion industry, and Japanese soap operas, comic books, films, and other popular-culture items can frequently be seen in Taiwan. Fetus ghosts are likely to be but one of these many popular-culture imports. The mid-1970s to mid-1980s was a peak period of commercialized fetus-ghost appeasement in Japan (Hardacre 1997: 94–95). Given the popularity and press coverage at that time, it is not surprising that religious masters in Taiwan would be inspired by the huge incomes being generated by this practice.

Yet, despite religious masters' desire to make money, fetus-ghost appeasement could not have come to Taiwan were there no demand for it. This point is supported by a number of people I interviewed who went to temples to burn incense in apology to their aborted fetuses without consulting religious masters. In such cases the worshipers were usually Buddhists who felt guilty for breaking the Buddhist prohibition against killing any life form. In these cases the patrons went to temples that did not normally appease fetus ghosts and burned incense for the dead spirits, often without consulting temple masters.[2]

The most important reason for the new interest in fetus ghosts is that it fills an important need. Since abortion was legalized in Taiwan there has been a marked increase in public discussion of the issue, and people seem at a loss as to how to cope with this moral problem, both for achieving their own peace of mind and placing it in a framework that fits their religious beliefs.

Practitioners of fetus-ghost appeasement are the only group of people with whom I have come in contact in Taiwan who consistently play down the Japanese influence. Teacher Lin,[3] a Daoist master who runs the largest fetus-ghost temple in Taiwan, denies that the practice came from Japan, strongly asserting that it is a traditional belief in Taiwan. He emphasized to me that in Japan the practice is a Buddhist one and that they have only one god, Dizangwang Pusa (Jizō), to assist fetus ghosts. In contrast, he pointed out, his own temple is Daoist and people pray to an array of gods to assist with *yingling*. Ms. Xu, the head of a Buddhist temple in Taibei, also denied that the practice came from Japan, stating that there was a long tradition of fetus-ghost appeasement in Chinese history, and that in fact the Japanese took this belief from China in the first place. Other religious masters from smaller temples also deny the connection, often saying something to the effect of "Japan is Japan and Taiwan is Taiwan. Just because there are some similarities doesn't mean they are the same."

Both camps are in part correct. On the one hand, there is some precedent for this practice in Taiwan. David Jordan has documented a case that occurred in Taiwan in the late 1960s in which a baby girl was worshiped by her surviving family members because her spirit was too powerful to exorcise and the ghost demanded worship as a condition of its good behavior (Jordan 1972: 165–166). Jordan also provides a case study of a girl who died at the age of one, the spirit of whom caused her older sister to get sick until they arranged a marriage for her (Jordan 1972: 143). Also, I have interviewed three middle-aged people who told me of infant spirits that were appeased in the 1960s. Each of the three people I interviewed about the practice at this time told me of children who died, either at birth or soon after, rather than being miscarried or aborted fetuses, which currently account for the vast majority of *yingling*. In this light it seems safe to say that the practice did exist, if only sporadically and in secret.

To the extent that it existed before the mid-1970s, it would seem that such appeasement was both far more simple and inexpensive. In each of the three cases I was told of that occurred before this time, the parents burned incense, a Daoist master said a short prayer, and that was the end of it. Also, before the 1970s there was certainly nothing near the kind of popularity that this ghost now has.

The boom of the belief in the mid-1980s was clearly with an eye to Japan, and one can see many practices involved in fetus-ghost appeasement in Taiwan that are Japanese in origin. Teacher Lin's temple, for instance, has a small representational statue to represent each *yingling*. I have not seen this for other ghosts in Taiwan, but it is quite common for fetus ghosts in Japan. Another example is the two heroines of the movie *Yingling* (Ding n.d.), both of whom have night-mares of fetus ghosts walking over "Hopeless Bridge" (Naihe Qiao) while a song is introduced with lyrics that are essentially the same as Japanese texts described by Helen Hardacre (Hardacre 1997: 41). Most important, the threats and promises associated with fetus ghosts in both countries are too similar to be coincidental. In short, Taiwan had some basis for fetus-ghost appeasement before the mid-1970s, but the practice was both underground and extremely rare. It in-creased dramatically in the mid-1980s as some temples began to adopt Japanese rituals associated with fetus ghosts.

In Japan there is one god, Jizō, who is in charge of fetus ghosts. In Taiwan, people also appeal to the Chinese version of Jizō, Dizangwang Pusa, for help with fetus ghosts. But this god does not take priority over other goddesses or gods such as Buddha (Shijiamouni Fo), Guan-yin, Xuantian Shangdi, or a host of others who may be appealed to, depending on the particular temple and the preferences of the wor-shipers. In fact, the range of gods in Taiwan that help to care for the *yingling* is virtually limitless. Fetus-ghost appeasement in Taiwan is primarily a Daoist and Buddhist practice, but the occasional Confucian or Christian will also appease fetus ghosts.[4]

Scholarship on Japanese fetus ghosts offers an interesting point of comparison for this study. LaFleur comments on the surprisingly public nature of fetus-ghost appeasement in Japan, pointing out that people use their family names on amulets on which they write apolo-gies to infant spirits (LaFleur 1992: 153). Hardacre's book reinforces this idea when she relates the account of a Japanese mayor who bullied his town's citizens into contributing money to buy fetus-ghost statues in order to attract tourism (Hardacre 1997: 214–215).

Certainly in Taiwan there is nothing like the tourism associated with the practice in Japan. There can, however, be a public dimension to the practice in Taiwan as well. As in Japan, those appeasing fetus ghosts in Taiwan will write their names on memorial plaques or idols. Unlike in Japan, however, it is rare for people to write their full names, and even when they do, the only people likely to see the names are other worshipers who are also appeasing their dead.

As Laury Oaks has remarked for Japan, a certain psychological

cleansing results from public rituals for fetus ghosts (Oaks 1994: 515).
To take Teacher Lin's temple's semiannual fetus-ghost appeasement
ceremonies as an example, worshipers are surrounded by others who
have shared the same experience and thus can derive comfort from
a sense of solidarity with the other participants at the ceremony. As
people go to the temple they are surrounded by hundreds of others
who are also there because of their abortions,[5] which potentially
reduces their feeling of being more sinful than others.

Yet this is an anonymous solidarity rather than one of personal
relationship, for those attending the ceremony live in different communities and are for the most part strangers.[6] Also, such solidarity
disintegrates when one leaves the temple, for most people at the
ceremony have no desire to make friends on the basis of their shared
abortion experiences.

Exploitation or Assistance? A Problem of Interpretation

Helen Hardacre, in writing on fetus ghosts in Japan (1997), takes a
particularly strong stance against fetus-ghost appeasement. She does
so on the grounds that those associated with the practice use images
of wrathful fetus ghosts to coerce women into paying exorbitant fees
to appease the ghosts.

> The situation of [declining fetus-ghost appeasement] in Japan today
> suggests that fetocentric rhetoric is rejected by the majority, even in
> the religious world. This is a hopeful conclusion, one pointing also to
> the majority's rejection of the fatalism and misogyny upon which the
> practice rests, a disdain for the use of fetishized images of the fetus to
> intimidate, a repudiation of religion's use to stigmatize and damn. This
> finding further suggests a reason to hope that pessimism and fatalism
> in Japan's religious world can be displaced by a more expansive and
> optimistic outlook. (Hardacre 1997: 258)

Again, without defending the practice of fetus-ghost appeasement in
all instances, I should point out that Hardacre's analysis has some
troubling points. The first is her emphasis that the majority of Japanese "reject the practice" (Hardacre 1997: 92, 258), or even that it is
a "small minority" that engages in fetus-ghost appeasement in Japan
(Hardacre 1997: xxii). She hints, as in the above quotation, that this
somehow invalidates the belief. By her own account, however, more

than 40 percent of all temples in Japan do appease fetus ghosts (Hardacre 1997: 92). This seems like a tremendously high percentage, especially considering that this includes temples from different religions. I am hesitant to address the issue of "pessimistic" or "optimistic" outlooks reflected in a religion, but if I were to do so, I would suggest that much in this study supports a view of making amends for one's perceived wrongs and easing the suffering of others. This could be argued to be a rather optimistic outlook, considering that one chose to abort the fetus in the first place.

Hardacre, perhaps unintentionally, hints at a benefit of this belief when she states that fetus-ghost appeasement "is dying out as it fulfills the basic meaning women give to it: assuaging feelings of irresolution and ambivalence" (Hardacre 1997: xxii). This is a surprising statement in a book devoted to condemning the practice. Also, the logic of this remark is problematic in that Hardacre overlooks the fact that new abortions will occur. If the practice serves the purpose she says it does, it seems reasonable to assume that people having new abortions will also seek to make amends. But Hardacre makes an important point, for in spite of her condemnation of the practice, the above statement seems to acknowledge its possible psychological benefits. Because Hardacre's study is on Japan, I will not discuss her research further here. As her book is one of the few English publications on fetus ghosts in Asia, however, and because her interpretation differs so markedly from my own, I felt it necessary to make these few points before proceeding to discuss the case of Taiwan.

To sum up, while there was some precedent for fetus-ghost appeasement in Taiwan dating back at least to the 1960s, the practice was both fairly underground and an extremely simplified form of the modern-day practice. Certainly, nothing like Dragon Lake Temple, which appeases more than five thousand new fetus ghosts a year, existed before the mid-1970s.

Many of the same issues surrounding the belief in both Japan and Taiwan serve as important foundational questions for the rest of this book: To what extent does the practice increase people's terror and/or guilt about the supernatural ramifications of abortion? Is the practice merely a group of male religious entrepreneurs exploiting women's fears to make a profit, as Hardacre (1997) suggests for Japan? What are the strategies to popularize this belief and why is it, in effect, so marketable in modern Asian countries such as Taiwan?

To my mind, the most important question for this analysis is the one least often asked: What does this belief provide to those participating in the practice that has made it so readily marketable? As I have already suggested, it would not be possible to promote this practice for profit were it not fulfilling fundamental psychological and social needs that are not being met by other religious beliefs and practices. With these questions in mind we can now turn to traditional religious beliefs in Taiwan.

4

Fetus Ghosts and Traditional Beliefs in Taiwan

FETUS-GHOST appeasement is in some ways an extension of more traditional religious conceptions, while in other ways it dramatically departs from the past. In the previous chapter I described the Taiwanese adoption and adaptation of this Japanese practice. Yet certain aspects of the belief are a better fit with traditional beliefs in Taiwan than in Japan. For example, in Japan when a spirit haunts a person, it is usually the ghost of a stranger; rarely is it the spirit of a relative (Ohnuki-Tierney 1984: 80). In contrast, in the traditional Chinese conception of the spirit world, disgruntled relatives' ghosts are commonly thought to wreak their wrath on the living.

Margery Topley, writing on her 1969 research in Hong Kong, noted that some women believed that if a woman had wronged someone who later died, that person's soul might return in the body of one of her children to seek revenge (Topley 1974: 245–246). This belief was used to explain both physical and behavioral problems (ibid.). Topley also records that a mother-in-law would be present during a birth, and if she "diagnosed resentment" of the fetal soul, boys would be given away and girls literally thrown away (Topley 1974). She also reports a widespread belief that when a child's fate was thought to be badly matched with another person, it would result in illness or other complications (Topley 1974). These Chinese religious precedents fit current ideas about fetus ghosts in Taiwan, for both women and spirit mediums associated with fetus ghosts often state that abortions are the result of mothers and their aborted fetuses not being fated together (*you yuan wu fen*). Unlike the situation in Topley's study, with fetus ghosts this explanation is offered after the decision to terminate the life of the fetus, not before.

Although belief in fetus ghosts has only recently gained widespread acceptance, it is very much an extension of traditional religious convictions. Illnesses, financial crises, and deteriorating familial relations in Taiwan are often explained as being caused by spirits angered by someone's improper actions, and illness can in turn be cured by symbolically rectifying that irregularity (Jordan 1972: xxii, 155). As Stevan Harrell has pointed out, ghosts are personifications of social and religious disruption, and as such become emblems for the randomness of suffering (Harrell 1986: 99–100). Conceptions about fetus ghosts' actions and motivations draw on culturally accepted norms that explain such structural anomalies through ghost hauntings. If a child suddenly becomes difficult to manage, or if someone falls seriously ill either in body or in mind, fetus ghosts can be used as a ready explanation.

One might expect women who have had abortions to express resentment toward a fetus for coming at a time that was not convenient for having a child. After all, Chinese parents were not traditionally famed for their patience with misbehavior on the part of their children. This is perhaps best exemplified by the tradition of a father's ritually beating a son's coffin to punish him for being unfilial by dying before his parents (A. Wolf 1974: 148; M. Wolf 1968: 47). In practice, however, though many women I have interviewed have expressed resentment about the situations that led them to have abortions (being unmarried, pressure to bear sons, etc.), I have not interviewed anyone who blamed the spirit of an aborted fetus for her predicament. In part this is because most women involved in fetus-ghost appeasement believe that they are in the wrong for having had abortions, but this also points to conceptions of spirithood, for the fetus's soul is thought to occupy the already existing physical form of the fetus. In other words, women first get pregnant and then the soul comes to that body. Therefore, the soul of the fetus is not thought to cause pregnancy but to be summoned by it.

Elizabeth Johnson has shown that women can use funeral laments to express unresolved grievances with the dead or with the living (Johnson 1988). Because fetuses are not given funerals, one might anticipate that the process of exorcising the spirit might provide a forum for such expression. But women who appease fetus ghosts do not use this opportunity to declare publicly their grief over having abortions or over the situations that led them to have those abortions in the first place. In general, even at temple ceremonies for fetus ghosts, the women are quite stoic, and when they cry they tend to do so silently rather than with the loud demonstration associated with funerals. Also, unlike funeral laments, in which women often create their own verses (Johnson 1988), spoken prayer for dead fetuses is usually prescribed by the religious master of a given temple. This is either in the form of written chants that are given to the women to read or, as at Teacher Lin's temple, with a written contract that the woman reads aloud for the gods and for her aborted fetus to hear. Women do use this opportunity with their families or lovers in private, however, using the topic of the appeasement as a way to remind others of their own suffering as well as the suffering of the fetuses' spirits.

Fetuses and infants are thought to have souls, yet their souls are distinct from those of adults.[1] Several scholars have written on fright syndrome in Chinese culture, in which souls are thought to flee their bodies if startled (Ahern 1975a; H. Chang 1996; Harrell 1986, 1991; Topley 1974). Newborn infants are considered to be particularly susceptible to fright syndrome in their first hundred days (H. Chang 1996: 433; Topley 1974: 237). Another belief particular to fetuses is that mothers must be especially careful about their actions during pregnancy because their fetuses' souls are thought to wander around the room. For this reason a pregnant woman has to be careful lest she harm her child (Ahern 1975a: 196–197; Harrell 1979: 524; Sung 1997: 170–171; Topley 1974: 237, 246).[2] This belief highlights the fact that fetal and infant souls, while human, are nonetheless distinct from those of older children or adults.

The greatest break with traditional thought is in the reversal of Confucian hierarchy. Stuart Thompson states, for food offerings, "Juniors always make offerings to seniors, never the inverse" (Thompson 1988: 74). Arthur Wolf makes a similar assertion that for parents to pray to their children would be "unthinkable" because it would reverse parent–child hierarchies so emphasized in Chinese culture (A. Wolf 1974: 159). This, Wolf postulated, would result in religious quandaries for the parents, because they would be left with the unhappy alternatives of either asserting that an offspring was an evil spirit to be disowned or living with the idea that their child was left to wander in the spirit world, both homeless and hungry (A. Wolf 1974: 147–148, 159).

Although Thompson and Wolf's assessment of this problem is true on a broader scale—in general it was not the practice to care for the ghosts of fetuses—they overstate their position a bit. As I noted earlier, Jordan's research, and my own, points to isolated cases of appeasement of infant spirits.[3]

Yet if Thompson and Wolf make assertions that may not be entirely correct, in a more general sense they have captured the sentiment of most people in Taiwan before the recent upsurge of fetus-ghost appeasement. Certainly, to be left in a position where one must pray to one's children is something that no Taiwanese or Chinese parent wishes. It is no doubt extremely uncomfortable when the logic of religious belief forces one into an action that is lacking in propriety.

Today, one can occasionally hear the same refrain that parents should not pray to their children; but although this sentiment still exists, it is increasingly rare. This change in conceptions of religious propriety reflects changing familial relations. As Thomas Shaw has pointed out, familial relations in recent years are shifting from one-way duty owed to one's parents to a growing expectation of mutual respect and assistance (Shaw 1994: 437). Hill Gates, with characteristic wit, makes a similar point:

> a broader public discussion of the family politics I often hear from working-class friends: that today's young people seem to be more filial if you don't beat them, threaten them, and govern them too strictly. "*Haizi pa ruan, bu pa yin*" ("Children are controlled better by kindness than by harshness") is often heard these days. (Gates 1996: 242)

The fact that fetus ghosts return to judge and punish their progenitors highlights these changes while simultaneously evincing a certain anxiety about one's children's increasing power over their parents and of shifting power structures between generations as a whole.

With the growing acceptance of fetus-ghost appeasement, parents no longer have to choose between believing that their "children" were malevolent spirits or condemned to eternal suffering. Now they can provide for their lost children. It is likely that this change is linked to the fact that medical care has substantially reduced infant mortality while at the same time providing ready access to abortion. Whereas it was once possible to say that a child died a natural death because it was an evil spirit, this solution is less viable now that fewer infants die of natural causes and a growing number of parents make the conscious decision to terminate the lives of their fetuses. Considering the dramatic increase in abortion rates, it makes sense that new religious beliefs would arise to provide for this situation.

Because people are having children at a later age, the age gap between grandparents and grandchildren or great-grandchildren is on average wider, and the distance between their views greater. Taking this distancing in conjunction with the fact that fewer adult children are living with their parents, one might guess that grandparents and great-grandparents have less emotional impact on their descendants than in the past. Thus, praying to one's ancestors may not have the same emotional force it once had, while the strengthening of the nuclear family and the shift away from parental relationships in which unquestioned obedience was the norm means that emotional bonds with one's children may in fact be stronger. In other words, praying to one's ancestors may be becoming more of an obligation with less emotional significance for those participating. Belief in fetus ghosts may therefore reflect a shift in the emotions involved in familial relationships in which one's filial devotion has become less guaranteed than ever before.

5

The Haunting Fetus

A few years ago I went to a hospital and killed the baby in my body. One day after several years I felt that something was wrong. I sensed that there was a boy who was always behind me. When I turned back to see, there was nothing. I didn't believe in ghosts until the spirit made me sick. My family took me to stay in a temple instead of a hospital. After one month [. . .] I recovered. I didn't see the child in the temple because Buddha protected me when I was there. But when I went home I still felt there was someone behind me. I went to see a fortune-teller [*suanming*] and the man gave me a talismanic paper. I stuck the paper on the door and burned incense to the ghost as the fortuneteller told me to do. The fortuneteller also told me to go to a temple and set up a memorial plaque for the dead child. He said it would be better for me if I went to the temple every year to see the dead child. I set a place for the child in a temple as the man said.

Now I am the mother of three children. I think that one of my three children might have the spirit of my dead child because I have never felt nor seen the child again. (A thirty-nine-year-old housewife, Taibei)

THIS quotation describes an experience typical of women who have been afflicted by fetus-ghost hauntings. Feeling anxious but unsure of the reason, ill with no explanation, women often turn to spirit mediums, fortunetellers, and Daoist and Buddhist masters for help. Like countless others, this woman hoped and believed that the soul of her aborted fetus would be given another life as her offspring so that they could fulfill their fate together as mother and child in an environment that would be better for both of them. Thus, she gains the psychological benefit of not killing life but postponing it, thereby still fulfilling her motherly obligations to that particular child.

Personal accounts such as this one are often far less frightening than one might expect. Often there is a sense of relationship, and of reconciliation, with the ghost that distinguishes this belief from ideas about the ghosts of adult family members who are no longer to be loved but only feared. Other stories of fetus ghosts, which are often told by people not directly involved in hauntings, evoke a vision of fetus ghosts that is far more dreadful:

> [Little Wen] didn't tell her parents but lived with a boyfriend and had four abortions. Later she married her boyfriend and got pregnant twice, but she had miscarriages both times and her husband went broke. Because over ten years earlier she had had abortions, the cruelly killed fetus ghosts, still not completely formed and covered in blood, could not erase their hatred and resentment. Because the fetus ghosts hated their mother's cruelty they came back to demand retribution. (A thirty-six-year-old male government employee, Taibei)

This account portrays an equally popular conception of the ghost in that it is both angry and vengeful. These two accounts of a ghost overlap yet are quite distinct. They are similar in that in both cases those who have had abortions are afflicted through either physical or psychological health, finance, or a more general sense of things going awry. The difference lies in the intent of the spirit, in the level of resentment, and in the ghost's willingness to forgive, forget, and most important, go away.

Because a fetus-ghost haunting can occur many years after an abortion, such visitations are used to explain a wide range of illnesses, both physical and psychological, real and imagined. For the diviner, this time scale obviously works to bring in a wider clientele, but it also widens the range of people who can use the belief to their own advantage. In many instances fetus-ghost appeasement marks an aim to heal the individual both in body and in mind. It provides strength and solace, especially to women who are by and large left to fend for themselves with both the physical and emotional strain of having an abortion.

The belief that one multiplies one's sins through repeated abortions is emphasized in the concept that each additional abortion can lead to an additional fetus ghost. In the above account, for example, a woman who had had four abortions had a number of fetus ghosts haunting her. Although this is an extreme, the idea that repeated sins lead to increased retribution has been a prevalent theme in my interviews.

Yingling come from both miscarried and aborted fetuses, and occasionally a child who died in infancy. In Taiwan, as in other areas of the world, the issue of when life starts is complex. Chinese count one's age from the year of conception, not of birth. Also, a quick look at some of the Chinese terms for fetuses and infants is in order. As in English, the Chinese word for embryo (*peitai*) is followed by fetus (*taier*). The term *yinger*, however, includes later-stage fetuses and newborn infants, and can expand to include children as old as two. The first character of the word *yingling* is from *yinger*. This crossing of prenatal and postnatal status means that my translation of the term *yingling* as "fetus ghost" is not entirely accurate. This is further complicated by the fact that *yingling* is used to describe the ghosts of both fetuses and some young infants.[1] On the whole, however, because of the rising abortion rates and a decrease in natural deaths of infants, the majority of fetus ghosts in Taiwan are caused by abortion. Thus, infant *yingling* are the exception, not the rule; the vast majority are associated with abortion. In part this has to do with the larger percentage of women who have abortions, in part it reflects the fact that abortions are chosen whereas miscarriages are unintentional. This is true in an emic analysis, in that many people believe fetus ghosts take their parents' intentions into account. In many cases an aborted fetus ghost is thereby considered more likely to cause problems than a miscarried fetus ghost. From an etic perspective, one can make a credible case that the choice of having an abortion could produce guilt, and the people involved are therefore more prone to interpret illness and other calamities as being caused by fetus ghosts.

Fetus ghosts are almost never thought to remain as fetuses in the afterlife. Instead they are usually represented as having matured to a physical age range of one to five years old. Usually their mental capabilities reach far beyond this, and they are often thought to be omniscient. Because they lack the maturity to balance this knowledge, this makes them especially dangerous.

John Lagerway draws an important distinction between how one approaches ancestors' ghosts as opposed to exorcisms of malevolent spirits, emphasizing that ancestors are thought to contribute to family fortunes, whereas the primary goal with malevolent ghosts is their expulsion (Lagerway 1987: 218). With fetus ghosts, the case is somewhat more complex. While it is true that one wants to rid oneself of this troublesome and often dangerous spirit, the ghost is in a middle ground between the ghosts of ancestors/family and strangers. Unlike ancestors' spirits, one would not want fetus ghosts to remain. Yet as familial ghosts there is a concern for their welfare, which is quite distinct from how one might treat other malevolent spirits.

The period of greatest risk is in the two or three years after an abortion when a woman is dealing with its physical and emotional effects. Unexpectedly, another common period of risk is many years later. Women are especially vulnerable when they reach menopause and their *yin/yang* balance begins to change.[2] Because this time in Taiwanese women's lives is also marked by their children nearing or reaching adulthood, it is also a period of adjustment bringing many shifting relations that might result in conflicts within a family. Fetus ghosts are commonly used to strengthen otherwise disintegrating familial ties. For instance, if a parent and child are quarreling, it may be decided that the child has been possessed by an older "brother" or "sister" who was aborted. The appeasement process then provides a chance to focus the blame outside of the family.

The largest age group of those appeasing fetus ghosts is from sixteen to the late twenties; the second-largest age group is from the early thirties to the mid-fifties. Occasionally I met people in their sixties or older who appeased fetus ghosts, but this was rare. Thus, while the age range is more spread out than one might have guessed for a practice associated with reproduction, the people whom I interviewed did tend to be a bit younger than the average temple goer in Taiwan.[3]

When an older person's aborted or miscarried fetus harms a younger family member, it is usually the inflicted younger person who appeases the ghost. If the possessed person is a child, her or his parents will appease the ghost. Less commonly, someone's aborted fetus can harm an older member of the family. In this case, the mother or father of the aborted fetus will appease the ghost. Thus, the majority of people appeasing fetus ghosts tend to be young to middle-aged.

It is most commonly the woman who aborted a fetus or her children who are vulnerable to the haunting fetus, but her other relatives are also at risk. Although a man can be haunted by a fetus ghost, it is often the case that this is a result of his relationship with the mother of the fetus rather than any direct relationship to the spirit itself. Note, for example, the use of the word "husband" rather than "father" in the quoted account. Also notice that the fetus ghosts' anger is directed at their "mother's cruelty" rather than their "parents' cruelty." In a comparative perspective, we can associate this with the physical and emotional bond between mother and child, and with beliefs about a woman's role as caregiver in contrast to the male's more distant role as financial provider.

A Ghost with Better Odds

An important component of the growing participation in fetus-ghost appeasement is the promotion of the belief by fortunetellers, spirit mediums, and exorcists. Abortion has become prevalent enough that an exorcist can explain virtually any problem as being caused by a fetus ghost. To cite one of many examples of this, I once saw a fetus-ghost exorcist talking with a potential client who was having difficulty coping with a number of problems in her life, ranging from her father's recent death to having been abandoned by her fiancé.

When she went to the exorcist, he gave her a penetrating look and said, "There is a fetus ghost following you, have you had an abortion?" She seemed startled and replied, "No, I haven't." He frowned slightly before giving her another penetrating look, "And your mother?" he said, slowly nodding his head up and down and raising his eyebrows knowingly. Looking somewhat apologetic, she replied, "No, no. I don't think she has." The exorcist then inquired about her aunts and sisters, none of whom had had abortions to her knowledge, after which there was a long pause. Both of them seemed at a loss as to how to make this thing work. After a moment she hesitantly said, "I did accompany a friend while she had an abortion once, but that was years ago."[4] The exorcist jumped up excitedly. "That's it then!" he exclaimed triumphantly, wiping a bit of sweat from his brow with one hand while reaching for a cigarette with the other.

This kind of probing is quite typical and, if one were a gambler, a bet with extremely favorable odds. This is the only case I have heard of in which a woman was being haunted by a friend's fetus ghost. It is extremely common, however, for someone to emerge from such an encounter without achieving the desired result, only to return home to discover that her mother or another family member had in fact had an abortion or miscarriage that had not been previously discussed. Keeping the high rate of abortion in mind, if one includes one's mother, grand-mothers, aunts, and sisters as possible causes for fetus-ghost hauntings, the number of families that cannot be linked with fetus ghosts in some way is probably close to zero.

For those in the trade, an equally attractive aspect of the *yingling* is that it is far easier to blame a malady on fetus ghosts than to fault an adult ghost. In part this is because funeral ceremonies are not conducted for fetus ghosts, so in effect every fetus ghost has a legitimate grievance, and conveniently the same one. Also, a spirit medium, fortuneteller, or exorcist is more likely to say things about a deceased adult that do not accord with their clients' experiences or expectations. In the case of adult ghosts, spirit mediums and fortunetellers are expected to produce factual or descriptive information about the mannerisms of the deceased, as opposed to quite general statements about unborn ghosts with fairly standard speech and the kind of accusations that one might expect from an angry child. Thus, the growing popularity of fetus-ghost appeasement in Taiwan works in two directions. The first is that, because of the increasing rate of abortions in the last half of the century, there are more women, and sometimes men, who seek to make amends for abortions. The second is that, because of the prevalence of abortion and the unformed state of the fetus, people in the business of the occult have found a ghost with better odds.

As an offshoot of this, in Taibei, and no doubt in other cities, some men who claim to have the ability to see ghosts[5] approach women and tell them that they have fetus ghosts following them. I have met women who were approached on the street or by taxi drivers who initiated a conversation and then quickly moved on to say that the women had fetus ghosts following them. The man with the "third eye" would then offer quick absolution for a price. This is not limited to fetus ghosts. I knew one woman who was told by a taxi driver that she would have very bad luck in the next year unless she appeased the gods. He went on to say that for NT$3,000 (US$90) he would say prayers on her behalf and burn incense and buy rice for the poor, which would sway the gods to give her better luck. She gave the man the money on the grounds that it was better not to take chances. Again, the relative ease with which someone could portray the feelings and emotions of a fetus ghost, and the statistical probability that a woman would have some connection with an abortion, would increase the success of such random approaches.

Opposition to Fetus-Ghost Appeasement

In Taiwan, fetus-ghost exorcisms became a hotly debated topic in the late 1980s and early 1990s. As in Japan, critics of the practice in Taiwan assert that women are frightened into paying money to religious masters who promise to send the spirits on to their next lives. Those who have spoken out against the practice in the Taiwanese press have also suggested manipulation of another nature, stating that unscrupulous religious practitioners of fetus-ghost appeasement financially exploit women by playing on their guilt.[6]

This opposition ranges from newspaper articles that criticize fetus-ghost exorcists for using women's "guilt" about having abortions to make money (Anonymous 1989: 6; C. Cai 1988: 3; Ping 1994: 11; Tao 1992: 22; Yu 1992: 13) to interviews and informal conversations about abortion and fetus ghosts in which the same complaints are voiced. The following are but two of many examples of Taiwanese newspaper or magazine articles that discuss the self-blame and/or guilt that those who have had abortions can experience:

> One psychiatric counselor also discovered that most women who have had abortions have deep psychological pain, especially those who did not wish to have abortions; for instance, those whose partners abandon them or do not accept that they were the ones who got the women pregnant, etc. After a period of time after an abortion, those who have had abortions slowly begin to limit the blame to themselves, and have sorrow and other suffering. To the women, after the day [of the abortion] this will influence relations with members of the opposite sex or their marriages.
>
> Recently, some people in the religious sphere use "fetus ghosts," openly starting "new business" and encouraging those who have had abortions to spend money to ask temples to establish memorial tablets to set the women's hearts at rest. This kind of action is especially for women who have had abortions and blame themselves. (S. Lin 1989a: 13)

and

> Thus, for example, people can ease their sense of guilt and do pen-
> ance through the ceremony of "making offerings to the infant spirit."
> (C. Chang 1996: 19)

Similarly, those I interviewed also broached the topic of guilt as a primary factor in this belief:

> I think people believe in fetus ghosts because they feel guilty
> [*zuiegan*]. When pregnant women have abortions they feel
> guilty. And doctors or nurses who help to abort the fetuses feel
> guilty too because they are the ones who actually kill the babies.
> If people feel guilty, they will be scared. If people feel fright-
> ened, they might hallucinate and see some strange things that
> might not be true.
>
> I have a good friend who was pregnant when we were
> seniors in university. All our friends thought that this was ter-
> rible, because we were still students and her economic situa-
> tion didn't encourage her to give birth to the baby, so she went
> to the hospital and had an abortion. But the thing wasn't
> over. Even now, she often tells me of that experience and that
> she feels guilty, and because she believes in fetus ghosts, she
> thinks there must be a fetus ghost following her and she is
> very scared. (A twenty-six-year-old female secretary, Taibei)

The fact that patrons gain psychological comfort from fetus-ghost appeasement is not lost on the Daoist or Buddhist masters involved
with the practice. Teacher Lin and Ms. Xu, religious masters in two
fetus-ghost temples in Taiwan, both told me that many people who
come to their temples often do so out of a sense of guilt (*zuiegan*).

One group of critics, while also concerned with the financial exploitation associated with the practice, tends to attack the conception
of fetus ghosts by pointing out the ways in which it contrasts with
more traditional religious practice or belief. One article in particular
(C. Cai 1988: 3) cited an unusually wide range of objections based
on religious orthodoxy. The reasons given included the already mentioned Confucian hierarchical belief that parents should not pray to
their children, and went on to argue that in Buddhist belief aborted
or miscarried fetuses are automatically reborn forty-nine days after
their deaths (C. Cai 1988: 3). This article then goes on to focus on the
unformed nature of a fetus, suggesting that the birth time and date,
the sex, and the appearance of an aborted fetus are not clear, thereby
making it impossible to properly envision it, thus precluding the ability to direct prayers for its merit to the correct soul (C. Cai 1988: 3).

At the height of the public debate over fetus ghosts, the leader of a Buddhist temple in Gaoxiong, a city in southern Taiwan, even took out an advertisement to condemn the practice (Anonymous 1990: 3; C. Cai 1990: 1). Surprisingly, a Taibei temple that he had accused by name sued him for libel; even more surprisingly, the temple won (Anonymous 1990: 3; C. Cai 1990: 1). This case was symbolic both in the fact that the courts sided with the fetus-ghost temple and in that the controversy extended from the largest city in the south of Taiwan to the nation's capital in the north. After this case, an uneasy truce seemed to emerge in which critics of the practice became less outspoken in their censure and practitioners became less public in their efforts to attract new clients.

In some instances the critics hold views further removed from common Taiwanese belief than those involved in fetus-ghost appeasement itself. One example of this is a newspaper editorial in which the author states that "an abortion is nothing more than cutting off a piece of excess flesh" (Yu 1992: 13). In other instances the level of analysis is more sophisticated, such as in the following news article written by a popular editorialist in Taiwan:

> [. . .] in a hierarchical society, women who have and raise children will gradually, and without realizing it, begin to feel guilty. For instance, when children in the process of growing up do bad things, regardless if it is family or common opinion, criticisms are all aimed at the mother. She internalizes all these external societal influences and, as a result, before she even thinks about it she has already been deeply influenced. To take abortion as an example, the suffering of the abortion operation dooms the mother to have nightmares. If the abortion is because of financial problems or only because of a desire to have a boy, having an abortion takes away one's own daughter's right to life and the mother will have subconscious guilt. She will have deep regret and guilt! Recently a popular folk religious belief called "*yingling*" uses such women's guilt to make money.
>
> In the final analysis, in our society women's experiences of giving birth have been distorted in many ways. Therefore, they are controlled by many external forces, including businessmen who illegally make money in this bad way. If we reach for the most important point, the patriarchal system has visible and invisible means of control. (L. Ping 1994: 11)

Another common criticism has focused on the financial exploitation associated with the practice. Though more vocal, those condemning the practice are far fewer than either those practicing fetus-ghost appeasement or those who do not care one way or another. Buddhists can roughly be split into three camps on this matter: (1) those who condemn the practice; (2) those who neither practice fetus-ghost exorcisms nor condemn the custom as long as it is not financially exploitative (C. Cai 1988: 3; C. Chang 1996: 19); (3) those who engage in fetus-ghost appeasement. Of these categories, the second is by far the most common. Criticism from Daoists or from those practicing folk religion is far more rare.

I have just outlined the criticism that fetus-ghost appeasement enables greedy religious practitioners to extract large amounts of money from gullible people. The actual picture is more complex. Teacher Lin's temple, for example, charges an annual fee of NT$1,200 (US$35) for three years. A worshiper at Ms. Xu's temple will usually appease a fetus ghost for one or two months, most commonly paying a total of NT$1,480 (US$43). Streetside Daoist temples usually have neither memorial plaques nor statues, often preferring to exorcise the spirit directly and be done with it. Such exorcisms are more individualized and labor-intensive for the Daoist or Buddhist master, and far more expensive for the client. For example, I interviewed one woman who had paid an exorcist NT$20,000 (US$882) for a three-day ceremony to appease a fetus ghost that was repeatedly causing her son to fall ill. Although this is more than the usual fee, no one I spoke with seemed to think that it was an excessive amount to pay for such services.

Even in these cases one should ask what the clients gain from such expenditures. Mrs. Huang, the woman who paid NT$20,000 to exorcise a fetus ghost, was raised on a farm. Ten years earlier a company had bought the land she had inherited and she became rich beyond her wildest expectations. Not having graduated from high school, and quite rustic in her speech and mannerisms, Mrs. Huang is quite anxious to assert her status as a woman of wealth and leisure. She frequently brags of her contributions to temples, as well as the fact that she is thinking of funding a new temple's construction, and that she paid such high prices for her fetus-ghost appeasement. This prestige expenditure attests to the fact that the very expense of the exorcism was valuable to her, in that through it she declared her financial power as well as placing herself in a spiritually and morally superior position to her kin. Unlike financing elaborate funerals or founding temples, however, it is rare for fetus-ghost appeasement to become such a point of prestige because of the stigma of abortion. This problem was sidestepped quite nicely in this case, for the haunting was attributed to Mrs. Huang's deceased mother-in-law's dead child.

On a smaller scale, it may be that larger expenditures help the person to feel that the significant expense signifies a higher level of repentance and moral reform. In the case of an offspring being haunted, it may also be that the amount spent can be used to demonstrate to the child the parent's willingness to sacrifice for her or his welfare. These points are part of my own interpretation, not an indigenous one, for when prices are suggested by a religious master it is normally taken as an acceptable expense for the services offered.

The financially exploitative nature of much of fetus-ghost appeasement has been the focus of most public criticism, and there are no doubt many cases in which this is true. But to truly understand the resistance to this belief, one must look at other factors, for Taiwan is full of spirit mediums, religious masters, exorcists, and fortunetellers who charge huge sums for their services. For some perspective, consider one news article covering the story of a pet cemetery in Taibei that charges NT$3,000 (US$88) a year to keep the ashes of cremated animals (Kyne 1998: 8).[7] Unlike Xu's temple, which usually appeases a ghost for two months, or Teacher Lin's temple, which does so for three years, the pet cemetery's annual fee has no set end point. To compare the price of fetus-ghost appeasement to other services offered by local temples, I know one woman who paid a Daoist master over NT$10 million (US$293,800) over a period of three years for assistance with a variety of problems ranging from advice on financial investments to her marital difficulties. In the end her investments failed, her husband left her, and the Daoist master, aware of who actually earned the money, sided with her husband. The costs of fetus-ghost appeasements that I have cited above pale in comparison. Also, because of the abstract nature of the results of fetus-ghost appeasement, practitioners are more likely to deliver on their promises.

Why should fetus-ghost appeasement draw criticism for its costs from people who ignore greater abuses? I suggest that it is primarily because fetus-ghost appeasement is relatively new. Most other forms of religious practice in Taiwan have been around as long as anyone can remember. If a fault is found, it is attributed to the rapaciousness of a practitioner or to the excess of his claims; the system itself is not called into question. In the case of fetus-ghost appeasement, however, accusations can be aimed not only against a few practitioners but also against the very belief itself. Nonetheless, for the most part fetus-ghost appeasement is tolerated, and a growing number of people in Taiwan have come to believe in *yingling*.

Six Portrayals of *Yingling*

As Duara has noted in relation to the mythology surrounding the god Guangdi, there is an "interpretive arena" for religious belief in that there are multiple competing images within any given one (Duara 1988: 780). In this way, older versions are transformed over time, with new elements gaining importance to meet contemporary needs (Duara 1988: 780).

One of the most exciting aspects of researching belief in fetus ghosts in Taiwan is that these changes in representation are occurring right now. Because of its newness, there is not yet a fully established or widely accepted view of fetus ghosts' actions or of the proper way to appease them. Thus, we can watch the shifts and contrasting developments of belief in ghosts and appeasement as they emerge. I will now address six different depictions of fetus ghosts. Although these are all thought to be *yingling*, their actions and characteristics differ quite dramatically.

Beneficent Fetus Ghosts

In rare instances, a fetus ghost is thought not only to love its parents but also to bring them good luck. I have only met three people involved in such cases, though I have heard of others. One of these was Little Huang, a twenty-nine-year-old unmarried female white-collar worker living in Taibei:

> LITTLE HUANG: My Daoist master has a third eye and can see the other world. He told me that if I turn around quickly when I am in the dark I will see my *yingling*.
>
> MOSKOWITZ: Did you look to see if it is there?
>
> LITTLE HUANG: No I didn't look. What if it's as ugly as me? Then I'd really be in trouble! [laughs] Actually, my *yingling* protects me. It

protects me from car accidents and other problems. My *shifu*[8] said I shouldn't eat meat. He said that this would help my fetus ghost go on to its next life more quickly.

Like most believers in fetus ghosts, Little Huang cannot actually see the ghost herself. Unlike a man I interviewed whose family intended to provide for their benevolent fetus ghost indefinitely, Little Huang was seeking to send her fetus ghost on to its next life in spite of the fact that it was helping her. When I asked why, she said: "Sure, it protects me, but it shouldn't be a ghost forever. It has the right to be reborn, don't you think?" Little Huang's concern for the welfare of her *yingling* does not conform to the criticisms I outlined in the previous section. In this account, Little Huang does not fear the ghost but gains comfort from it; she does not appease it because she has been coerced by the threatening nature of the spirit, but does so out of concern for its welfare.

Location-Associated Fetus Ghosts

Although more common than beneficent *yingling*, fetus ghosts that haunt a location rather than a person seem to be more common in ghost stories than in actual experience. I have heard many stories of fetus ghosts haunting places, but in all of my interviews I have never heard a firsthand, or even a secondhand, account of this kind. This form of fetus ghost is not connected with a particular person. Instead, the ghosts stay at a particular location, usually the hospital they were aborted in, either because their parents have died or because their fate with their mother was not strong. Such fetus ghosts are usually thought to be mischievous rather than malevolent. A twenty-two-year-old male university student told me the following:

> This is a true story. A man had a toy store but there was something mysterious going on there. He cleaned the store every evening, but it was always a mess in the morning. Why? He always thought about this. One day, he put a video camera on the wall and watched the VCR in the morning. He was surprised because he saw many children playing with the toys. He asked his neighbor what had been in the building before he had a store there. The neighbors told him that there was a gynecological clinic there before his store. Many fetuses had died there.

Another example is a chapter in a book of "true" stories about fetus ghosts that relates a similar account in which more than twenty fetus ghosts haunt a house because it was once a hospital where they had been aborted (X. Zhong 1994a: 44–83). In this story the man who had recently bought the house could not sleep because he kept hearing someone jumping around on the roof. The most grievous thing these ghosts did was to shout a few insults and dirty words at the author. In both the account given in my interview and that given by the author of this book, the vision of fetus ghosts is one in which they are less harmful than annoying, doing nothing that any group of children allowed to play alone at night would not do. The next four categories of fetus ghosts are far more often encountered than the two I have just presented. The malevolent fetus ghost is perhaps the most common, but the other categories also come up frequently.

Malevolent Fetus Ghosts

A very common depiction of a haunting fetus is as a vengeful spirit who is angry about having been murdered and losing its chance to enter the world. This perception of the ghost is especially widespread among those who are not involved in the practice in any way. I met one woman who believed that her chronic cough was caused by such a ghost. Her illness was so severe that she could not complete a sentence without having a coughing fit. I met another woman who told me she had a mental breakdown because of her angry fetus ghost. One woman I interviewed had recurring nightmares of her fetus emerging out of the darkness. Its face had become black and its large white eyes bulged as it silently pointed an accusing finger at its mother. She was understandably very upset about these nightmares, which were taken as a legitimate haunting by her family members. She later sought a fetus-ghost exorcism, after which the dreams stopped. In this form, the *yingling* is a malevolent spirit that has come for revenge in the form of causing nightmares, illness, insanity, and/or death. In such accounts, fetus ghosts are thought to be vengeful and highly dangerous.

The malevolent fetus ghost is the closest to traditional Taiwanese conceptions of ghosts. Stevan Harrell, for instance, says of more traditional ghosts that a ghost that has died from unnatural causes "remains angry and will prey on the innocent living, not so much in desperation as out of resentment and desire for revenge" (Harrell

1986: 99). An interesting point to consider is that the image of fetus ghosts that most commonly comes under criticism in the press is in fact the closest to other traditional ghosts in their malevolence.

Fetus Ghosts That Harm without Intent

Malevolence is not always attributed to fetus ghosts. Sometimes the ghosts have no intent to harm, but their excess of *yin* energy naturally causes illness. At other times the victims are unsure of the ghosts' motivations but nevertheless have been negatively affected by the ghosts. A female factory worker in her mid-twenties told me the following:

> I met a man who can see some things we cannot see. There are some statues in his house and many people go there to pray. I was feeling muscle pain without reason, so I went to his house to pray too. After I prayed, he murmured something and yelled: "Get away, go back to your seat. Do not bother this woman anymore!" He said to me: "When you were young you had an abortion but you didn't arrange the proper religious rites for it so it is coming back to you now. I told the ghost to stay away, so from now on you should be all right."

When I asked her why the ghost was harming her she said, "I don't think it wanted to hurt me, but it's bad for people's health to have ghosts hanging around."

Fetus ghosts that harm without intent and malevolent fetus ghosts cause many of the same illnesses. One difference is that those that harm by their presence rather than out of malevolent intent tend not to cause nightmares. Nor do they usually cause psychological or behavioral problems. Like the malevolent fetus ghost, however, they can cause severe physical illness, sometimes leading to death.

Pitiful Fetus Ghosts

Robert Weller has suggested that the status of those who died will also influence the perceptions about their ghosts, reasoning that, while people worship gods and ancestors out of respect and fear, ghosts, as marginal kinsmen, are worshiped out of pity rather than terror (Weller 1987: 66). Though one should not underemphasize the degree to which people do indeed fear ghosts, Weller's provocative stance that a growing perception of "pitiful kinship ghosts" in Taiwan has evolved from a like change in the disenfranchised living population (Weller 1987: 85, 1994: 125) also applies to the case of fetus-ghost appeasement. In general, fetus ghosts, by virtue of their aborted status, are natural candidates for pity. In accounts of pitiful fetus ghosts the spirit is not thought to be powerful or all-knowing but, rather, highly vulnerable. Such accounts often portray *yingling* as being cold, hungry, and scared, not understanding why they were "abandoned" by their parents. In such a view, fetus ghosts are also vulnerable to older and larger ghosts, who might steal their food or just pick on them for fun.

We can see a good example of pitiful *yingling* in one of Teacher Lin's morality texts:

> *Yingling* are very pitiful. The place they inhabit does not have sunlight, they don't have a place with a roof over their heads, so when it rains they get soaked and when it snows it is so cold their skin turns red. This gets so bad that one can see them huddling together for warmth. They suffer in this way day after day, and only after fifty years of this will they go on to their next lives [unless someone provides for them]. (S. Lin 1996c: 72)

Sometimes the categories I have outlined overlap. For instance, a location associated with a fetus ghost might also be portrayed as a pitiful *yingling* that, because of its excess of *yin*, harms its relatives without intending to.

Anxiety-Related Fetus Ghosts

In the previous five sections, people's experiences with fetus ghosts were fairly concrete in that they either had direct contact with the ghosts or were directly affected by them in some way. An equally large group of people appeasing fetus ghosts have never had these experiences; rather, they have a generalized feeling of guilt and wish to do something to atone for their abortions.

Ms. Liu lives in a small town in southern Taiwan. She is a "little wife" (*xiaolaopo*), a term used to signify a married man's mistress. Usually such a woman's partner would make a life commitment to the younger woman, buying her a house and helping to raise their children. But the father of Ms. Liu's children found yet another lover, roughly fifteen years younger than Ms. Liu. He had long ago bought Ms. Liu her own house and continues to provide money for their children, but Ms. Liu, who has had no formal work experience and has not attended university, is acutely aware that her partner's new mistress has left her in a precarious financial situation, so she is now looking for a legal husband. Ms. Liu is thirty-five years old with an eleven-year-old daughter and a six-year-old son and realizes her marriage prospects are not good.[9]

> Ms. Liu: You know, men are really rotten. They always want younger women; that's their father for sure, left me for a twenty-year-old and now I have to look for a new husband at my age and with two kids. So that's why I go to the temple to appease my fetus ghost. I already have two children and I don't have a man anymore. When I got pregnant what could I do [but get an abortion]?
>
> Moskowitz: Why did you decide to go to —— temple?
>
> Ms. Liu: I don't know. I had heard about the temple from a friend and I felt bad about the abortion. I mean, I had to do it but I still don't feel good about it. I love my children and I'd do anything for them, but every time I look at them it reminds me of the abortion that I had. That's why I go to the temple [to provide for the ghost of the aborted fetus]. I hope my baby can be reborn and I hope that it will be happy.

As in the above account, many of those I interviewed expressed feelings of helplessness and self-blame for their abortions. In these cases, appeasing the ghost relieves a general sense of guilt.

In many instances, fetus-ghost appeasement is like other ghost appeasement in which an afflicted person will more or less buy off a ghost to alleviate her or his own suffering. In these situations it is easy to criticize the practice, for women are frightened into paying money to alleviate fears that have, in a sense, been created by the very exorcists who offer assistance. But the anxiety-related haunting fetus also brings out more altruistic motivations. Those appeasing the ghost are concerned with the fate of their aborted children and provide for them, not only to buy them off as with other ghosts, but also to ease their suffering. In fact it is this category that shows the practice in its best light, both in bringing to the surface the humanity of those who have had abortions and in producing the positive psychological effects of the practice and belief. This version of fetus ghosts is perhaps the least closely associated with traditional thought but seems to be growing.

Fetus Ghosts as Antiabortion Propaganda: Morality Tracts

In the mid-eighties, Daoist and Buddhist masters left antiabortion fetus-ghost tracts in the waiting rooms of clinics, hospitals, and bus stations. Now, although one can still find other religious tracts in such places, fetus-ghost tracts are conspicuously absent.[10] I suspect this is part of the uneasy truce between critics and practitioners of fetus-ghost appeasement that I noted earlier.

I will now provide excerpts from three morality texts. Cai Wen's morality tract is fairly typical in length, only six pages, which are in fact folded out of one sheet of paper. The other two texts are book-length and are sold at bookstores.

Ms. Xu's Text

The following excerpt is from a book-length morality text written by Xu Qiongyue, who refers to herself as Ms. Xu.

> European and American nations are Protestant and Catholic nations and do not believe in *yingling*, karma, or reincarnation. But if we look at it from the Buddhist perspective [*guandian*], when an unmarried or married woman accidentally gets pregnant and then has an abortion, the aborted child's spirit will continue to stay by its mother's side. And because abortion is the killing of life, it is like murdering one's son or daughter with one's own hands. Because of this, the heart of the soul of such a son or daughter is full of hatred and resentment. Such a spirit is always by its mother's side, waiting for the moment when its mother gets pregnant again so that it can take the first opportunity to enter its mother's womb [to be reborn as her next child]. When a woman has an abortion she creates bad karma, which exists in the form of the killed fetus's hate and resentment. This is why when most women who have had abortions later decide to give birth, their children's hearts are full of hatred and rebelliousness beyond that of other children. (Xu 1995: 5–6)

Ms. Xu's vision of the malevolent fetus ghost conforms to the portrayal used by critics of the belief and practice. Yet Ms. Xu's temple is one of the most affordable that I have seen. In several of my interviews with her she spoke of the resentful and hateful aspect of fetus ghosts. Each time, however, she was careful to emphasize that fetus ghosts knew the reasons for which they were aborted and understood the sincerity of the parents' repentance. Thus, in Ms. Xu's vision of fetus ghosts there is a sliding scale of resentment and retribution according to the parents' actions and the sincerity of their regret.

Ms. Xu is very much concerned with using such stories to discourage abortion. Almost every interview I had with her concluded with her thanking me for helping to spread the news of fetus ghosts to the United States, reasoning that this would discourage Americans from having abortions. Ms. Xu's text is a perfect example of the images upon which critics of fetus-ghost appeasement have focused. Yet, as with many accounts of fetus ghosts, Ms. Xu's conception of *yingling* contains a tension in which hatred and love coexist.

Cai Wen's Tract

Four different Daoist temples are associated with this next tract, three in Gaoxiong and one in Taibei. Cai Wen is the head of all four of these temples.

> The term *yingling* belongs to a category of not yet fully developed souls. It cannot harm anyone, and an infant who dies at birth has fate with its parents but not a fate that can endure [*you yuan wu fen*]. This is not a true relationship between relatives. Naturally there is no fetus ghost that specializes in looking for its parents to "haunt" them.
>
> Because people misunderstand, the term "fetus ghost" has come to mean an evil spirit. This makes women panic. In society there are a lot of sorcerers [*wushi*] and you cannot avoid asking yourself if you are doing the right thing or not. In civilized countries, men and women must work hard together to protect their children. Unlucky infants who die at birth have no way to become people and we should of course give special blessing to fetus ghosts. We hope that they can go on to their next lives earlier so that they may continue their fates in this world. Under heaven, if fetus ghosts truly have souls and have knowledge, then they should know their parents' hearts and that their parents are painfully sorry for their fetus ghosts. Thus, the ghosts couldn't add to their parents' troubles. (W. Cai n.d.: 2)

As in the materials I discussed earlier in this chapter, fetus-ghost appeasement in the above account is presented as a comfort to both parents and ghosts. This morality tract emphasizes that abortion is wrong while simultaneously trying to dispel the fears of the progenitors of the fetus. The above statement that the fetus ghosts "should know their parents' hearts and that their parents are painfully sorry for their fetus ghosts" once again emphasizes a relationship of love and forgiveness with the ghost rather than one of fear. If one takes this as a manipulation by the Buddhist master in order to earn money, one should also note that it relies on the conception of mutual care and pity, offering services to protect the ghost rather than asking the parents to contribute money out of fear.

Rather than blaming the parents, Cai Wen asserts that parents and their aborted fetuses do not have "a fate that can last," and that the spirits were aborted because they are "unlucky." This connects with my earlier presentation of traditional beliefs explaining infants' deaths. Along the same lines, the parent–child hierarchies outlined earlier also come into play here. The fetus ghost is portrayed as a vulnerable child who deserves special care, thus emphasizing the parent's role as protector of her or his offspring. Yet when Cai Wen states that the fetus ghosts should "know their parents' hearts" and "sorrow," the spirits are essentially asked to understand that their parents sometimes must make decisions in circumstances beyond their control. This implies that the parents should have the right to make such a decision if the situation warrants it. On the other hand, in explaining the parents' lack of control, the fetus ghosts are put in a position of judging their parents, assessing the parents' motivations and feelings, and deciding not to "add to their parents' troubles." Though Cai Wen seems to believe that the spirits would naturally decide to forgive their parents, the fact that the children are in the position to forgive, and therefore to judge, provides further support for the idea that this belief marks a reversal of traditional conceptions about parent–child hierarchies.

Teacher Lin's Tract: The Worm Mutilator

Lin Jianyi, who refers to himself as Teacher Lin, is the head of Dragon Lake Temple, which is the largest fetus-ghost temple in Taiwan. In the last few years, Dragon Lake Temple has appeased over five thousand fetus ghosts a year. Teacher Lin is the author of dozens of book-length morality texts and wrote the following account, in which he quotes an anonymous woman who presumably came to him for help.

> I am the mother of three boys. My two oldest children are normal,
> their grades are okay, nothing to worry about. But my youngest son

made me worry. He was not like other children. When he was two years old he was only able to say a few sentences. He was at an age when he should have been able to start speaking. I didn't know why but he wouldn't speak, and when he did speak it was only to say "no" [*bu yao*]. He wouldn't say anything but that. If others spoke with him he would never laugh. He preferred to spend his time watching television by himself. The only time he would laugh was when he was cutting worms to pieces, it was really weird.

When you have a child you will of course have strong feelings for him, and when you don't know how to teach him you will be very worried. He was growing up; he went to kindergarten and then to elementary school but he was still a loner without friends. And at this time he had begun to throw rocks at the neighbors' cats and dogs or used sticks to hit them while laughing loudly to himself. What was this all about? I didn't know what to do until one day a friend introduced me to Dragon Lake Temple. [. . .] Many years ago, because I was sick I went to a hospital for a medical examination. Because I was afraid I would give birth to a deformed child I had an abortion. Whenever I think about this I am very sad. Although I very much regretted getting an abortion I was so busy looking after my children that I forgot to pray for the fetus ghost properly. It was only after I heard the explanation from the temple that I knew that my child was being stirred up by a resentful fetus ghost. This explained why he was acting the way he was. After the master at Dragon Lake Temple explained that my child was possessed, they exorcised the spirit. It made my heart glad to hear their chanting, and it was not long before my entire body felt comfortable. My heart was so happy and I was very happy to return home. As soon as I opened my front door my child gave me a bright smile and said, "You've come home." I had never seen my son smile in this way, I was shocked. So many years of problems that no medicine could cure were wiped out as soon as the spirit was expelled. After this, the child became more and more lively and quick and that dark period in our life disappeared. Suddenly my son would happily tell our family that it was time to study and he would go to do his homework without anyone asking him to. He even stopped killing worms and hunting small animals and he began to take part in every kind of organized activity. It was like he had changed into a different person, I could not have been happier!

From this we can see how horrible it can be when a fetus ghost possesses someone. For the good of other women I have told my own experience. I hope that every young woman and married woman will remember this well. Don't casually have abortions, you should protect the lives of the young. (J. Lin 1996a: 100–102)

Whether one takes this story to be true as is intended, or as a representative situation meant to prove the effectiveness of fetus-ghost appeasement (and of Teacher Lin's temple), it is very telling. In either case, and in spite of the exaggerated speed and completeness of healing, it provides us with a feeling for the conceptions of personality change that fetus ghosts can cause. The woman in this account is intended to serve as a warning to others, who are in this way told that their abortions could not only lead to suffering for their aborted fetuses but also cause their other family members serious ills as well.

Like Cai Wen's tract, this account exhibits marketing strategies that are far more sophisticated than has previously been acknowledged. In these texts we can see an approach that exploits patrons' fear and guilt while simultaneously offering comfort, not only in the form of protection against malevolence but a means of fulfilling one's desired role as a parent by caring for the aborted "children" whom they feel they have wronged. In looking at the issue from this perspective we can better understand the unstated marketing strategies of the practitioners as well as what this new practice has to offer to satisfy needs that were not being met by more traditional religious beliefs.

Critics of the practice might point out that all of the quoted texts serve to generate income. Cai Wen's tract was paid for by a contributor, and its last page is a form asking for voluntary contributions to help publish more fetus-ghost morality tracts. The other two texts do not ask for money directly but, like Cai Wen's tract, do include the addresses of the temples. In effect, then, all three of these texts act as advertising. In fairness, however, they also have the goal of helping people and improving society's ills. Cai Wen's text attempts to alleviate fears of the more stereotyped version of fetus ghosts; and while the other two tracts include a component of fear of the ghost's malevolence, in interviews both Teacher Lin and Ms. Xu emphasized the comfort that fetus-ghost appeasement provides to their patrons as well as their hope that their tracts will help to discourage future abortions.

This chapter has had two aims. The first has been to describe this new practice in Taiwan. The second is the hope that in presenting a fuller range of beliefs concerning fetus ghosts we can gain a well-rounded view of the practice. This is not to deny accusations that have been leveled against it—I have outlined a wide range of marketing strategies used to manipulate potential clients—but rather to suggest that the practice is more than just a few religious extortionists using a group of women who are passive and easily deceived victims. As Margery Wolf has so eloquently pointed out, it is a mistake to "accept the stereotype of Chinese women as so many uterine pawns in a male system" (M. Wolf 1974: 159).

The dramatic nature of ghost malevolence often leads to an undue focus on the ills that ghosts create. As Li Yih-yuan has pointed out for ancestor worship, however, the most basic component of such rituals is that they enhance already existing emotional bonds with their ghost relatives (Y. Li 1985: 267, 270). Religious masters who deal in fetus ghosts do not create guilt out of a vacuum as much as they accentuate already existing feelings that are derived from a range of traditional beliefs about parenthood, the spirit world, and morality. In presenting the issue in such black-and-white terms, critics of the practice seem to overlook the fact that this new phenomenon is based on more traditional beliefs that also rely on what might be called a commodification of sin, in which it is possible to make amends for one's wrongdoings by sacrificing one's money (in its many forms) as a sign of sincere repentance.

In reality, the marketing of the belief in fetus ghosts and their appeasement is less sinister, and far more sophisticated, than it has been portrayed. In addition to images of the malevolent fetus ghost and issues of guilt that are so often mentioned in critiques of the practice, other portrayals emphasize a concern for the welfare of the spirit of the aborted fetus and the love between mother and child. This belief provides an arena for women to share their reasons for having abortions, to express remorse, and to actively redress past wrongs; thus they can strive to gain comfort and restore familial harmony. If the practice has swindlers and crooks, it also has people who are sincerely striving for such moral aims as preventing abortions, comforting women who have had them, and ending the suffering of the souls of deceased fetuses. One does not have to agree with the religious premises, the gender assumptions, or the stance on abortion on which the practice of fetus-ghost appeasement is based to acknowledge these positive elements.

Hase-dera Temple, Japan. Jizō statues wearing garments hand-knitted by the people appeasing the ghosts.

Dragon Lake Temple courtyard. Worshiper burning money for the fetus ghosts and the gods.

Above: Dragon Lake Temple courtyard during the semiannual ceremony. Worshipers follow a Buddhist chanting group.

Below: Praying on the main floor of the fetus-ghost building at Dragon Lake Temple.

Fetus-ghost statues and gifts on the lower floor at Dragon Lake Temple.

Above: Fetus-ghost statues at Dragon Lake Temple.

Below: Dragon fountain at Dragon Lake Temple.

The cover of one of Teacher Lin's morality tracts. The drawing shows a little girl doing mischievous things because she is being controlled by ghosts.

Outside of Ms. Xu's temple, Taibei.

6
Written and Visual Media

I N the previous chapter I outlined six different personas of fetus ghosts and used examples from urban myth, people's own accounts, newspaper articles, and morality tracts. I now turn to visual media and other written accounts of the ghost. These accounts provide a further illustration of the diversity of portrayals of fetus ghosts. Also, as did the morality tracts I have already presented, these accounts help to shape people's views of the spirit and provide potential appeasers with conceptual frameworks of how one should deal with the ghost.

Yingling: **The Movie**

A movie came out in the early 1980s entitled *Yingling* (Ding n.d.). I was expecting a horror movie where fetus ghosts maimed, mutilated, and destroyed. Instead, it turned out to be a drama that set out to discourage abortion and to present conceptions of fetus ghosts and ways to appease them. In this movie the fetus ghost was by and large portrayed as a victim rather than a malevolent or harmful spirit.

The plot of the movie revolves around two women. One is an unmarried college student named Mingming who is impregnated when she is raped by her classmates. The other woman is Mingming's boyfriend's older sister, Mrs. Li. The movie begins when Mingming sneaks out of her house to join her boyfriend, Wang Kai, at a disco. Wang Kai is greeted by a female friend and goes to dance with her. Mingming, left on her own, is given drugged chocolate by two classmates, who later lure her to their van and rape her.

Later, a group of students is sitting in a sex-education class including Mingming, Wang Kai, and the two students who raped her.

Wang Kai, who has left Mingming because she had sex with the others in spite of the fact that he knows she did not consent, ignores her until her rapists begin taunting her in front of the class, at which point he steps in to fight with them. During the fight, one of the rapists trips and his forehead is impaled by another student's pen. He staggers toward Mingming and dies on her lap, leaving a rather ominous blood-stain on the midsection of her dress—subtlety is not a characteristic of this movie.

Later, Mingming returns to the hospital she went to after being raped and learns that she has been impregnated by one of her rapists. She asks the intern to give her an abortion but he refuses because he is not yet a doctor. In a later scene Mingming is eating with the intern. Noticing that she is adding quite a few hot peppers to her soy sauce, he warns her that it would not be good for the baby. She responds: "Good, I want to burn it to death . . . I tried jumping rope, falling down the stairs, boxing, taking a hot bath, none of this was any use." Apparently the intern is finally moved, either by her story or by her reckless abandon in eating hot peppers, for in the next scene he gives her an abortion while indulging in his neurotic behavior of brushing his teeth when he is nervous. This emphasizes his distress over having given Mingming an abortion, and he continues to brush his teeth in every scene for the rest of the movie. It also contrasts him with the real doctor, who casually says: "I've [given abortions] hundreds of times. To me it's just like brushing my teeth."

Mingming tries to reapproach Wang Kai, who rebuffs her, saying, "Go ahead and eat more drugged chocolates, see if I care." Later, she disappears at the beach and everyone assumes she has drowned. She appears at the end of the movie, however, revealing that she had been saved by a group of fishermen and had spent the preceding few months on their boat. Apparently, being surrounded by fishermen was good for her, for she no longer talks to herself, seems calm and relaxed, and returns a wiser woman who understands fetus ghosts.

Running parallel to this story is that of Mrs. Li and her husband. Mrs. Li is pregnant, but both she and her husband feel overwhelmed by the two children they already have. The husband presses Mrs. Li to have an abortion but she refuses. Later in the movie, Mrs. Li falls down a staircase and is rushed to the hospital. The doctor aborts the fetus in the process of saving her life. Although she did not choose to have the abortion, she very much blames herself for it. To illustrate this point, in one scene her boss points to a crucifix on his wall, telling her to swear before the crucifix that she has not had an abortion. After a moment's pause she states, "In the name of Jesus I confess that I killed my third child."[1] This was not in fact true, as she both opposed having an abortion and was unconscious when it took place.

The movie makes some pointed statements about the nature of male–female relationships in Taiwan, both intended and otherwise. The following is Mrs. Li's angry condemnation of her husband after he has raped her.

> When you want [sex] you definitely have to have it. What do you think you are? You want it, but what about me? If I get pregnant you still won't let me have the child, you still won't accept responsibility. You forced me to secretly have an abortion. What do you want from me? I'm just a machine, a tool. You want me to have sex with you day or night, when you are angry, when you are drunk, even when you win the lottery you want to have sex. Damn you! You're not made of flesh and blood. I refuse you in the name of [the aborted fetus]. I refuse you, you selfish father!

The husband is close to being schizophrenic in the way he pendulates from being a sympathetic and loving husband who says he cares about his wife and the fetus ghost to a man who tries to rape her several times (once successfully), strikes her, and locks her in the bathroom while he prepares to detect and then exterminate his fetus ghost.

The husband's intellectual approach to the ghost shows the same erratic nature as his emotional reverses. At times he makes speeches on how fetus ghosts do not exist. At another point he states that as a father he is naturally concerned for the fetus ghost. The rest of the time he refers to the spirit as "the enemy" and describes how he will defeat the ghost for the betterment of mankind and to prove that he as the father and patriarch has the right to do what he pleases with his offspring.

As the movie progresses, Mrs. Li's husband becomes more and more obsessed with the idea of disproving the existence of the fetus ghost, or destroying it if it does exist. In the climax of the movie, he asks for the help of his neighbors, Wang Kai, the internist, and approximately ten scientists (working with infrared video equipment and cameras, a sound sensor, a ghost-warning alarm, and other ghost-

detecting gadgets as well as a 10,000-volt ray gun that is fired several
times in the house to destroy the fetus ghost). He also enlists two
policemen, who run around the house with machine guns, and representative priests from three religions—Daoism, Buddhism, and Christianity. A police car and a manned fire engine wait outside just in
case something goes wrong. Yet he criticizes his wife for being a fool
to think that fetus ghosts exist despite the facts that he believes he
has been hit by a ghost motorcyclist and that he has amassed this
small arsenal to destroy the spirit. The husband's speeches and incon-
sistencies makes him a caricature incapable of real empathy or
predictability. As a whole, the movie implies that such is the nature
of men.

The movie is equally telling in the assumptions it makes about
other gender relations. As in other depictions of fetus ghosts, there
is a strong mother–child/ghost bond that contrasts with the men's
relationships with the ghost, which range from nonexistent to antago-
nistic. Although the movie is sympathetic to both Mingming and Mrs.
Li, their position is often unquestioned. For example, the morning
after Mingming is raped, her mother, who does not know what happened, warns her against going out with her short-skirted friend,
saying that no good will come of it. Thus the movie implies, intentionally or unintentionally, that Mingming more or less got what was
coming to her.

Another example is Wang Kai, who repeatedly fights with Mingming's rapists because of their act but also ostracizes Mingming. Although the movie is clearly sympathetic to Mingming in her abandon-
ment, at no point does anyone point out to Wang Kai that she did
not plan on being raped or that he might be more supportive to her.
In general the movie is not lacking in pointed statements, so the
absence of such a speech stands out. Instead, both Wang Kai's violent
behavior toward the rapists and his ostracism of Mingming seem to
be presented as natural male instincts.

The relationship between Mrs. Li and her husband is equally revealing. In several scenes the husband tries to force his wife to have sex
with him (once he succeeds; once she manages to kick him off the
bed; and once she knees him in the groin, thereby dropping him to
the floor, and tells him she wants a divorce). Toward the end of the
movie, however, Mrs. Li and her husband are shown as reconciled,
for he carries her to the bedroom as she semiplayfully hits him in pro-

test. While this is going on, her brother looks on in smiling approval —the line between domestic strife and domestic bliss in this portrayal is a thin one indeed.

The movie presents several conflicting images of the ghost. In one scene Wang Kai is talking to Mrs. Li and her husband. He heatedly tells them that he had just seen Mingming who said she wanted to kill herself. "And over what? Because of a *yingling*. [. . .] If a woman has an abortion the fetus becomes a fetus ghost. It will always follow her and keep tormenting her! It will make her sick and make her feel bad, and can kill her! A fetus ghost was driving Mingming to drown herself!" In another scene, Mrs. Li and her husband go to a Buddhist temple, where the Buddhist master says: "In Buddhism, fetuses have souls too. Read the canons and you'll find those who have abortions go to hell. The aborted fetus becomes an angry ghost." Mrs. Li's husband says, "I've heard the fetus won't forgive its parents and even brings calamities on them." To this the Buddhist master replies: "If the parents practice the Buddhist rules, ghosts and disasters can't harm them. But if the parents continue to sin, they will have no end of disasters and ghosts. So Buddhists have to cultivate themselves [*xiuxing*] and provide salvation for angry ghosts." Later Mrs. Li and her mother go to a different Buddhist temple that appeases fetus ghosts.[2] The Buddhist master tells them:

> Married or not, regardless of destiny, a person who kills a fetus is repaid
> with a short life. Ghosts will chase the guilty causing trouble, breaking
> up families, and even causing death. Are your shoulders numb, your
> back hurts? [. . .] That is because it hangs on your back and neck all
> day, of course your back and neck are uncomfortable.

Mingming's aborted fetus never really gains individual status. Instead Mingming has a few dreams in which she sees many fetus ghosts on Hopeless Bridge (Naihe Qiao),[3] where an unnamed being from the underworld waves his sword menacingly. The Lis' fetus ghost plays a larger role, but it is fairly passive in the movie. It never speaks and is shown only toward the end, when it crawls up the stairs like a normal child, though glowing in a ghostlike way. The fetus ghost also makes toys move, the fetus-ghost statue glows, and the fetus itself glows after being thrown in a dumpster after the abortion.[4] The married couple's fetus ghost does not bear resentment toward its family for the abortion. On the contrary, in a dream it leads its mother to the house where its kidnapped older sister is being held. If antagonism exists, it is purely on the part of the living (Mrs. Li's husband), not the ghost.

The couple's lives do dramatically change for the worse after the fetus is dead, however. For one thing, there is a marked tension between Mrs. Li, who wanted the child, and her husband, who exerted pressure for an abortion. Also, Mrs. Li, who was up for promotion, is fired by her Christian boss, who does not approve of her abortion. While pregnant, Mrs. Li attributed their narrow escape from a car accident to protection from the fetus in her womb. After the fetus is aborted, however, the husband is hit by a ghost motorcyclist, and they discover that the doctor left something inside Mrs. Li during her operation. Also, their son is seriously injured, narrowly escaping death after falling off a tricycle he was standing on to reach the kitchen counter while boiling water and whacking at a frozen piece of chicken with a butcher knife. Their daughter is kidnapped and at last found looking disheveled on a bed in a dirty hovel, with the implication that she has been sexually abused. Toward the end of the film, Mrs. Li reviews these disasters, suggesting that they were direct supernatural results of her abortion.

Despite the array of images of the vengeful fetus ghost, the only concrete actions that the ghost performs are to knock a man off a ladder, to lead Mrs. Li to rescue her lost daughter, and to flee its pursuers. In the final scene, that of Mingming's triumphant return from her adventures with the fishermen, Mingming makes the following speech to a crowd of onlookers including Mrs. Li and her husband, the internist, Wang Kai, and the neighbors:

> I came to bring a message from [the name of their fetus ghost . . .]. He said he is very sad he can't be with either of you but he knows he has made the right choice. He knows you had good reasons to refuse him. He doesn't resent or hate you. He loves you, and will even help you in the future. He's waiting for another chance. He believes the world is beautiful and good and when he has the opportunity he will definitely come back [to be reborn. . . . In speaking of the realm where the fetus ghosts live she says:] Every child is waiting there. It was an unimaginable experience. They all very much want to come back. What they feel for their parents isn't hate. It is hope and love.

In the end of the movie all the main characters are united and happy, and outside there are two piles of rocks, referring back to an earlier scene in which Mrs. Li explains that fetus ghosts spend most of their time piling up stones—one for their father and two for their mother—which are knocked down by malevolent spirits.[5] As there are only two piles of stones, one can assume that the ghost had had just about enough of its father.[6] These rocks, combined with Mrs. Li's statement and the theme song explaining their significance, suggest that the fetus ghost has defeated the scientists, religious personnel, police, and its own father. It is a "happy" ending, in that the mother's attempt to save her fetus ghost has succeeded.

Like many of the portrayals of fetus ghosts that I presented in the previous chapter, this movie's goal of discouraging abortion creates a sympathetic view of fetus ghosts paradoxically combined with the dangers that the spirits could potentially bring. One has a sense that the moviemakers wanted to cover every possible point to which a viewer might relate. As the differing images are all presented by different characters in the movie, the fact that there are so many disparate images is less jarring than one might expect. The movie thus acts as advertising for fetus-ghost appeasement as well as aiming to discourage abortion. It also serves to reflect, and possibly to form, popular belief about the spirit.

Although Mrs. Li's husband repeatedly says that it is his right as a father to decide the fate of his children, born and unborn, a great portion of the movie is devoted to proving him wrong. This brings us back to our discussion of the changing balance of power between parents and their offspring, and the parental anxiety that seems to accompany this shift. Another striking point of the movie is the relative benevolence of the fetus ghost. This sympathetic portrayal of the ghost personifies the *yingling* as a childlike being with adult comprehension of its parents' intent. By portraying it in this manner, the movie serves as a warning to take the life of a fetus seriously, while at the same time the film acknowledges that there are some situations where abortion is understandable. In Mingming's case, the fact that she was raped leads the intern to perform an abortion in spite of his misgivings. The anxiety and doubt that follow for both Mingming and the abortionist are quite serious, but in the end of the movie both are cured. Similarly, Mrs. Li is absolved from her part in the death of her fetus, in part because the abortion was necessary to save her own life and in part because of her sincere repentance coupled with her willingness to appease the ghost. Thus, the movie both condemns abortion and presents a means of redeeming oneself through fetus-ghost appeasement.

Two Short Stories

A very different portrayal of an infant's spirit can be seen in Li Xiu's short story "A Small Boy's Resentful Spirit" (X. Li 1996a), which tells of a ghost that torments a female tenant in his building. The story begins like this:

> "Mama——mama——hold me——mama——."
> "Ah . . . Whose child are you? I am not your mama! I am not your mama!"
> "Mama——Mama——."

This is the story of a woman named Qiulian who is repeatedly pursued by the ghost of a small boy "raising his little head, which was bloody and cold" and accusing her of abandoning him and of ignoring his physical pain (X. Li 1996a: 88).

> Qiulian was watching television when she heard the indistinct sound of someone sniffling. The sound of the grieved crying seemed as if it wanted to enter the very marrow of her bones making her entire body shudder. [. . .] Under the curtains she saw a pair of feet wearing a pair of black leather shoes. Black-red blood slowly flowed down to become a puddle of blood. The smell of blood entered her nose. (X. Li 1996a: 91)

In despair, Qiulian tells a coworker about her predicament and her coworker gives her an incantation that she can use as a magic spell against the ghost. Not long after that, earthworms and two rat tails appear in the soup she is eating. She looks up and sees the boy there. The boy says, "Mama, it's no use—even if you cast your spells many times I still won't go on to my next life" (X. Li 1996a: 92). As she starts to faint she uses her last strength to shout, "I . . . am not . . . your . . . mother . . . you've mistaken me for someone else" (X. Li 1996a: 93).

Later, she wakes up under the table, then runs up the stairs where she sees the ghost. He is standing atop the fifth floor, jumps off the ledge, and is crushed on the pavement below (X. Li 1996a: 94). He then reappears in front of her, and with her last strength she says, "You've mistaken me for someone else," and the boy suddenly disappears. In the end of the story the narrator explains that three years earlier a woman had lived with her child in that apartment. The woman often left the child alone, and one day the boy fell to his death. The story concludes with the narrator's statement that ever since the boy died every young woman who lived in that apartment met the ghost and would run for her life.

The same author also wrote "A Drowned Little Girl's Ghost" (X. Li 1996b), in which the protagonist, Huang Juanjuan, is also haunted by the ghost of a child who died in her apartment before she lived there. Throughout the story she hears the sound of water, and she finds her own emotions becoming like those of a child. She also begins buying toys without realizing she is doing so. Toward the end of the story she goes into the bathroom and sees a doll floating facedown in the water and is suddenly confronted by the child ghost.

> With a vicelike grip, a baby grabbed Huang Juanjuan's hand with her small hand which was like cold ice water. Her small face was an ashen white hue and blood dripped out of the corner of her mouth and eyes as the ghost looked at Huang Juanjuan with a deathly ghostly stare! "Mama——Mama——." (X. Li 1996b: 112)

The story concludes as the narrator tells us that a woman and her baby used to live in the apartment. The woman would come and go without speaking to anyone and one day just disappeared. The landlord went into the apartment and found a dead baby floating facedown in the bathtub. Since that time no one dared to live in the apartment until Huang Juanjuan moved in.

Both of these stories tell of the ghosts of very young children rather than fetuses. Yet, the malevolence of these child ghosts toward their mother figures is an important reminder of the anxiety that parents seem to feel toward their offspring. Unlike the movie *Yingling*, which aims to discourage abortion and promote repentance, these two short stories are written purely for entertainment rather than instruction. This shapes the dramatic character of the ghost. The pure malevolence of these spirits plays on parental anxiety about the death of the young. These accounts also serve as a valuable point of contrast for the movie and for the stories in the next section. Indeed, the two stories I have just discussed are far closer to what one would traditionally expect of ghosts, further highlighting the complexity of other accounts.

An Exorcist's Books

The exorcist Zhong Xing has written two books of "true" short stories of his experiences in helping those afflicted by fetus-ghost hauntings (X. Zhong 1994a, 1994b). I have seen his books on sale in bookstores in Taibei, Taizhong, Tainan, and Gaoxiong, and he has made several television appearances to talk about his experiences with fetus ghosts. Thus, as is the case with Ms. Xu's and Teacher Lin's morality tracts, Zhong Xing's books are popular enough that they not only reflect common attitudes about the ghost but are also a force shaping popular opinion about the spirit.

These stories are told in the first person with a highly dramatic flare—lots of tears, lots of statements that can essentially be summed in the phrase "Mama, I love you," again and again and again. The stories in both books are somewhat overly dramatic by Western standards. In these accounts the mother and/or father begin crying in the first few pages and continue to do so until the end of the story. This strongly sentimental style, though not usual for ghost stories, is quite in keeping with traditional Taiwanese-language operas and modern Taiwanese soap operas. This stylistic choice in itself reflects a desire not to frighten but rather to bring out emotions concerning abortion with which the author's readership can identify. This serves to increase Zhong Xing's book sales, to bring him patronage as an exorcist, and to legitimize his work as a social service.

In Zhong Xing's stories he often explains the harmful effects of ghosts' *yin* energy on the living. In both books, his portrayal of fetus ghosts is one in which they do not harm out of spite but as an unintentional effect of their presence. I have already suggested that, paradoxically, belief in fetus ghosts both exploits and empowers the believers. The following story demonstrates some of the emotions involved and the comfort that exorcising the spirit provides. These stories are too long to translate in full, but I will now provide a summary of one to give a better feel for what we are dealing with here.

Daughter Butterfly

Chapter 7 of Zhong Xing's first book (1994a) is entitled "Daughter Butterfly." It opens when Zhong Xing meets with some old junior high school friends. One of his friends asks him for advice, telling Zhong Xing about his older sister, Shangping. Shangping has already had three daughters, and her mother-in-law issued a final ultimatum saying that if Shangping did not give birth to a son in the next three years the mother-in-law would tell Shangping's husband to find another wife to bear a male child to continue the family line. The friend asks, in chagrin, "What age do we live in that we still think men are so important and women are unimportant [*zhong nan qing nü*]?"

At his friend's request, Zhong Xing goes to visit Shangping. On arriving at the house he immediately senses a change in his energy field (*cichang*) with which he senses the ghost. Not long after that he sees an older male ghost and a three- or four-year-old female fetus ghost.[7] When he meets Shangping he senses that her body's *qi* energy, or life force, is abnormal. After talking for a brief time with Shangping, he asks her if she has recently had an abortion. She is predictably shocked, but Zhong Xing explains that he has seen the fetus ghost and an older ghost that followed her husband when he left the house. She then admits to having had four abortions in the previous two years. She explains that her mother-in-law wants her husband to divorce her if she has another daughter and laments that she believes her husband would follow these instructions. She then states: "I know I killed my four children, but if I had given birth to them I would have lost everything. My mother-in-law would have cruelly broken up my marriage. [. . .] I don't want anyone to come and destroy my family" (X. Zhong 1994c: 187).

Zhong Xing explains that if fetus ghosts are present they can influence the entire family's energy field and suggests that, when the ghosts return with her husband, Zhong Xing should take them away and exorcise them. The older ghost turns out to be Shangping's father-in-law, who says that he knows his *yin* energy is bad for his family, but "when I saw how my wife was treating my daughter-in-law it touched my heart" (X. Zhong 1994c: 193). He goes on to explain that he wanted to tell his wife that she was in the wrong but she could not hear him because he was a ghost. He also wanted to prevent Shangping from having the abortions, but he could do nothing about it for the same reason. He says that three of the four aborted fetuses did not have a strong fate with Shangping but that the fourth had an especially strong one with her and that this was the fetus ghost by his side. Zhong Xing then has the fetus ghost, named Butterfly, stand in front of Shangping, who says to it: "I don't know what to say, I only feel full of guilt [*zuiegan*]. I'm sorry I aborted the four fetuses that might have become my children. Yes! Help me ask her if she wants some clothing, candy, or toys" (X. Zhong 1994c: 197). Although he says nothing to her, Zhong Xing narrates that many people think fetus ghosts need clothing or toys because they are afraid of the cold or the dark, but in fact the only thing they fear is that the mother and child will not be able to take care of each other.[8] Later, Shangping says: "Butterfly, I'm sorry. I can't see you or hear you but my heart is very sad, very sad" (X. Zhong 1994c: 200), and she begins to cry. When the fetus ghost sees her mother crying she says, "Mama, don't cry, it scares Butterfly" (X. Zhong 1994c: 200).

Zhong Xing tells Shangping what the fetus ghost said and the mother tries to be cheerful. Then Zhong Xing suggests that he take the fetus ghost away to send her on to her next life, at which point the spirit appeals to her grandfather, saying that she doesn't want to go. Shangping also asks that the ghost be allowed to stay, but Zhong Xing tells her that this would be wrong. He then explains that she should allow him to send the spirit on to her next life, because if the *yingling* were to stay her ghostly presence would harm Shangping's health and emotions. He concludes by saying that it would also be better for the child, who would otherwise forever wander the earth without being reincarnated. In the end Zhong Xing takes the two ghosts off to send them on to their next lives and hints to the reader that they are likely to be reborn into the same family.

This account differs from Zhong Xing's other stories in that it is the only instance, in either of his books, where an adult ghost appears. But aside from this it is quite like the other accounts I have presented. I chose this story because it relates so closely to the other issues I have discussed in connection with real cases recounted by people whom I have interviewed.

Lin Fangmei, in writing on abortion in Taiwan, points out that "Stories from a Man Who Has Spoken with Fetus Ghosts," Zhong Xing's first book, has significance beyond mere ghost stories because we can take them as representations of human relations in connection to abortion and fetus-ghost appeasement: "This book discusses abortion and places it in the context of the relationship between the two sexes and the entire situation of family life, the structure of exorcisms, mutual activity, and mutual recognition of parent-child relationships" (Lin Fangmei 1996: 17). In fact, Zhong Xing often explains the importance of exorcisms for the living and the dead, but in none of his stories does he actually describe the process or structure of the exorcisms themselves. Rather, the stories end with Zhong Xing walking or driving away with the *yingling*, to be exorcised later. But Lin is correct, I think, in that these stories can be taken as emblematic of the choices women must face in having abortions and the strain that the abortions have on their relationships within their families. Zhong Xing's stories certainly resonate with many of the interviews I conducted in which women and men told me the factors they felt were beyond their control that influenced their decisions to seek abortions.

If we reexamine the story "Daughter Butterfly," we find a strong critique of Taiwanese women's weak positions in their families. The story sets this tone almost immediately when Zhong Xing's friend incredulously remarks that the sexist preference for male heirs continues today. Shangping's statement "I don't want anyone to come and destroy my family" reminds us of the precarious position in which women are left because of the divorce law. In this light we can see that Shangping potentially risks being financially stranded and completely separated from her children with no visitation rights. The fact that she has had four abortions in the hope of having a male child is very much connected with the structural weakness of women and the pressure to produce male heirs. It also emphasizes the nature of what is often a strained relationship between daughters-in-law and their mothers-in-law, a point that Margery Wolf has documented so well (M. Wolf 1968, 1972, 1975).

If we look more closely we can also see that Zhong Xing, in his role as a spirit medium, gives Shangping ammunition to do battle with her mother-in-law. Spirit mediums are often taken very seriously in Taiwan, and for Zhong Xing to say that he has spoken with the ghost of the father-in-law, and that this patriarch of the family disapproved of his wife's treatment of his daughter-in-law, could potentially tip the familial power scale in Shangping's favor. In the end of these stories, as in many true-life situations, belief in fetus ghosts provides resolution and comfort on a personal level for the mother, and potentially for the family as a whole.

Like his first book, Zhong Xing's second book is related in the first person in a highly melodramatic style. Unlike in the first book, however, Zhong Xing goes to greater lengths to emphasize that these accounts are truth, not fiction. In an effort to emphasize this point, he includes seven letters: from a reporter, a television host, a business person, three teachers, and an author. In these letters the writers comment on their ideas about fetus ghosts and attest to Zhong Xing's accomplishments. This is followed by six chapters giving accounts of Zhong Xing's experiences with fetus ghosts. At the end of the book he includes ten letters from people relating their experiences with abortion. These letters are responses to Zhong Xing's introduction to his first book, in which he invites readers to write to him if they would like him to send their fetus ghosts on to their next lives. Placed next to the first page of each letter is a photocopy of the handwritten letter on its own individually styled stationery. Presumably this is intended to emphasize that these letters really did come from different people. By stressing that the stories are true, Zhong Xing reminds the reader that he is a real exorcist should they require his services, and that the ghosts and the services are also real.

As in the first book, each story takes place in a different setting (visiting a factory, going to a conference, going to a friend's house, etc.) and a different situation (some people know they are being haunted, most do not). In all the stories the parents are extremely remorseful. Once they know that they are being followed by their "children,"[9] the parents of the fetus ghost in question do not want Zhong Xing to send it away but tearfully beg to be allowed to stay with their child forever. Zhong Xing must then reason with the parents, pointing out that they are not being fair to their children, who deserve to be sent on to their next lives so that they can live a normal existence. The parents inevitably succumb to Zhong Xing's reasoning out of a love for their children and tearfully allow him to take the fetus ghosts with him, usually (again tearfully) begging the spirits to forgive them and to come back by being reborn as their future children.

The accounts in both books are very telling in their assumptions about gender and familial relations. The emphasis is on a woman's position in society that forces her to have abortions, her remorse for her deeds, her continuing love for the ghost, and even her plea to allow the ghost to stay with her. These elements are all present in virtually every one of Zhong Xing's stories. Only one story in either book (X. Zhong 1994a: chap. 3) is purely about the relationship between a father and his fetus ghost, and in this story the woman is dead and therefore absent. In the second book, two of the stories have remorseful fathers of aborted fetuses, but in both of these stories the real relationship is inevitably one of mother and child. In one chapter, for example, the father repeatedly apologizes to the spirit, which responds "Mama." The ghost only acknowledges its father when the father essentially says, "What about me?" after which the ghost says "Daddy" and then seems to forget all about him again, turning its attention to its mother (X. Zhong 1994b: 102–103).

Although it is true that the ghosts in Zhong Xing's books are often portrayed as mistrustful or even hostile to living adults, this is presented as resulting from the ghosts' fear of being harmed again rather than their intent to seek revenge. Thus, Zhong Xing portrays them as ongoing victims rather than ghosts that now have the upper hand.[10] Along the same lines, although Zhong Xing sometimes describes a particular fetus ghost as being more mature and understanding than a normal child of that age, the fetus ghosts in these depictions are hardly the omniscient beings that most Taiwanese people believe them to be. Often Zhong Xing does not even realize they are ghosts at first, by which one can infer that although others cannot see them they look exactly like normal children in the spirit world. In these cases, Zhong Xing knows they are ghosts because they are aware of his presence through a closed door, because his energy field senses they are ghosts, or because there is some other clue that they are not living children. Often the children smile, laugh, and play like normal, well-adjusted children.

In each story Zhong Xing must overcome the ghost's or ghosts' mistrust of adults, suggest that he could send them on to their next lives, and explain religious terms such as "to send a ghost on to its next life" (*yindu*) to the ghosts. In keeping with this picture of fetus ghosts as innocent children, Zhong Xing refers to himself as "uncle" (*shushu*) when he talks to them. When he refers to them in his narration he uses the terms "fetus ghost" (*yingling*) and "fetus demon" (*xiaogui*),[11] but he mixes these freely with terms also used to refer to living children, including "young girl" (*xiaonühai*), "young boy" (*xiaonanhai*), and "small child" (*xiaohai*). All of these terms are used interchangeably, thus minimizing the otherness of fetus ghosts and appealing to the reader's sympathy for them. In keeping with this, there is a noticeable infantilization of their speech: the fetus ghosts in these stories generally speak in simple sentences, often haltingly, and use childish words. When the people in the stories show fear of the ghosts, Zhong Xing uses this reaction either as a humorous relief of tension or as an opportunity to explain why the living should not be afraid.[12]

The stories also emphasize the women's lack of power over their life situations, both by stressing their regret over the abortions and by the way in which Zhong Xing refers to the ghosts as children who are not fated to be with their parents. As a last point, Zhong Xing opines that his having met ghosts or their living relatives must be a reflection of the will of the "Old Man in the Sky" (Laotianye), who wants him to help in this way.[13] Thus, Zhong Xing presents himself as an emissary from heaven.

In a sense these stories serve as a how-to manual for both exorcist and client alike. In them we see how and where Zhong Xing meets clients, how he might respond to their inevitable surprise and/or disbelief, and possible explanations for the haunting that could in turn be used to maneuver one's passage through a family conflict. The stories also show the ways in which a spirit medium or exorcist might "prove" his claims by exhibiting knowledge of a very little information (such as how many abortions a woman had had or the sex of an aborted fetus) that could be gleaned from friends or hospital records. Like my interviewees, the characters in these stories are searching for an explanation of concrete problems. They seem to want to believe in the solution and are not really that difficult to convince.

In addition to offering a better idea of how such religious masters operate, these stories provide ways of thinking about the ghosts, detailing Zhong Xing's views, which can on occasion consciously contradict other popular conceptions.[14] As I mentioned in the beginning of this section, Zhong Xing is perhaps the best-known fetus-ghost exorcist in Taiwan, which lends these views added weight.

In comparing the diverse accounts of fetus ghosts in this chapter, one is again confronted with the variety of motivations and actions of fetus ghosts. Li Xiu's stories portray child-spirits that are both malevolent and unjust. This is hardly surprising, for the ghosts' antagonism is what makes the stories interesting. In the movie, and in Zhong Xing's accounts, however, the ghosts are portrayed as being far more sympathetic to the living. In the movie there is a clear intention to discourage abortion, and the film uses every approach possible to make this point. A good portion of its dialogue contains pedantic lectures on the evils of abortion, and on the existence and nature of fetus ghosts. In contrast, Zhong Xing's characters make passing comments condemning abortion, but on the whole he makes every effort to comfort rather than to frighten, suggesting that with his help everything will be fine. This approach emphasizes that the ghost is a victim that needs his help, and that the living will benefit from his services. I have already described different versions of fetus ghosts that reflect people's particular problems and personalities. Here we see accounts of fetus ghosts that were consciously manipulated to meet the storyteller's purpose, whether that was entertainment, antiabortion propaganda, or advertisement.

7
Religious Masters and Their Temples

Twenty years ago, Taiwan could for all intents and purposes have been called a third-world country. Thriving on agriculture, the rural village was the home of most families in Taiwan. Today, the urban landscape is spreading: skyscrapers, Western suits and prices, traffic jams, and the all-important 7-Eleven store on every third block are taken for granted as natural parts of life. Taiwan has experienced a frenzied modernization that is hard to describe or even to comprehend. Yet amid all these changes traditional temples tucked in corners and alleys remain; one cannot walk more than ten minutes in any direction without seeing one.

Temples are both generalized and specialized. They are generalized in that most of them can provide a wide range of services that do not greatly differ from those of others. They are specialized in that each temple has a particular patron god and performs distinctive duties that lend it its own unique atmosphere. To take the area around my apartment in Taibei as an example, one could walk for three minutes down my alley past a very small home-run temple and another four minutes along come to a large Daoist temple that offers funeral processions. Facing this was another small individually run temple.

Across the street from my house in the other direction was a Buddhist temple. This temple did not provide funeral services, but it had clubs for middle-aged women who gathered once a week to chant Buddhist sutras (badly, I'm afraid) and offered English classes and outings for children, among other services. Four blocks farther down the street there was a Buddhist temple that helped to appease fetus ghosts and had a small store on the first floor in which one could buy books, candles, and incense for offerings, postcards, or other knick-knacks. Approximately two miles away, and countless temples later, in the famous temple Xingtian Gong, one could have one's fortune told or wait in one of several long lines to be blessed with incense by one of the Daoist nuns there. These nuns dealt with problems ranging from children's illnesses to unemployment, all through a thirty-second blessing with incense.

As I noted in the Introduction, the majority of Taiwanese people's experiences with fetus ghosts are at smaller street-corner temples. Although these temples are often not much larger than the living room in an average American home, there are hundreds upon hundreds of them scattered through every city in Taiwan. Also, many of the newer temples are not "temples" in the traditional sense. Property values in Taibei are currently among the highest in the world. As a result, the majority of new temples in the city are in fact what I call "apartment temples" (*shentan*),[1] apartments that have been converted into places of worship. Such temples are quite small and have no room for the large statues or stone pillars that one might find in more traditional temples. They are packed with small statues of gods, incense, divination sticks, morality tracts, and other religious paraphernalia. Various people from the community come to the religious masters either for help with a specific problem or just to chat because they were walking by. None of these smaller temples (that I have found) would consider themselves to be fetus-ghost temples because they also provide a range of other services. But if someone were to walk up to a Daoist master at virtually any small Daoist temple and offer money to appease a fetus ghost, it would be rare indeed if she or he were turned away.

A Buddhist Temple in Gaoxiong

In central Gaoxiong there is a large, majestic Buddhist temple that appeases fetus ghosts. In addition to the temple itself, there is an office, library, and living quarters for the monks and nuns. The main god is the historical Buddha (Shijiamouni Fo).

The head monk was very charismatic, relaxed, and confident in himself and his authority. He did not claim that he could see ghosts, but rather that he could assess when people had a spirit harming them if other treatments failed. He told me the following:

> People's hearts are not peaceful so they have wrong thoughts, and their problems are not necessarily *yingling*. Usually if someone is sick I will advise them to first go to a clinic to get medicine. Everything has a spirit, and aborted fetuses also have them, but they won't necessarily do bad things. People shouldn't worry; *yingling* that do bad things are very few. If it does turn out to be a *yingling* that is causing the problem, one of our monks can recite passages from the scriptures [*songjing*] for two hours and that will be fine. Sometimes we will have to do this more than once, maybe four or five times, but usually one time is enough.

He also told me that it was up to his clients to decide how much they wanted to contribute to the temple for this service. He declined to estimate an average contribution amount, but the majestic nature of the temple, its obvious wealth, and the fact that a monk would read the scriptures for two solid hours, would likely make a worshiper feel embarrassed to contribute too little.

The Noodle Vendor

I have already mentioned that some people approach women on the street and offer to help them appease their fetus ghosts for a small price. The Noodle Vendor is a similar example of a layperson generating income from this practice. The Noodle Vendor sells noodles and cooked vegetables in a night market in Taibei. In his profession he often talks with customers as they sit at his stall to eat. In the course of these conversations he comes to know about his regular customers' lives—their wants, their desires, and their frustrations. As a result, he has started a sideline production, so to speak, working out of his home to appease ghosts, which he claims to be able to see.

Like many of the religious masters I discuss here, he does not have a set fee but relies on his clients' donations. I suspect the modesty of his station would garner far smaller donations on average than, say, the Gaoxiong Buddhist Temple. But this too could add up to significant amounts. The client I interviewed, for example, only paid two or three hundred NT dollars (US$8–12) on each visit, but he went to the Noodle Vendor's home two or three times a month, and they had not set an end point to the appeasement process.

The Noodle Vendor's home cannot even be called an apartment temple in that it has not been renovated to look like a temple.

Instead, on entering his apartment one must first walk through the living room to reach a small room in the back of the house that is devoted to worship. This room contains several small statues of gods, the most prominent of which is a three-foot-high statue of the god Guangong. To appease a fetus ghost the Noodle Vendor has his clients burn incense for them. After that he has the appeasers kneel on a pillow and bow three times for each ghost. That is it: quick, easy, and inexpensive.

A Daoist Temple in Douliu

In Chapter 5, I briefly mentioned a woman I interviewed who paid her Daoist master NT$20,000 for a three-day ceremony. She attended all three days of this ceremony at an apartment temple in the city of Douliu, about 70 kilometers south of Taizhong. Each day's ritual lasted for four to five hours. During this time, the Daoist master wore special ceremonial robes, burned incense and money for the fetus ghost, and led his client through a series of chants and prayers directed to the many gods of the temple and to the fetus ghost itself.

This Daoist master also claimed to possess the ability to see ghosts. He was the only religious master with whom I have spoken to say that the appeasement process does not send the ghost on to its next life. Instead, the appeasement process was just that, an appeasement, and the ghost would remain in the spirit world and could possibly return at a later date to be appeased again. Also, he said that, as was the case with other ghosts, *yingling* would return during ghost month (*gui yue*) during the seventh lunar month,[2] and that it was necessary to make food offerings and burn spirit money on the ritual days of this month for their behalf. Because this master emphasized that the ghost would continue to exist in the spirit world and would require at least a minimum set of offerings during ghost month, we can see that each ghost had the potential to supply him with income for some time. As is true at most of the temples I discuss here, this was just one of many services this master offered.

Daoist Master Bob's Temple

Daoist Master Bob, whom I will discuss again later in relation to fetus demons, has an apartment temple located in Gaoxiong. He and his wife live on the second floor of the temple. The patron god of his temple is Santaizi, but Daoist Master Bob often tells his clients that they have their own patron gods to whom they should pray for help. After collecting his own fees, he escorts his clients to temples with different patron gods. One may assume that they return the favor.

Like the two religious masters just described, Daoist Master Bob claimed to be able to see and talk with fetus ghosts and other ghosts. His conception of fetus ghosts was far less distinct from other ghosts than that of other masters. All of the other religious masters told me that fetus ghosts could not age beyond three to five years regardless of how long they had existed in the spirit world. The ghost of a fetus that was aborted forty years ago, for example, is most often thought to look and act like a three- to five-year-old child.

In contrast, Daoist Master Bob believed that fetus ghosts age indefinitely just like other ghosts and told me that, whereas Buddhists believe that spirits cannot age in the afterworld, Daoists believe they can. This is more in keeping with traditional views of the spirit world in which marriages are arranged between dead unmarried ghosts and living people in order to relieve their structurally anomalous positions and to protect the living. Although *yingling* today, including those who died in their first two years of life, are almost never thought to need this service because they are not believed to pass beyond childhood in the spirit world, Daoist Master Bob's vision of the ghost adheres more closely to traditional beliefs about ghosts. He told me that at the age of twenty a *yingling* wants to marry, and naturally expects its parents to help. In addition to exorcising the spirit, therefore, Daoist Master Bob also assisted in performing marriage rites for fetus ghosts that had grown to adulthood.

Like the Douliu Daoist master, Daoist Master Bob also incorporated ghost month into fetus-ghost appeasement, saying that special offerings needed to be made for fetus spirits at this time. He said that during ghost month, the spirits of fetuses—both fetus ghosts and fetus demons—wandered the earth like other ghosts, but that because of their larger size the adult ghosts would take all of the food and spirit money offered to wandering spirits. Accordingly, he asserted, one had to set out offerings specifically for *yingling* to prevent wandering fetus spirits from going hungry, becoming angry, and wreaking their vengeance on the living. Thus, in addition to appeasing fetus ghosts and performing marriage ceremonies for those he had not sent on to their next lives, he also left time for the service of providing for wandering fetus spirits. Daoist Master Bob told me that, if a *yingling* was making someone sick or bothering them in some other way, he would go to the mountains to cast spells (*zuofa*) to help the fetus ghost to be reborn in another life.

I knew two of Daoist Master Bob's clients. One paid him in excess of NT$10 million (US$293,800) for religious services that were not related to fetus ghosts in any way. Another client, though declining to tell me how much she had paid, said that she had also paid very large sums for his services, part of which were associated with a fetus ghost.

Daoist Master Bob, always a man of his own particular style, made a huge income from his clients. In the case of the woman I interviewed, she did not pay him large sums to appease the fetus ghost; rather, he used his ability to see the ghost as part of a wider sales campaign to make her believe in his powers. Once he had gained her trust, he charged her huge sums to help her pray to have a child. Sporting his gold Rolex watch and gold rings, making a show of buying a house with cash, and casually mentioning his million U.S. dollar property holdings, it was clear that this semi-illiterate son of farmers from one of the poorest regions of Taiwan had found a route to financial success.

Cai Wen's Temples

The Daoist master Cai Wen resides in Gaoxiong and spends most of his time at his main temple located in the heart of the city. He visits his Taibei temple once a week, but I was unable to arrange an interview with him there, though I did interview him in his Gaoxiong temple.

The Taibei temple is an apartment temple. One floor is devoted to the printing of religious tracts and houses its own library and other temples' religious texts. The floor above has three altars: a central altar and separate altars to its right and left. At the Taibei temple they denied appeasing fetus ghosts despite the fact that this temple was one of the four listed on Cai Wen's fetus-ghost morality tracts, saying that they just printed the leaflet for Cai Wen. Over the course of our interview, however, it became fairly clear that this was not the case.

About twenty minutes into the interview I asked the man working there how they appeased fetus ghosts at their temple. Apparently he had forgotten that he had previously told me they did not appease *yingling*, because he led me to the center of the temple and said: "First you would have to burn incense in front of our patron god, like this. Then you would contribute money to the temple so that we could print morality tracts and donate to the poor." When I asked him how long the appeasement process lasts and how much it costs, he answered: "Each case is different. The person would consult with Cai Wen to decide these matters." Although this could hardly be called a rich ethnographic interview, one does get a sense that the process is a relatively simple one, and that the ceremony and the costs are adjusted to meet the needs, and the means, of particular clients.

Another of Cai Wen's Gaoxiong temples is a huge multistoried building in the countryside of Gaoxiong County, a few miles from the famous Buddhist temple Foguanshan. With the exception of special events, this temple is not active. Rather, it is something of a tourist attraction, with people congregated at the steps below waiting to sell drinks and snacks. This temple is usually staffed by one attendant, who does not seem to have much interest in religious matters. Like the Taibei temple's staff, he told me they did not appease fetus ghosts, adding that this was a Japanese practice rather than a Taiwanese one.

Cai Wen's main temple, in the heart of the city of Gaoxiong, houses the gods Guangong and Qingshuizhushi. Unlike those at the Taibei temple, here the staff immediately admitted to appeasing fetus ghosts. When I interviewed Cai Wen he told me that he disagreed with temples that prolonged the appeasement process, and that one should be able to appease the ghost in one day. "Sometimes," he said, "one day is not enough, but at most two or three days should be fine." I asked how many people came to him in one year to appease fetus ghosts, and he said he helped about seven hundred people a year. When I asked how much they paid he said that it was up to them; if they wanted to make a contribution to the temple of a few hundred NT dollars, that was fine.

Cai Wen's temples are very much for the local community. In addition to their morality tracts, they have their own newspaper-length newsletter that covers the events the temples sponsor for people of all ages.

Ms. Xu's Temple

Xu Qiongyue, who calls herself Ms. Xu (Xu Xiaojie), manages a small Buddhist temple in Taibei. It is affiliated with another Taibei temple under different management.[3] At the time of this writing, Ms. Xu's temple dealt with only a little over one hundred fetus ghosts a year, although there used to be more. Because Ms. Xu's temple was just a few blocks away from where I lived in Taibei, I was able to drop by both for interviews and to informally say hello or buy gifts for friends. Although Ms. Xu stresses that appeasing fetus ghosts is but one of the temple's many functions, I have seen her morality text on fetus ghosts in bookstores in Taibei, Taizhong, Tainan, and Gaoxiong. Because of this widespread distribution, her book has helped to shape many people's conceptions of the spirit.

Ms. Xu's temple has two floors. The ground floor is a bookstore and curio shop selling everything from small statues of Buddhist gods to incense and candles to burn for dead spirits, postcards, and other knickknacks. The second floor consists of a few more books for sale, a short table and cushions where one can sit and talk, and an area for prayer with several small altars for gods and goddesses.

Those who come to Ms. Xu's temple select one patron Bodhisattva of their choice to help take care of their fetus ghost. Ms. Xu explained: "In Buddhism there are many gods, but they are not strong enough to deal with *yingling*. But you can choose from any one of the hundreds of Bodhisattvas for help with fetus ghosts." The most popular four Bodhisattvas for fetus-ghost appeasement at her temple are represented by statues in the temple's place of worship. According to Ms. Xu, the Dizangwang Pusa is the one most commonly appealed to for fetus ghost appeasement, but the other three, Yaoshi Fo, Buddha (Shijiamouni Fo), and *Guanyin*, are quite popular as well.

Unlike Dragon Lake Temple, which I will soon describe, Ms. Xu's temple does not have small statues to represent fetus ghosts, but it does have small, yellow wooden memorial plaques. These plaques are exactly the same as, and are mixed in with, other yellow plaques for deceased parents and ancestors. In addition, there are red plaques for living people who are ill or in other difficulties.

Ms. Xu is quite modest in her claims, freely admitting that she cannot see ghosts. When I asked how much she charged to appease a fetus ghost, she shook her head:

> We couldn't take money for this, if we did then the *yingling*
> would cease to be their parents' problem but would bother us
> instead. Also, fetus ghosts know if parents just want to buy
> them off by paying temples a lot of money. What they really
> want is sincere repentance from the heart. They can tell the
> difference you know.

Although Ms. Xu's temple does not charge for the rite of fetus-ghost appeasement as other temples do, worshipers must buy oil lamps at her temple to burn in front of a Bodhisattva's statue. An oil lamp (*youdeng*) is made up of a small, rounded fishbowl-shaped glass with liquid oil and a wick. The lamp ranges from NT$200 to NT$850 (approximately US$6 to US$25). The vast majority of burning lamps at the temple are of the NT$200 variety. One must also buy oil at the temple. A quart of oil costs NT$160 (US$5) and lasts for one week. For one month one would pay at least NT$840 (US$25) (four bottles of oil and the glass container), and for two months one would pay a minimum of NT$1,480 (US$42). In very rare instances someone might decide to pay for a longer time period. Ms. Xu showed me one lamp that had been lit for a year. In such cases the expenditure would increase accordingly. Some worshipers take the oil lamps and memorial plaques home with them to pray to them there, though most do not.

Those appeasing fetus ghosts pay for everything on their first visit, after which workers at the temple will take care of refilling the lamps with oil. There is a corner with partially used oil bottles with people's names written on them. When I expressed surprise that worshipers came only once, Ms. Xu shrugged with a sad expression, "people are busy." After writing the name of the person appeasing the ghost[4] and the name of the fetus ghost on the label of a oil lamp and lighting it, she or he will burn incense and then either bow three times or kowtow three times, according to individual preference, while saying a prayer.

Although at first glance Ms. Xu's temple seems to be more casual than other temples, this does not mean that people do not take it seriously. On my first trip to Ms. Xu's temple I saw a man in his late thirties who seemed close to tears as he kneeled down on his hands and knees, reverently kowtowing in front of one of the altars.

Dragon Lake Temple

Dragon Lake Temple is situated in the countryside on the outskirts of the city of Houlong in Miaoli County, just off the western coast of

Taiwan between the cities of Taibei and Taizhong. The train, for reasons of its own peculiarities of time and space, inevitably takes longer to get from Taibei to Miaoli than to get to Taizhong, which is geographically twice as far away. To get there one must drive roughly six kilometers from the nearest train station, past rice fields and open land. Because of the remote location of the temple, its popularity throughout Taiwan is perhaps surprising. Yet in a sense it is this very remoteness that has made it popular, for appeasers can go there without announcing to their friends and neighbors that they have had abortions.

In 1975 Teacher Lin (Lin Jianyi) retired from his job as an elementary school teacher and used his life savings to build a temple on the edge of "Dragon Lake," so named because a passing taxi driver had once seen a dragon flying over the lake some years before. In keeping with Taiwan's traditions, Teacher Lin founded his temple by adopting a patron statue from an older temple—in this case, a statue of Xuantian Shangdi from a 150-year-old temple just up the street.[5]

Teacher Lin saw a need for an organized form of fetus-ghost appeasement in Taiwan. Now, over twenty years later, he can proudly boast that Dragon Lake Temple is by far the largest, best-known, and oldest temple to openly appease fetus ghosts. There are approximately 16,400 fetus-ghost statues at Dragon Lake Temple. Since parents must appease their fetus ghosts for three years before they can go on to their next lives, this means that there is an average of a little more than 5,400 new fetus ghosts each year just at this one temple alone. The number of actual patrons is somewhat less than this, as some people will have more than one abortion in a year.

There is an annual fee of NT$1,200 (US$35) to appease a fetus ghost for three years. Worshipers are also expected to pray to their fetus ghosts and to visit them on each of the semiannual religious ceremonies held at the temple. Many people come more often. For instance, I know one married couple that goes to the temple every Sunday, burning incense and setting out small snacks for the ghost of their miscarried infant.

Those who decide to appease fetus ghosts will go to talk to Teacher Lin, or the head of the founding temple, who will choose a name for each fetus ghost if it does not already have one. They must then attend the next biweekly ceremony, in which the new patrons begin the appeasement process. After that they must come to the semi-

annual ceremonies. If they wish, they can also come during any day
of the year for more private meetings either with Teacher Lin or with
their fetus ghosts. People appeasing fetus ghosts can come on any day
of the semiannual three-day ceremony, but they are required to
attend on at least one of the days.

Approximately half the worshipers bring fruit for the gods and
offerings of food and toys for the fetus ghosts.[6] Once a patron has set
out fruit for the gods and left offerings in front of her or his particular fetus-ghost statue, she or he will go to register. Registration is a
quick and easy process. One goes to a desk labeled "Fetus-Ghost Service Desk" and pays the NT$1,200 annual fee per fetus ghost.[7] On
payment, one of the women at the service desk will stamp the red
contract.[8] The red contract is a large piece of paper that contains
what is essentially a legal petition to the gods and fetus ghosts. This
includes a standardized worshiper's appeal to the gods with an admission of guilt, an apology, and an agreement to appease the fetus
ghost for three years. In exchange for this the gods are asked to mediate with the fetus ghost on the appeaser's behalf.[9]

After receiving a red contract, the patron will go to a small room
to the left (as one faces the temple) of the main temple to pick up
spirit money and incense. There is a large packet of spirit money to
burn for the gods and a small packet of spirit money to burn for the
ghosts. Worshipers then go to the main temple to burn incense to
the main god and to say a prayer. They then burn incense at the
altars at the right- and lefthand doors of the temple and in the main
temple, after which they burn incense in a large incense pot in the
middle of the courtyard. Once all this is done, the person appeasing
the ghost will go to the main fetus-ghost temple, where she or he will
kneel on a cushion or stand while burning incense and reading the
red contract out loud to the gods of that floor. The newer fetus ghosts
are kept on the main floor, while the ones from previous years are
moved to the floor below. If the appeaser's fetus-ghost statue has been
moved downstairs, she or he will then repeat this reading (standing
this time) for the gods on the bottom fetus-ghost floor. She or he will
then quietly read the red contract out loud one last time in front of
the particular fetus-ghost statue, which can be located by looking for
the identification number on both the red contract and the statue.
After doing this, the worshiper will go outside to the front of the main
fetus-ghost floor and burn the red contract to deliver it to the spirit

world. The last step is to burn the spirit money, first for the gods in the right furnace and then for the ghosts in the left furnace.

After this series of steps the appeasers are done. Some will stay for a few more minutes, perhaps returning to say one last prayer either to one of the gods or to their fetus ghosts themselves. They might also peruse the religious tracts, which are usually sold in bookstores for NT$200 each but are free on the special ceremonial days. Most people leave soon after they have finished the appeasement steps. In fact, these go quite quickly, only taking twenty minutes to half an hour.

Teacher Lin was kind enough to allow me to spend the night at the temple on a number of occasions. On each day of the semiannual ceremonies the temple begins to open at four in the morning when the female staff gets up and begins opening the temple doors and gate, lighting candles and incense, ringing the gongs, and making preparations for the cooking of the day. The members of the Buddhist chanting group are usually up and around by six in the morning, as are Teacher Lin and his family. Some members of the chanting group stay at the temple during the ceremonies. The temple is already starting to shut down by six or seven in the evening.

The semiannual ritual days themselves are three one-day events during which a Buddhist chanting group is hired to chant and play music. They also chant at the smaller rituals held for new members on every other Sunday. On the afternoon of the last day of the ceremony, prayers are also made to wandering spirits, and locals from the surrounding area come to give food to the gods. The ceremony ends with the temple donating large bags of rice to poor people from the surrounding area.

Although everyone appeasing fetus ghosts at Dragon Lake Temple is expected to attend these ceremonies, this does not mean that there is a crowd of sixteen thousand people at any one time. Although there are a few worshipers who come on more than one day of this event, most leave after approximately half an hour. In general they come, they register, they make the rounds to leave gifts for their fetus ghosts and pray to the gods, they read and then burn the red contract, they burn incense and money for the gods and the ghosts, and then they are gone. The last day is perhaps an exception because this day is considered to be the most important, and more people stay to watch or to participate by bowing or kowtowing at the appropriate times while the Buddhist musicians play music and chant in front of them.

Teacher Lin lives on the temple grounds in a house to the right of the main temple with his youngest son, his daughter-in-law, and their two children. His other two sons do not live with him but are often there on the weekends. He also has three daughters, but, in keeping with the Chinese tradition that aligns them as part of their husbands' families, they visit only on special occasions such as birthdays, holidays, or the fetus-ghost appeasement ceremonies, when they come to help at the registration desk.

Dragon Lake Temple consists of three large buildings: the main temple, Teacher Lin's house, and a large side building. The side building has two floors that house statues of gods and fetus-ghost statues, a floor dedicated to star gods, and a floor for the cafeteria and kitchen. The layout of the buildings mimics that of a traditional house. Traditional Chinese living quarters were centered around a main house. As the sons grew up, the family would add a left wing, and then finally add a right wing for younger brothers, creating the shape of an upside-down rectangular horseshoe, thus leaving a courtyard in the middle. Dragon Lake Temple holds to the same configuration: the main temple is in the central position, the fetus-ghost temple serves as the left wing, and Teacher Lin's house is on the right, though unconnected, wing, also leaving a courtyard in the middle. Thus, a symbolic hierarchy exists, with the patron god's residence in the center, the fetus ghosts' residence where the oldest sons would be, and Teacher Lin and his family at the lowest point of the hierarchy.

The main temple contains a patron god, Xuantian Shangdi. On the right side is a statue of Amida Buddha (Emituo Fo) and on the left side there is a statue of Dizangwang Pusa. In the back of the temple, on the righthand side, there are shelves with dozens of eight-inch-high statues of gods, most of which are Xuantian Shangdi but some of which are Guanyin. These statues never leave the temple but can be sponsored by worshipers.[10] At the left rear of the temple there is a map on the wall showing star gods. There are also statues in the yard representing star gods, zodiac signs (the dragon, the snake, etc.), characters from the novel *Journey to the West*, the goddess Guanyin, aboriginal religious art, and others.[11]

The main floor of the building is devoted to fetus ghosts and contains shelves filled with statues of them.[12] There is a second room for fetus ghosts on the floor below.[13] Unlike Ms. Xu's temple where a client would choose one Bodhisattva to help appease the ghost, or other temples in which one would also direct one's prayers to one god, at Dragon Lake Temple patrons are expected to read the red contract aloud, once in both of the fetus-ghost rooms for the gods and once in front of the fetus-ghost statue. Some also read the contract in the main temple.

The fetus-ghost statues are approximately one foot high and quite heavy, consisting of solid metal. On the front of each statue, the staff writes the name of the fetus ghost, the name or names of those appeasing the ghost, and the date on which the appeasement process began. Like most Daoist temples in Taiwan, Dragon Lake Temple draws upon a mix of Daoist, Buddhist, Confucian, and folk religious traditions, and its members worship a wide range of gods. This floor and the one below it has hundreds of fetus-ghost statues lined up on shelves.

The top floor of this building is not actually devoted to fetus ghosts but rather to star gods and money gods. Below the second fetus-ghost room is a cafeteria where workers and followers go for free vegetarian food for breakfast, lunch, and dinner. From the window one can see a Buddhist nunnery and a four-story statue of Guanyin, which has remained in the same state of construction for the last two years because the Buddhist nunnery that was funding the building ran out of money. I have described a good deal about the temple that is not directly relevant to the topic of fetus ghosts, but because part of the attraction of the temple lies in its amusement park quality it seems worth mentioning.

Teacher Lin has written dozens of morality tracts that give general ideas about the nature of the relationship between the living and the spirit world, always being sure to include stories about temple goers' experiences with ghosts. Through these religious tracts Teacher Lin has been able to reach a wide following throughout Taiwan, uniting an otherwise diverse group of people.

As I noted earlier, there is an average of approximately 5,400 new fetus-ghost statues added each year. If we multiply this by the NT$1,200 that people must pay annually to keep their statues at the temple, this comes to NT$6,480,000 (approximately US$231,400) a year for fetus ghosts alone. In addition to this, at the semiannual ceremonies one can see that there are approximately two hundred people a year who pay the same fee to appease wandering ghosts, ancestors' ghosts, or other ghosts. Occasionally a client will voluntarily contribute large sums of money or gifts, such as some of the stone statues or stone pillars that line the entranceway to the parking lot and the temple.

Clearly Dragon Lake Temple is financially successful. But it is important to point out that the per-person charge is quite inexpensive compared to those of many other temples. Teacher Lin's genius was to set up a system that takes relatively little time and effort both for himself and for the individuals concerned, in effect mass-marketing the appeasement process in such a way as to allow an affordable package for individuals while still generating a sizable income.

Yet one should also note that maintaining such a temple entails considerable expense. In addition to supporting his family, Teacher Lin must pay for a permanent staff to run the temple. On the six annual ceremonial days he has to hire additional people to help with cooking and cleaning, as well as the group of six Buddhist musicians. On these days he provides free religious tracts to anyone who wants them and free rice to the poor.[14] The temple also makes contributions to the city, including a fire engine it donated to the city, street lights for the stretch of road in front of the temple connecting the cities to the north and the south, annual contributions to the local fire department and schools,[15] and a stipend for the head of the temple that provided Dragon Lake Temple's main god. Also, there is upkeep, electricity, water, taxes, and other expenses.

As we have seen, some people go to Dragon Lake Temple because a spirit medium or fortuneteller has told them that the source of their problem is a fetus ghost. Others may not actually experience problems but feel guilty after an abortion and wish to do something to make amends for what they think of as a sinful act. Some people go directly to Dragon Lake Temple, where most problems would be attributed to fetus ghosts. Fortunetellers, spirit mediums, and worshipers at Dragon Lake Temple also recommend it to others. In the last case there is a strong element of self-diagnosis, in that the worshiper chose to go to Dragon Lake Temple rather than another that is not associated with fetus ghosts.[16] This is true even in the first scenario, for if they did not know they had a fetus ghost haunting them, they nevertheless chose to go to someone who would explain their malady in a framework of spiritual causes rather than going to a doctor, for example, who would have a quite different set of explanations for the same problem.

People's emotions at the temple vary tremendously. If a ghost is from a relative's abortion, or if someone is appeasing the ghost for relief from a specific physical or economic malady rather than from a sense of guilt, the worshiper may breeze through these activities while joking with a friend or family member on the way out. Others, especially those who have come alone, are more solemn. Though I have never seen anyone sobbing out loud, on these occasions I have seen many obviously distraught men, and an even greater number of women wiping tears from their eyes.

In addition to the red contract, incense, and spirit money, which every worshiper burns for the fetus ghosts and gods, some people also bear additional gifts for their fetus ghosts. There is no set offering for those who want to bring such presents. This flexibility provides people with an opportunity to choose a gift that allows room for a personal expression of what might have been. The following is a list of some of the toys and food that I saw on one walk through the temple on the third day of one of these ceremonies:

> A Snoopy and Woodstock pillow, baby clothing, a toy yak from McDonald's, a mini bowling set with plastic pins and a bowling ball, candy, oranges, a teddy bear, a wind-up shoe, toy guns, pineapple cakes, cookies, jelly candies, a toy fishing kit with plastic fish and fishing pole, plastic soldiers, a baby's wool cap, a box of chocolates with a picture of a boy Tarzan on the package, edible molds (to make jelly grapes, fish, etc.), bathing trunks and a shirt with a baby bear embroidered on it, a pink toy cement truck, Minnie Mouse, a baby rattle, toy dalmatians, Mickey Mouse, a toy rabbit, jelly, crackers, cookies, several large cans of milk powder, flowers (which are set out both by the temple staff and by parents), a toy bird, a pacifier, apples, strawberry candies, yogurt, M&M's (peanut), baby shoes, potato chips, instant noodles, an action play set, three shot glasses full of milk, juice, a stuffed toy bear, rabbit, chipmunk, dog, cat, a musical dog, a toy telephone.

And the list goes on. These toys are set out on the ledge in front of the shelves and, when possible, on the shelf bearing the worshiper's fetus ghost. If there is no room on this shelf, the toy or food is placed on the ledge below. This is seemingly like Weller's account of the 18 Lords temple, in which templegoers offer untraditional gifts such as cigarettes to the gods (Weller 1994, 1996), but there is an important difference here. In Weller's account the cigarettes were offered as a bribe, a means of ingratiating oneself with the gods to get them to do one's bidding. In the case of fetus ghosts, the appeasement process could be seen as a bribe to induce the spirit to stop harassing the living, but the toys and other gifts are voluntary, a means of making the spirit more comfortable, as one would try to comfort a child. Thus, while both cases represent a new development in what is allowable in sacrifice, the emotional import of the gifts could not be more different.

Less commonly, people will go to Dragon Lake Temple to appease wandering spirits, ancestor spirits, or spirits they knew in previous lives. Instead of statues, simple paper slips for these ghosts are pasted to the outside wall of the fetus-ghost building. The paper has the same format as what is written on a fetus-ghost statue. One goes through the same process, burning the red contract, incense, and spirit money. In addition, one can pray to money gods; star gods; or a tree god, which is actually one tree growing on another different genus of tree, thus representing the tree god for married couples. Like other temples, one can also use divination blocks,[17] pray for good fortune, or appease ancestors. But these are all of secondary importance because, unlike other temples, the main function of Dragon Lake Temple is to appease fetus ghosts.

The majority of people who appease fetus ghosts are women, who comprise approximately 70 percent of the people at the Dragon Lake Temple at any given time. While it is common for women to go alone or with their female friends, one also sees men who have come by themselves. I have never seen a man come with male friends only. The majority of men who come to the temple are accompanied by their spouses, girlfriends, or lovers. Many men who accompany women seem to feel uncomfortable and out of place, and it is common to see a man heading for the rest area while his wife or girlfriend makes the prayer rounds for their fetus ghosts. Often, however, when a man tries to sneak off to the rest area he is roughly chastised by his partner, after which he goes with her to appease the ghost.

It is not that men do not have a stake in this process. Although fewer in number than their female counterparts, there are indeed men who come on their own. They, as well as men who accompany their partners, have told me of their extremely deep feelings both toward the fetus ghosts and about their part in the abortion that created the ghost.

Sometimes whole families go to the temple to appease fetus ghosts. For example, one fifty-year-old woman and her husband brought their three teenage daughters with them to appease her *yingling*. Another man in his late twenties, who did not seem to care much about the appeasement himself, was accompanying both his girlfriend as she appeased their fetus ghost and his parents as they appeased theirs. In a fetus-ghost temple in Japan, I saw a woman tell her eight-year-old child to pray for his older brother. I have never seen Taiwanese children asked to participate in such rites. They are, however, quite often brought along while their parents perform the appeasement ritual.

The fact that the temple performs other services also gives people an excuse for being there if they happen to run into someone they know. Many of the worshipers first heard of Dragon Lake Temple through friends, so such encounters are more common than one might think. Because of the remote location of the temple, however, it is rare for worshipers to meet other acquaintances there by accident; still, I have seen it happen. Even when there is a chance meeting, however, people are not likely to ask too many questions, as most are there for the same reason and are mutually anxious to avoid talking about the issue.

A Comparison of the Temples and Their Services

Each of the temples I have described has its own style of appeasement. Yet certain patterns do emerge. Most of the temple masters told me that it is up to the worshipers to decide how much they want to contribute. But it is worth noting that the Daoist master in Douliu also said this, although one of his clients had told me that he had specifically instructed her to pay NT$20,000. Daoist Master Bob told me the same thing; but, as mentioned earlier, I know that one of his clients paid him NT$10 million (US$293,800) for services not associated with fetus ghosts, and another client paid him large sums for a range of services, including providing for a fetus ghost. In both of these cases Daoist Master Bob suggested appropriate contribution amounts, though often in a roundabout way. Thus, it seems likely that the sliding scale is in fact manipulated by the masters rather than being an entirely voluntary process. This is not to say that payment is always more expensive than set fees. The Noodle Vendor, for instance, charged two or three hundred NT dollars per visit, and I know of another woman who paid her Daoist master a similar fee. Overall, my data suggest that such inexpensive costs are rare, and that if practitioners do not all charge such extortionate sums as Daoist Master Bob, other examples, such as the Douliu temple, still point to quite large fees for these services. Even in the cases where the per-visit charge is quite small, repeated appeasements would result in costs accruing.

In most cases, people do not take fetus-ghost statues, plaques, or other religious offerings home but leave them at the temple. The advantage of leaving offerings at the temple is obvious, for their presence in a home would announce the abortions in question to all visitors. Another advantage of leaving offerings for ghosts outside of the home is that the offerings are thought to draw the ghosts away from their families and bring them to the place where they are left (Harrell 1986: 107). This is certainly in keeping with popular thought about Dragon Lake Temple, for instance. A good example is the fact that many people warned me to be careful when spending the night there because the presence of all the fetus ghosts would create an excess of *yin* energy that could be harmful to me if I remained too long. Also, keeping memorial tablets at temples provides a way of caring for the ghosts of societally anomalous relatives without placing them on domestic altars, which would risk offending the ghosts of patrilineal ancestors (Sangren 1983: 18).[18]

The differences between Dragon Lake Temple and Ms. Xu's temple are quite significant. The most striking is that Ms. Xu is a woman. Although most of those appeasing fetus ghosts in Taiwan are female, with the exception of Ms. Xu all of the Daoist and Buddhist masters, fortunetellers, and spirit mediums associated with this practice that I met were male. In addition she is quite young, in her mid-thirties in contrast to Teacher Lin's seventy years.

Another point of interest is a simple difference in the personalities and backgrounds of the founders. Teacher Lin's methods are innovative yet are also based on a traditional religious model such as adopting the patron god from a more established temple. Although in one of our interviews Teacher Lin denied that he has this ability, many worshipers at his temple believe that he can sense, see, and/or communicate with ghosts. Worshipers also told me that he and the master of the founding temple receive divine inspiration when naming worshipers' fetus ghosts. In contrast, Ms. Xu makes no claim to be able to commu-nicate with beings in the spirit world, basing her practice on the Buddhist scriptures.

Teacher Lin's temple is located in a rural area in which citizens are easily won over by the temple's gifts to the fire department and schools. Ms. Xu's temple is less able to gain public goodwill in this fashion because of its smaller income and the urban nature of its environment. Also, one should not forget that Taibei is home to the federal government, which has been known occasionally to crack down on religious organizations. Thus, Teacher Lin has much more leeway, and Ms. Xu, who operates in the emperor's domain so to speak, must be more conservative in her claims.

Ms. Xu's temple is Buddhist, although it might not be accepted as such by some of the certified Buddhist temples. As I outlined in Chapter 5, some Buddhist organizations have been quite vocal in their condemnation of fetus-ghost appeasement, saying that this is not a truly Buddhist practice. Thus, if Ms. Xu were not modest in her claims, she would run the risk of being condemned both by orthodox Buddhist organizations and by the government.

As a last point of difference, Dragon Lake Temple is large enough that it has room to expand its housing of fetus-ghost statues and other religious paraphernalia as well as the crowds of worshipers who attend the ceremonies. Ms. Xu's temple, while in many ways more tasteful, lacks the sense of heat and noise (*renao*), or bustling activity, which is so prized in Chinese and Taiwanese culture. In contrast, Dragon Lake Temple's array of gods, statues, and other religious points of interest, combined with crowds of worshipers, creates just this atmosphere.

Although Dragon Lake Temple and Ms. Xu's temple are very different in the respects I have just described, they also have some important similarities that should not be overlooked. The environ-ment of both temples provides a certain anonymity for its patrons. Dragon Lake Temple does so because it is essentially in the middle of nowhere. Ms. Xu's temple does so because it is on a small street in Taibei, the largest metropolis in Taiwan, and thus possesses a certain urban anonymity. Both temples reflect Taiwan's growing urbaniza-tion and religious specialization. In the last twenty years, Taiwan has been transformed from an agricultural community with closely linked village ties to an urban one with widely extended ties in the work force, schools, and other meeting places. Whereas the traditional temples I discussed at the beginning of this chapter often serve the community around them, both Dragon Lake Temple and Ms. Xu's temple have an extremely diverse membership that does not attend the temples frequently.[19] Those who appease fetus ghosts at Ms. Xu's temple come from all over Taibei, and a few worshipers from other areas of Taiwan. Dragon Lake Temple's patronage is even more diverse, coming from all over the western coast of Taiwan. Thus, both temples reflect Taiwan's urbanization, drawing not on a community of neighbors but on a loosely organized group of strangers.

Finally, both temples have expertly made use of written media to attract clients, and both offer fairly quick, easy, and relatively inexpensive redemption. In contrast to other temples, which often have a religious master who takes charge of exorcising a fetus ghost, Teacher Lin and Ms. Xu both stress the element of self-help, in which people take responsibility for their actions, both in their admission of guilt and in making amends for their wrongdoings.

In the preceding pages we have seen a range of methods for appeasing fetus ghosts and the varying costs that are involved. In the temples I have described there seems to be a general tendency for Buddhist masters to be more modest in their claims because of their tenuous position in relation to orthodox Buddhism, as opposed to Daoist masters, who often claim to have more agency in expelling the ghosts. While some of the beliefs seem to have a logical consistency, others display the ways in which beliefs are tailored to fit the needs of a particular temple or religious master. This gives us a clear view of religious transformation as it is taking place, including a cast of players with their own distinctive personalities and the tools they use to achieve a better performance. With this background in mind, we can now proceed to look at what temple goers gain from the beliefs.

8

Illness, Healing, and the Limitations of Fetus-Ghost Appeasement

O FTEN a person's refusal to seek Western medical treatment in favor of traditional medicine or religious solutions is seen as illogical or even superstitious. Gananeth Obeyesekere, for example, maintains that we underestimate Taiwanese peasants when we assume that they are unable to use "simple instrumental rationality" in making the choice to visit Western practitioners (Obeyesekere 1975: 421). Yet I suggest that quite often it is precisely instrumental rationality that leads many Taiwanese to seek other options. Arthur Kleinman's study, for example, lists fairly comparable results for medical and religious healing systems; 86 percent of patients treated by physicians reported improvement as compared to 82 percent of people treated by shamans who felt they had improved (Kleinman 1982: 411).

To better understand why people in Taiwan turn to traditional medicine and ghost appeasement to cure illnesses, it is perhaps best to look first at the failings of Western medicine as it is practiced in Taiwan. Once we do this, it seems fair to say that, in many cases, for a patient to turn to alternative forms of medical treatment is a rational choice indeed.

Medical and Spiritual Treatment

Most spiritual solutions in Taiwan are sought in conjunction with other forms of medical treatment rather than as a substitute for it (Harrell 1991: 46), and for serious illnesses most people in Taiwan will first go to Western or traditional Chinese doctors. It is only after these doctors fail to cure the illness that patients look into other options (Gallin 1975: 275; Jordan 1972: 139; Martin 1975: 123–124).

In her study of Taiwan, Emily Ahern notes that a significant number of patients reported that they felt a clear explanation of their illness was very important to them (Ahern 1975b: 100). Yet there is a strong reluctance on the part of practitioners of Western medicine in Taiwan to answer patients' questions (Martin 1975: 134–135). Practitioners of traditional Chinese medicine and religious healing offer an important service, in that they give explanations for illness that ease the worries of the ill and their loved ones (Martin 1975). As Arthur Kleinman has pointed out, illness occurs at a biological level but is experienced as a personal and social reality (Kleinman 1975: 600). Thus, to be able to know the nature of one's disease brings comfort with the feeling that one can take action against a visible enemy rather than struggling against a vague, amorphous force that does not follow causative rules of reason (Ahern 1975b; McCreery 1979; Turner 1967). Emily Ahern states:

> Whether the sick person himself acts or whether action is taken on his behalf, one of the most important effects of seeking a cure is that the patient and those around him are given a language with which to describe and understand the illness. Whether or not the treatment succeeds in curing the illness itself, it will have succeeded for a time in affecting people's *experience* of the illness, a result scarcely less vital than achieving a final bodily cure. (Ahern 1975b: 108)

Even when it is offered, the diagnostic terminology used in Western medicine may not go far enough in explaining an illness in comprehensible terms, whereas the idea that one has fallen ill because of one's sins is immediately understandable, tangible, and, with the help of religious practice, thought to be potentially resolvable (Obeyesekere 1975: 424). This links illness with the patient's whole life rather than a few symptoms, as healing is thought to require moral reform to influence the individual, which in turn is thought to affect the family and society itself (Gallin 1975: 274; Unschuld 1976: 304). Conversely, problems within the family can cause sickness for individuals (Jordan 1972: 93).

There are several other shortcomings of Western medicine as it is practiced in Taiwan. Because patients tend to complain that they have not been given proper treatment if they have not received a good deal of medicine, doctors are known to prescribe a wide array of pills or shots for almost any ailment. Also, many Taiwanese people I have spoken with feel that good Western doctors are trained in the West and that most skilled practitioners remain in the countries where they have studied. For the most part, they told me, the doctors who return to Taiwan are second-rate. I cannot say if this is true or not, but the popular perception that it is true is no doubt another factor in people's willingness to experiment with other options. In addition to this, many patients feel uncomfortable in the presence of Western-style doctors, who are far more educated and are accorded the highest level of respect in Taiwanese society (Martin 1975: 133).

Physical Illness

> An unmarried young woman I know got pregnant but for many reasons had to have an abortion. After she did this, strange things began to happen. Every midnight, she heard the sound of a female baby crying, and sometimes she saw a white shadow running around her living room and laughing. It looked like a normal one-year-old baby. Because the ghost was around her, she became thinner and thinner and began to have some very serious health problems. Because of this she asked an exorcist to make the ghost go away. She then became safe again. (A twenty-six-year-old college-educated woman)

Symptoms attributed to fetus ghosts usually include severe weight loss and fatigue. This could tie in with the national obsession that women be slender. It might also connect with a more generalized depression. Other common ailments associated with fetus ghosts include severe pain in the shoulders or stomach. In many cases, such localized tension is likely to be the result of stress. It is also probable that some afflictions stem from the very real physical side effects of obtaining abortions at private clinics, for a great many clinics are unsanitary and have unskilled practitioners. Less commonly, people might appease fetus ghosts to relieve severe coughs, which are prevalent in Taiwan's highly polluted environment; illnesses that are likely to be caused by aging; or terminal ailments that Western or traditional Chinese medicine had failed to cure.

Ohnuki-Tierney has suggested that appeasers of fetus ghosts in Japan often suffer from "what we might call psychosomatic illnesses, often of a mild nature" (Ohnuki-Tierney 1984: 78, 80). John McCreery makes a similar point when he suggests that, when an illness is psychological or psychosomatic, religious healing may play a major role in the healing process (McCreery 1979: 53). The psychological comfort that fetus-ghost appeasement provides should ease the symptoms of such illnesses.

It seems imprudent to dismiss people's deeply felt beliefs that appeasing fetus ghosts helps to heal their illnesses. An etic analysis might label this as "the placebo effect," in which patients recover because they believe they are receiving the proper treatment. Proving the medicinal benefits of this religious belief is obviously difficult, but I have repeatedly been told of people's improved health after appeasing fetus ghosts. To apply this to the specific maladies that I have already mentioned, the psychological comfort that fetus-ghost appeasement provides could ease muscle tension or stomach pains as well as symptoms arising from depression.

The relief of other maladies may simply be a matter of the body healing itself over time but being attributed to the fetus-ghost appeasement. In instances where the illness is real, belief in the ghost and its appeasement process provides a tangible cause for an illness and the promise of a cure. Because most illnesses do abate over time, the appeasement process eases normal anxieties associated with illnesses. Also, because it is likely that stress inhibits the healing process, it seems plausible to suggest that the reduction of stress in this manner may in fact aid one's recovery. For whatever reasons, in addition to the psychological comfort that fetus-ghost appeasement provides, there do seem to be some positive physical effects.

Behavioral Problems

In Chapter 5 I included the story of "The Worm Mutilator" from a religious tract, in which a child whose fetus ghost was appeased miraculously changed from an antisocial, animal-abusing, and reticent child into a socially responsible, hard-working, and loving son. Less dramatic, though more common, are typical children's behavioral problems, which more experienced parents might simply attribute to a stage associated with a particular age. One example of this is the case of a construction worker from a small town in central Taiwan whom I met during one of the Dragon Lake Temple semiannual ceremonies. He told me of his three-year-old son, who was being "influenced" (*yingxiang*) by the ghost of the fetus that his wife had aborted five years earlier. When I asked how he knew his son was afflicted, he replied, "He's been very naughty in the last year." Then he paused for a moment and looked at his son with concern: "He's always going through drawers and throwing their contents on the ground and he never listens to what I say. If he does something wrong and I scold him he seems to be sorry for what he's done, but five minutes later he will be doing something else that he shouldn't be doing." I asked if appeasing the fetus ghost had had any effect. His face lit up. "Oh sure, he's been much better in the last couple of weeks"; grabbing the boy playfully, he addressed his child: "Haven't you? Haven't you?"

A similar case is a woman I also met at Dragon Lake Temple. She was a twenty-three-year-old secretary at a company that sold photographic equipment in Taibei. She sat on a bench in the rest area cradling her seven-month-old child in her arms. Like many temple goers, she asked me if I was there to provide for a fetus ghost. I explained what I was doing there and asked, "And you?" She nodded to the baby in her arms, "We're here for her." I asked, "Is she all right?" She said, "Her health is fine but she's always crying, my husband and I can never get any sleep and we're worried about her." I asked if appeasing the fetus ghost was working, and she responded: "What? Oh, yes, I guess. We only just started so I suppose it's too early to say for sure." The uncertainty with which this mother responded is common. Often, just as people might turn to Western medicine if traditional Chinese medicine proved ineffective (or vice versa), many of those who appease fetus ghosts for a specific purpose will give it the benefit of the doubt but wait for the final results before attesting to its effectiveness.

In the above examples, belief in fetus ghosts helped to alleviate parental fears about the behavior of their offspring. It is striking that parents would seek help for such "normal" problems. One possible explanation for this is that they are overly anxious about their children because of a lack of experience: a steadily growing number of people are opting not to live with their parents after they are married and thus may lack the constant source of information about child rearing they would have had if they stayed with them. Another factor is the belief in the "fright syndrome," the belief that startled souls can leave their bodies. This phenomenon is thought to occur especially in infants, another explanation for the prevalence of parents who worry about normal infants' activities. It is possible that when fetus-ghost appeasement reduces parents' anxieties, their children are relieved of parental pressure, which in turn could influence their behavior. Thus, we can see both the harmful and curative effects of fetus ghosts.

The following excerpt is from one of Xu Qiong Yue's religious tracts that was written to discourage abortion and provide information about fetus ghosts and their exorcisms.

> I know an older member of our temple who was raising her two children. They had a happy life and a stable business. Of her two children she had a closer predestined relationship[1] with her older son. But her older son had a rebellious personality and would often do things that angered his mother. One can tell if a father or mother has a strong fate with a particular child; one can get this feeling at just a glance. Some children have come to collect debt from previous lives and some come to repay a debt owed to their parents. It is very rarely that a child will have the kind of karmic relationship in which someone does not need to repay a debt or collect repayment from past lives. Just think of your own family, whether as a child you were closer to, and had a stronger fate with, your father or mother should be clear. This strong feeling is one that you don't have to analyze, it just comes naturally. I believe you readers have all had this experience.
>
> Both this mother and others could sense that she and her son had an especially close relationship because they were fated to be together. All parents under heaven will say, "I love all of my children equally, whether they are male or female, older or younger." Of course, that parents love their children is a natural characteristic, but if you observe closely, you will notice that there is always one child who is especially dear to his or her father's or mother's heart. Perhaps this is because you owe a debt to this person from another life.
>
> This year her older son is graduating from junior high school and is getting ready to take the entrance examination for high school. So his mother was of course more strict with him. Although they had a strong predestined relationship, when they were together the son would unexpectedly have outbursts of furious temper, and a loathing built in his heart day by day. His mother did not understand how her son could have such a rebellious character. In this way the mother and son had a life together that was filled with contradiction; love and hate mixed together. And where did the fury that was growing in her older son's heart come from? He was also at a loss to explain it. And late, late at night, when everything was quiet, they both knew deep in their hearts that they still cared for each other very much. [. . .] When

an unmarried or married woman accidentally gets pregnant and then gets an abortion, the aborted child's spirit will continue to stay by its mother's side. And since abortion is the killing of life, it is like murdering one's son or daughter with one's own hands. Because of this, the heart of the soul of such a son or daughter are full of hatred and resentment. Such a spirit is always by its mother's side, waiting for the moment when its mother gets pregnant again so that it can take the first opportunity to enter its mother's womb [to be reborn as her next child]. When a woman has an abortion she creates bad karma which exists in the form of the killed fetus's hate and resentment. This is why when most women who have had abortions decide to give birth, their children's hearts are full of hatred and rebelliousness beyond that of other children. (Xu 1995: 3–6)

Because the spirit of an unappeased aborted fetus is thought to be likely to be reborn as its mother's next child, children's behavioral problems can be blamed on abortions or miscarriages that occurred many years before. Through this displacement it is possible to strengthen parent–child ties that have otherwise come under a great deal of stress.

As we can see from the above quotation, the problems and medicinal effects of the *yingling* extend far beyond the relationship between mother and aborted fetus. An etic analysis might place the blame on outside structural pressures, noting that the older son was preparing to take one of the hardest tests in his life—a test that would shape his future far more dramatically than the university examinations he would take later. The fact that his mother "became more strict" at this time shows that she only added to this pressure.

Another etic explanation might suggest that the son was going through puberty, thus placing the blame not on the nature of the child but on unavoidable biological functions. In the United States the concept of puberty entails a disturbing separation of one's physical characteristics and one's personality, not unlike spirit possession. A temperamental teenager is given quite a bit of leeway for her or his actions under a culturally legitimized concept of puberty that is thought to be when the child's body takes control over her or his mind. Nonetheless, as the body and mind are still perceived as comprising one unit (the person), the teenager is still held responsible for her or his actions, although under mitigating circumstances.

C. K. Yang's Durkheimian analysis of Chinese religion suggests that the ritual expression of grief for a family member helps to reaffirm family ties precisely when a death might weaken them (Yang 1961: 36). David Jordan also suggests a structural interpretation, noting that in Taiwan violations of harmony, ranging from sickness and financial ruin to deteriorating family relations, are often blamed on ghosts (Jordan 1972: xxii). Belief in *yingling* removes the problem from the child completely, firmly placing it on a dead spirit that cannot be harmed if hostilities and prejudices are aimed in its direction. In this view, to blame sick children for their temper tantrums would be the equivalent of blaming someone who was ill for her or his fever. In the above account, for example, belief in fetus ghosts allows the mother and son to place the focus of blame outside of their own relationship. By expelling the ghost, they can assert their love and begin again without blame for previous actions.

Mental Illness

My mother and two cousins have gone to the same spirit medium; all of them were haunted by fetus ghosts. My mother had an abortion almost twenty-five years ago and only recently discovered that the fetus ghost was still following her. She set up an urn for it in a pagoda and goes to pray to it once a year on tomb sweeping day.

I also have a cousin who was having mental problems. She was going crazy and almost killed herself because she felt that she "was not herself." My aunt talked her into going to a spirit medium, and he told my cousin that she was being haunted by her uncle who had died a few months after he was born. The uncle asked that she act as his granddaughter and perform the appropriate rituals for him. After she did this she got better. The same thing happened to a male cousin. In that case, the male cousin's aunt who had died shortly after being born was haunting him.[2] (A twenty-three-year-old female graduate student)

As one man I interviewed put it, "In the West you have psychologists; in the East we have spirit mediums." Much of my argument pertaining to people's dissatisfaction with Western-style medicine in healing physical illnesses also holds true for psychological illness. In this area we see the same use of incomprehensible terms, the same educational and class difference between doctors and patients, and in many cases a similar lack of effectiveness.

Just as the language of Western medicine is foreign to most Taiwanese, so psychological conceptions that we take for granted as part of our understanding of the world are foreign to Chinese understandings of psychology and cognition (Gallin 1975: 279). Also, to go to a psychologist is considered shameful, both for the individuals involved and for their families, because it suggests individual weakness and the possibility that the patient had bad parenting. On a more pragmatic level, being diagnosed as having a mental illness could potentially mark that person, or even the person's family members, as unfit for marriage or producing heirs (Kleinman 1975: 606).

As I outlined in Chapter 5, fetus-ghost appeasement can have a financially exploitative element for women who are already held responsible for the physical, financial, and emotional price of abortion. But in addition to demonstrating the level of exploitation involved, the willingness to pay a high price for this service is an indication of the importance of this process for the person paying the fee. Belief in *yingling* confers many of the same psychological benefits that religious confession or psychotherapy provides, in that it allows the discussion of a fairly taboo subject. By helping people to feel that their aborted fetuses are being cared for in the spirit world, or that the spirits have been sent on to their next lives, the guilt about the appeasers' perceived sinfulness is very much alleviated. For women this is especially poignant, as many women lack emotional support when they get an abortion. If one compares appeasement to the cost of psychological therapy in the United States, for example, or to the threat of eternal damnation that one might face in other religions for that matter, it is a relatively inexpensive and quickly achieved process. Although belief in fetus ghosts can accentuate the guilt of those who have had abortions, and of those involved in the decision making that led to those abortions, the same concept can be a strong healing force for those who believe.

Comfort, Healing, and Their Limitations

I used to have muscle cramps in my shoulders.[3] Also, I have a severe stomach ailment and I have a hard time eating. Before appeasing my *yingling* I had lost a lot of weight. Since my wife and I started providing for our child I've still had stomach problems, but it's much better. I have gained eight kilograms since I started providing for my child and the problem with my shoulders is gone! (Mr. Wang, October 1997)

> My stomach? Oh, you know, it still bothers me. It looked like
> it was getting better for a while, but I'm still having a problem
> eating. (Mr. Wang, February 1999)

Mr. Wang, a middle-aged businessman, initially felt that appeasing his
fetus ghost was curing him. Yet more than a year later the tenure of
his appeasement had almost expired but his ailment persisted. Mr.
Wang assured me that he still believed in his fetus ghost, but his tone
of voice was less enthusiastic and seemed to hint at a lack of the certainty he had once possessed.

Mrs. Li

Mrs. Li is a woman in her early forties. She adores children, and
the fact that she has no offspring of her own is clearly a sad element
in an otherwise contented life. The fact that she teaches at a high
school in Tainan is both a pleasure and a pain to her in that she has
the opportunity to be around young people, but this satisfaction is
limited by the fact that they are not her own children. In 1987 she
met a Daoist master who told her that she had a six- or seven-year-old
fetus ghost following her.[4] Although she had never had an abortion,
she had missed her period for two months approximately seven years
before. Taking this to be the fetus ghost to which the Daoist master
referred, Mrs. Li was impressed that he could know about what she
had interpreted as a miscarriage known only to herself, her husband,
and her sister.

The Daoist master told her that her daughter (the spirit of her
aborted fetus) had protected her over the last several years. Mrs. Li
took this as referring to some well-paying investments she had made
and to the fact that she had a good husband who was hard-working
and did not gamble or run around with other women. The Daoist
master also told her that her fetus ghost had a particularly close relationship with the goddess Guanyin, who had adopted the ghost, and
that the child was happy and being taken care of in the spirit world.
The Daoist master went on to predict that she would have a child
within the next two years and that the *yingling* would be reborn as
that child. Mrs. Li clearly took comfort from the fact that she already
had a child of sorts, and her face was positively radiant when she
spoke of her "child." I had known Mrs. Li for many years, but I had
never seen her as happy as she was in the following six months. She

often referred to her child and said that she had felt a sense of security since the Daoist master told her the child was protecting her. Most important, this ghost-child filled a void in her life.

Unfortunately, her Daoist master was too bold in his claims. In the ensuing six months he wrongly predicted that Mrs. Li's friend would give birth to a boy, he approved several of Mrs. Li's investments that failed, and he predicted that the wrong candidate would be the winner of a local election. Perhaps most important, he had treated a friend of hers shabbily. After six months, Mrs. Li became completely disillusioned with this Daoist master, and as a result of that disillusionment she stopped believing in her fetus ghost. Mrs. Li was characteristically optimistic about the matter, saying that the bad experience proved to her the values of her Christian belief, from which she said she had begun to stray when she met the Daoist master. I do not think that she is less happy now than before she met the Daoist master, but any comfort she had derived from the thought of her fetus ghost is now gone.

Although she never told me the exact amount she paid the Daoist master, she hinted that she had given him large sums to provide the fetus ghost with clothing and money, and to begin a process to send the spirit on to its next life.[5] Yet, to hear her speak of the matter, the money was relatively unimportant to her. On the whole, those in charge of fetus-ghost appeasement seem to have a fairly keen perception of what their clients are willing to pay. Even in Mrs. Li's case, she could afford the costs of the appeasement rituals, although they were not cheap. The greater the claims of Daoist and Buddhist masters, the more likely clients are to be disillusioned, because they have concrete facts against which they can check the master's credibility. This Daoist master's mistake, therefore, was less being greedy than being overconfident in his own abilities. When talking with this master, I had the feeling that his greatest strength, and weakness, was a certain impulsiveness, which charmed his clients but also put his credibility at risk.

Religious masters who make more modest claims, such as Teacher Lin or Ms. Xu, generally charge less money per patron, but they lose less of their clientele and gain a good reputation from word of mouth, which results in their attracting a larger number of clients. Even then there are limitations, however. If a client goes to a temple out of a general sense of guilt, it is usually the case that that guilt is alleviated after the appeasement process, but in other situations the solution is not a perfect fit to the problem.

Mr. and Mrs. Wu

Mr. and Mrs. Wu regularly frequent a Daoist temple in Taibei. Mr. Wu is the very essence of the traditional concept of a Chinese scholar. He is soft-spoken and cordial, and I have never heard him speak unless he had something important and insightful to say. Some years ago he graduated from National Taiwan University, the most prestigious university in Taiwan, and then went on to earn an M.B.A. at Yale. On returning to Taiwan he started working for a computer company with four hundred employees. In 1998 the owner retired and Mr. Wu became CEO of the company. Although he was a dedicated Buddhist for many years, he now frequents a Daoist temple in Taibei, where he and his wife visit to burn incense and leave small offerings of milk for their fetus ghost. Often they will remain at the temple so that Mr. Wu and the Daoist master can exchange ideas about morality and religion, sharing wisdom from their different religious backgrounds.

Mrs. Wu has a B.A. in English literature. After marrying she left her job to become a housewife. Far more outgoing than Mr. Wu, she loves to gossip and talk about current events. Mr. Wu is approximately fifty years old, and Mrs. Wu is a decade younger, but to their sorrow they have no children. Three years ago she had a miscarriage. Mrs. Wu once told me, "I can feel a presence behind me," which she happily asserts is her "child." It is for this "child" that they go to the temple.

Watching the couple together, you would scarcely know they were married. Both of them are quite willing to talk to others, but they seem at a loss for things to say to each other. When in a group I have never seen them stand or sit beside each other but always create a buffer by putting others, including myself, between them. In part this is because of a disparity in their interests. Mr. Wu is constantly reading religious books and looking for other men to discuss the latest idea that he has read about; Mrs. Wu once confessed to me that she only went to university because she knew it would increase her marriage prospects. Now that her mission has been accomplished, so to speak, she makes no pretense of showing an interest in such matters.

The couple's marriage has little to hold it together, with two exceptions. The first is a dedication to tradition and to the concept of marriage as a lifelong commitment. This dedication is equally strong on both sides. The second is their fetus ghost, which plays the role of a living child in that it acts as the adhesive to mend the cracks of an otherwise brittle relationship. Although they are unsure if their fetus ghost is female or male, the one thing they can reliably share in their conversations is their "child." And when they talk about this, it is the one time you can see them smiling together.

Clearly, the fetus ghost has filled an important gap in the Wus' lives. The problem, of course, is its imminent loss, in that both of them believe that after another year their child will be reborn and they will again be left on their own. They have told me they will continue to go to the temple after their fetus ghost has gone on to its next life, but the question remains as to what will happen once their "child" is gone.

Jeffrey

Jeffery, in his late thirties, is a white-collar worker in a small company in Taibei. I first met him at Dragon Lake Temple where he told me, "My wife and I have been coming to this temple for two and a half years now, but when we finish here we may continue to appease [the same] fetus ghosts at another temple in Taibei." I replied with surprise that I thought Teacher Lin said that the fetus ghosts would be reborn after three years and asked him, "If the fetus ghost was reborn, whom would you be praying for?" He replied: "Most people can appease their *yingling* in three years. My wife and I are appeasing three fetus ghosts you know. . . . I don't know . . . my wife and I just feel that we haven't done enough . . . maybe the appeasement isn't working, I don't know." To continue to appease a fetus ghost after the first appeasement is very rare, but it does happen, which points to the limitations of this process.[6]

On the whole, I was struck by how well-adjusted those appeasing fetus ghosts were. Most of them possessed an appealing friendliness that was a pleasure to work with. Jeffrey was not like this. Jeffrey was a short, thin man who peered out at an angle from glasses he rarely washed. His every statement was vague and he was often rude. Despite his eagerness to meet with me, Jeffrey proved to be the most difficult person I had ever interviewed. Simple questions such as "When did you first start appeasing your fetus ghost?" were met with vague answers such as "Oh, a while now [long pause], a while now." At one point he told me that his coworkers were surprised that he had received my call. This did not seem surprising in and of itself, and I asked, "Why, because I'm a foreigner?" He replied, "Oh that, yes, but just that I got a call in general. . . . I don't usually get many calls."

Many of Jeffrey's statements contained obvious hostility. For example, he told me, "At work they don't like me, but they don't really know who they are dealing with." He told me that, in addition to frequenting Dragon Lake Temple, he was also appeasing his fetus ghosts with a Daoist master in Taibei, "I go to this master to help me with things." We sat in silence for some time. I then asked, "What kinds of things?" He replied, with a self-satisfied grin, "Oh, just things." At the time I was just beginning to research the belief in fetus demons, so I asked, "Have you heard of any religious masters who raise fetus demons?" He replied, "Oh yes," smiling knowingly. I asked him if he knew anyone who did so, and he again replied, "Oh yes." We sat in silence for some time, after which he continued, "You'd be surprised how many people raise fetus demons. You might even know some-one who does this and you might not realize it."[7]

Later in the interview Jeffrey said, "You should really meet my Daoist master sometime, he is very powerful." I told him that I would be delighted to, asking if the master appeased fetus ghosts. Once again, he smiled knowingly and slowly said, "Oh, yes, he does that, but he also does other things." When I asked him what kinds of things the master did, Jeffrey once again replied with a smirk, "Oh, just things." Toward the end of our interview he told me, "I go to my Daoist master for protection." I asked what kind of protection, and he said, "Oh, just protection, I need help sometimes."

One might assume that Jeffrey's interactions with the second Daoist master catered to his need to feel important and potent in spite of a life of being friendless and unempowered. As opposed to Mr. Wang and Mrs. Li, who seemed to be well-adjusted people who received comfort, in one form or another, from appeasing their fetus ghosts, Jeffrey seemed to have deeper psychological problems that appeared to be continuing strongly in spite of his religious activities. Most important for this study, however, is the fact that he was not satisfied with the fetus-ghost appeasement process. Despite his going to the second master, there was no evidence that this was helping him either. In short, as with any therapeutic method, there are some cases that are so complex that the appeasement process is not enough.

In this chapter I have examined people's choice of turning to fetus-ghost appeasement as a form of physical or psychological therapy, and shown that this choice stems as much from the failures of Western medicine as it does from the perceived effectiveness of spiritual healing. In most cases, the people participating in fetus-ghost appeasement reported success in curing physical and psychological maladies as well as relieving a more general sense of guilt.

In speaking of the role that fetus-ghost appeasement plays in resolving familial tensions, one is faced with the possibility that such techniques have the potential to be either eufunctional or dysfunctional. In the cases where the problems being faced are short-term points of stress, it seems likely that the practice is eufunctional, in that belief in appeasing fetus spirits brings comfort and displaces blame for problems that will naturally heal over time. To apply this to the examples I have already provided, behavioral problems of very young children, teenagers going through what we call puberty, or middle-aged women going through menopause, as well as external pressures such as the college entrance exam or financial hardship, seem to be made more tolerable by belief in fetus-ghost appeasement.

On the other hand, if the problem is more enduring, such as a domineering parent or a child who has long-term behavioral problems, the belief may be dysfunctional in that it only serves to displace blame without addressing or resolving the real underlying tensions. In these cases, one religious solution after another might be tried without any real long-term results.

This also leads to a related point—the tenure of the appeasement process. There is a wide range of possible time investment for the appeasement process. A longer investment of time might help appeasers to feel that they have sufficiently proven the sincerity of their repentance when they cannot afford the higher price of other temples. Also, if we can assume that many physical and behavioral problems will resolve themselves over a period of time, then longer-term investments, such as the two-month tenure at Ms. Xu's temple or the three-year period of appeasement at Dragon Lake Temple, are more likely to be thought to produce positive results. In contrast, a few-hour ceremony requires quick resolution of the problem lest the afflicted person move on to try other forms of healing and accredit the disappearance of their affliction to that new method.

In Chinese culture, to openly express one's feelings is rare. When people are depressed, they are far more likely to say that they have colds than to say they are sad. Often, family members are hesitant to talk about embarrassing matters. In this setting the *yingling* plays an essential role in allowing people to discuss otherwise taboo topics. By talking about fetus ghosts, those appeasing the ghost can begin to raise issues of abortion, sexuality, guilt, anxiety, and illness.

Yet there are also limitations. More obvious cases include terminal illnesses, where belief in fetus-ghost appeasement might provide comfort but not a cure. To address other limitations of the practice, I gave four examples of people who were psychologically and financially invested in the process. Yet, when appeasers lose faith in their religious masters because they fail to heal the physical maladies in question, or when the problems in question are serious enough that they persist beyond a period of a few years, the process can fail.

9

Sexuality and
the Haunting Fetus

CONTINUOUS motifs in this evolving analysis of fetus ghosts have been the guilt experienced by the living, the censure expressed by some outside commentators, and the anger often attributed to the ghosts themselves. Important to all three of these is a concern about sexual excess and sex merely for pleasure. This chapter will therefore focus on the traditional Chinese and modern Taiwanese fear of sexual excess and the ways in which this fear plays itself out in beliefs concerning fetus ghosts. Intertwined with fear one can see shifts and tensions in the relationship between the individual and society. My analysis of this phenomenon will include three interconnected elements: (1) a focus on individual sexual fulfillment and health; (2) an anxiety concerning physical self-indulgence that leads to illness; and (3) a fear of sexual immoderation that is perceived to lead to a breakdown of familial and social order, thus leading to chaos.

In the following pages I suggest that, in traditional China, Daoist tracts on sexuality allowed for a discussion of, and even an emphasis on, the individual in an environment of Confucian emphasis of social obligation. In contrast, as people in modern Taiwan are becoming more individualistic and more sexually permissive, belief in the haunting fetus is emerging as a means of reenforcing social responsibility.

Sexual Excess and the Health of the Individual

In traditional China, ancient Daoist literature on sexuality emphasized self-control, linking it to the health of the individual. Van Gulik translated the following passage from a Sui Dynasty (A.D. 586–618) text:

131

The way to make the semen return to enforce the brain is thus. When, during the sexual act the man feels that he is about to ejaculate, he must quickly and firmly press with fore and middle finger of the left hand the spot between scrotum and anus, simultaneously inhaling deeply and gnashing his teeth scores of times, without holding his breath. Then the semen will be activated but not yet emitted; it returns from the Jade Stalk and enters the brain. (van Gulik 1961: 145)

The Dynastic History of the Later Han Period (A.D. 25–220) says the following:

> Master Jung-ch'êng was adept at nurturing and controlling (his physical functions). He absorbed (new) semen from the Mysterious Vagina (literally: vale). The main point of this art is to prevent the Spirit of the Vale (i.e., one's potency) from dying by preserving one's vital essence and by nurturing his vital force *(ch'i)*. Then one's gray hair will turn black again and new teeth will replace those that have fallen out. This art of having sexual intercourse with women consists of restraining oneself so as not to ejaculate, thus making the semen return and strengthen the brain. (van Gulik 1961: 71)

The following is van Gulik's translation of the *Yixinfang*, published in 1854:

> Every man must regulate his emissions according to the condition of his vital essence. He must never force himself to emit semen. Every time he forces himself to reach orgasm he will harm his system. Therefore, strongly built men of fifteen years can afford to emit semen twice a day; thin ones once a day, and the same applies to men of twenty years. Strongly built men of thirty may ejaculate once a day, weaker men once in two days. Strong men of forty may emit semen once in three days, weaker men once in four days. Strong men of fifty can ejaculate once in five days, weaker men once in ten days. Strong men of sixty may ejaculate once in ten days, weaker men once in twenty days. Strong men of seventy may emit semen once a month, weak ones should not ejaculate anymore at that age.
>
> Yang-shêng-yao-chi—"The Taoist Liu Ching said: 'In spring man can allow himself to emit semen once every three days, in summer and autumn twice a month. During winter one should save one's semen and not ejaculate at all. Indeed the way of Heaven is to store up Yang essence during winter." (van Gulik 1961: 146)

These texts, old as they are, are startlingly congruent with current beliefs in Taiwan, especially beliefs held by those forty years of age and over, concerning the avoidance of overly frequent sexual activity.[1]

I should emphasize that such materials did not directly prohibit sexual activity. On the contrary, abstinence was thought to be as dangerous as indulgence, potentially leading to mental instability and even death (Wile 1992: 7–8). Yet again and again we see in these texts a call for strict control. By stressing that there were proper and improper ways to engage in sexual intercourse, these guidebooks provided a method to indulge in pleasure without the loss of order.

Van Gulik maintains that one effect of withholding their emissions was that men could have sex more often, achieving the goal of helping the female partner to reach orgasm (van Gulik 1961: 46, 109). He then uses this information to formulate a characteristically eccentric, and somewhat charming, argument that this served the purpose of maintaining family harmony in households with multiple wives (van Gulik 1961: 155). Van Gulik reasons that, by following the bedchamber manuals' guidance not to ejaculate and to have sex with as many women as possible, a man would be more likely to fulfill his several wives sexually (van Gulik 1961: 60).

Charlotte Furth points out, correctly I think, that van Gulik's analysis is flawed, in that the bedchamber manuals more often than not contain a common "Chinese metaphor of sexual intercourse as combat, with its representation of the partners as 'enemies' destined for victory or defeat," in which the final prize was a limited supply of *qi* energy (Furth 1992: 134–135). Douglas Wile makes a similar point for what he calls the ominously adversarial language of "the battle of stealing and strengthening" found in the bedchamber texts (Wile 1992: 14). Yet, though Furth's analysis seems more credible, van Gulik's attempt to come to terms with what would appear to be conflicting signals that are, if you will pardon the pun, embedded in the texts, is an important one.[2] Also, while van Gulik might have overemphasized the importance of female orgasm in the texts, the concern was present. Wile provides a wonderful example of this in his translation of the Sui-Tang classics in which Su Nü explains to the Yellow Emperor the many ways to assess whether a woman is experiencing pleasure, and how to increase that pleasure, during intercourse (Wile 1992: 87–88). As van Gulik points out, the woman's orgasm itself was considered to strengthen her partner's vital powers (van Gulik 1961: 46). This emphasis on women's orgasm in combination with men's desire to take women's life essence would seem, paradoxically, to both refute and support Furth's argument.

Furth asks the important question: "Psychologically, how are we to understand this organization of the erotic around a performance of masculine self-discipline and self-denial?" She suggests that a Freudian interpretation would suggest a fear of female power in which "the female 'enemy' and her 'deep abyss' represent castration anxiety" (Furth 1992: 137). She dismisses this argument, however:

> The female "other" is not a socially threatening or engulfing mother but simply the instrument drawing males to a boundary where the sense of self is lost. The bedchamber texts are stunningly direct in linking the abandon of coital climax with death as the loss of all selfhood. [. . .] The loss of semen, then, is experienced metaphorically as death, and associated with disease and decline into age. If the microcosmic body replicates cosmic processes in generative acts, production and destruction are mutually dependent, and the moments of climax, like the critical transitions in the movements of universal change, destroy phenomena ceaselessly even as they create. In the final analysis, therefore, for males the art of love is transformed into a work of regeneration, toward the production of an immortal, deathless self. (Furth 1992: 137)

It is hard to argue with such a convincing and eloquent analysis. Yet further questions remain. Furth sums up the essential battle of the art of sex and the representational fear of loss of self and of death; but is that all? If one of the primary goals is to prolong life, is death the ultimate fear, or do death and loss of self in turn represent a larger fear? I will come back to these questions in a moment.

There is a marked absence of external intervention on sexual activity in the bedchamber manuals. Instead, the threat or promise of changes in health stressed personal well-being and encouraged individuals to be self-regulating. Foucault notes a similar phenomenon in ancient Greece and Rome, which he calls "the cultivation of the self" (Foucault 1984b: 41).[3] The texts that Foucault and van Gulik worked with are strikingly similar in this respect. In fact, Foucault provides an extremely brief comparison between van Gulik's work and his own study (Foucault 1984a: 137–143). In it he mentions the dread of the sexual act found in China (Foucault 1984a: 137) while also noting the emphasis on conjugal pleasure (Foucault 1984a: 143). Unfortunately he makes no attempt to reconcile these seemingly opposing forces.

Foucault's analysis seems to arise from a surprisingly unquestioning view of the Daoist tracts, in which he tends to romanticize other cultures and imply that they did not have the same complexities of control and regulation of sexuality that we see in ancient Greek texts. He speaks of the erotic art of China, Japan, India, Rome, and the Arab-Moslem societies, in which "truth is drawn from pleasure itself," as opposed to medical texts of the modern West, which are essentially texts of power and regulation (Foucault 1978: 57). Yet it does not take very close scrutiny of the Daoist bedchamber manuals to see similar themes of regulation—and, moreover, exactly the kind of self-regulation that Foucault suggests for modern Western medical texts that emphasize regulation and self-control.

The answer to the seemingly paradoxical contrast between such views of sexuality lies within the framework for which Mary Douglas has become so famous, where she outlines a basic human need to create and maintain order (Douglas 1966). In Douglas's model, particular rules are less important than the need to have rules—any rules. This applies well to the ordering of sexuality that we are grappling with here. In this framework it is perfectly understandable that one can both celebrate and fear sexuality. After all, the more one believes in the healthful benefits of sex, the more it makes sense to fear its potency.

The differences between the materials that Foucault studies and those van Gulik provides lie not so much in the concern with regulation of sexual activity in relation to the individual as in the environment in which this surfaced. Foucault's study focuses on a period that could arguably be called the birth of Western democracy and individualism. But in traditional China, Confucianism stressed that each individual was part of a greater whole in which a person played his or her own role in relation to the family, which in turn served as a microcosm of the state. In other words, Foucault's model of sexuality explored one aspect of an integrated system of emphasis on individuality in ancient Greco-Roman culture. We can see a similar attention to individual well-being in China, but this was both distinct and dramatic in its direct contrast to the larger movements of that society. Although the Chinese bedchamber manuals are clearly obsessed with prolonging life, I suggest that the tracts not only express a fear of an individual's death or sense of self, as Furth suggests, but also a fear of complete chaos. In Chinese culture there has long been an obsession with avoiding chaos (*luan*). The loss of individual control is important precisely because "man" is thought to be a microcosm of the universe, and thus individual loss of control suggests the possibility that all is chaos.

The simultaneous promotion and fear of the individualism that I have just presented occur repeatedly in the Daoist bedchamber manuals. *The Art of the Bedchamber* from the Former Han Dynasty (206 B.C.–A.D. 23) states: "If one regulates his sexual pleasure he will feel at peace and attain a high age. If, on the other hand, one abandons himself to its pleasure disregarding the rules set forth in the above mentioned treatises one will fall ill and harm one's very life" (van Gulik 1961: 70–71). The following excerpt is from *Fangneipuyi*, which was published in the Song dynasty in 1066 and reprinted in the Yüan period in 1307 (van Gulik 1961: 193):

> A man must not engage in sexual intercourse merely to satisfy his lust. He must strive to control his sexual desire so as to be able to nurture his vital essence. He must not force his body to sexual extravagance in order to enjoy carnal pleasure, giving free rein to his passion. On the contrary, a man must think of how the act will benefit his health and thus keep himself free from disease. This is the subtle secret of the Art of the Bedchamber. (van Gulik 1961: 193–194)

In both of these passages, the goal is to achieve personal health and longevity through regulation and avoiding loss of control. This strain (in both senses of the word) of sexual individualism coupled with a fear of passion as an emblem of excess can be seen again and again in such materials.

Frank Dikötter's study on Republican China notes conceptions of health drawing on "Western" medical knowledge that were essentially modern medical versions of the traditional beliefs of sexual practice and health that I have outlined above: "[A book entitled *Sex Knowledge* claimed] that 'the brain can easily be flooded with blood during the time of sexual excitement.' Undesirable results of intercourse included sexual neurasthenia, physical decay, anemia, psychosis, indigestion, respiratory problems and impotence" (Dikötter 1995: 56). Dikötter outlines the ways in which Western science was used to validate moral antagonism toward sexuality. If we substitute the language of Western science for *yin/yang* essence, the underlying fear that sexual excess would lead to deteriorating health is more or less the same as that found in the traditional Daoist sexual tracts.

Sex education and family-planning materials in both mainland

China and Taiwan further exemplify this link between chaos and individuals' sexual excess leading to societal decay. Another example is a sex treatise published in mainland China in 1926 by a medical doctor, Chang Ching-sheng. One of the more interesting aspects of Chang's depiction of sexuality is its emphasis on moderation and morality. His is not the speech of a prude, nor of a traditionalist. In his book he discusses the fluids of sex, sexual impulses, and pleasure with surprising openness. But this discourse is within a moral structure of sexual moderation within a marital union. It is a medical treatise that draws on "Western medicine" but uses the word "harmony" as a metaphor for orgasm (C. Chang 1927: 45), that stresses the preservation of "life force" (C. Chang 1927: 108), and that further suggests an ideal sexual pattern of engaging in intercourse once a week (C. Chang 1927: 46, 64). Once again, staying within these bounds is presented as a scientific necessity rather than as a moral claim, depicting the lack of sexual moderation as a certified medical danger:

> According to a famous Peking physician, some of the young persons whom he treated may have died because of a suicidal cruelty toward their reproductive organs. [. . .] Flower-like maidens suddenly lose their fragrance; intelligent youths contract tuberculosis. [. . .] Both sexes reduce their bodily vigor through giving vent heedlessly to their lusts. (C. Chang 1927: 17)

More than fifty years later we can see these same concerns. Harriet Evans has pointed out that, although modern medical beliefs in mainland China attempt to distance themselves from traditional *yin/yang* conceptions of sexuality and health, ideas about the harmful effects of "excessive loss of semen" continue to be a central facet of modern medical understanding in China (Evans 1997: 73). Similarly, Honig and Hershatter have addressed mainland Chinese medical warnings against fashion that use medical science to support their moral claims:

> The warnings about health hazards were couched in scientific terms, and they included almost every accoutrement of 1980's fashion. Heavy makeup was criticized for interfering with the excretion of wastes through the skin and burdening the kidneys and lungs. Gold and silver jewelry were pinpointed as a cause of contact dermatitis. Shoes with heels higher than three centimeters were faulted for cutting off circulation to the toes and leading to toe deformities. Tight-fitting jeans were identified as a source of pressure on the nerves of the lower back and pain or numbness in the thighs. (Honig and Hershatter 1988: 48)

In modern Taiwan we can see these same themes of sexuality, moderation, and self-control in family-planning propaganda. As an example of this we can look to Chen Chao-nan's translation of lectures given by Taiwan's Family Planning Institute. One of these lectures refers to sexual intercourse by stating: "Whether you are engaged or not, a suitable distance must be maintained between each other. Do not drown in the flood of emotion" (Chen 1983: 129). This is then followed by a four-part list of the "sad consequences" of premarital sex:

> Pre-marital sex relationships frequently lead to sad consequences because:
> 1) Girls are devalued by boys. Attraction to each other decreases. Girls may be suspected of not making a good wife [sic].
> 2) Pre-marital intercourse may make you feel guilty.
> 3) Pre-marital intercourse may have the following side effects: pregnancy, VD, and guilty feelings.
> 4) If a boy cannot control his sex impulse, can he be responsible for his family in the future? A girl who can properly control her sexual needs may be seen as more idealistic by boys. Love must be sincere and responsible. Love requires you to properly control you [sic] needs. (Chen 1983: 129)

Like Chang's work there is a peculiar blend of science and morality here, combined with the continuing theme of moderation. Note the prevalence of the issues of self-control and guilt. Even number three, which begins by addressing physical consequences such as pregnancy and VD, concludes with "guilty feelings," which was already covered in number two. From this we can see the growing concern with the psychological effects of sexuality as well as what one can only assume to be a reflection of the societal condemnation of sexual indulgence that would lead to this guilt.

Order and Chaos: Looking Beyond the Individual

Individualism and sexuality are topics linked to the age-old and often strident broader call for moral order in China; and avoiding chaos has always been one of the stronger concerns there. As I noted earlier in this chapter, an interesting tension arises in that, while traditional Daoist tracts were emphasizing the benefits and ill effects of sexuality for the individual, both the government and Confucianism have traditionally supported a rigidly defined family unit in order to maintain social and political stability.

There are several approaches one might take to analyzing the relationships among the individual, family, and state. The first is to examine the effects of state policies on issues such as marriage and sex. This method adopts an analytical framework in which one examines the effects of the macrocosm (state or economic structure) on the microcosm (family and the individual). This ties in well with Rosaldo's model of public and private spheres (Rosaldo 1974, 1980) in which the public (male) sphere is seen to control the private (female) sphere.

A second approach is to examine the imagery involved in the public realm's influence on the family. Jeffrey Weeks, in his study of Victorian sexual trends in England, is characteristically elegant when he speaks of the perception that "The decency and morality of the home confronted the danger and the pollution of the public sphere" (Weeks 1981: 81). One can also look at state control of religion as a means of curbing potentially chaotic mass movements (Weller 1994: 170).

For the purposes of this analysis, however, I believe that it is more profitable to examine the ways in which individual actions are perceived to influence society. To return to Dikötter's work on the Republican Era, sexuality's link with individual health extended to strong nationhood and modernity (Dikötter 1995: 1–2). At the same time, however, sexuality also posed an ominous threat to the Chinese race:

> Conservatives advised young people to inhibit their sexual instincts, pointing out their duties with regard to the future of the race: "If the sexual desire is not curbed, the sexual organs will weaken through wear and tear. This in turn will affect the physical strength of our sons and grandsons, eventually leading to the disappearance of our race." (Dikötter 1995: 56)

This "wear and tear" on youth's sexual organs extended individual concerns with sexuality and health to their consequences to society as a whole. This suggested mutually influencing systems in much the same way as Confucianism posited a causal relationship between the individual, family, and the state.

Even the title of the abortion law "The Eugenics and Health Protection Law" (EL 1984) reflects a fear that individual sexual activity can lead to weakness for the race and the nation. I have also noted that family-planning education has been severely hampered by its emphasis on avoiding sexual activity rather than thorough training in the use of contraceptives. The following excerpt, published by the Taiwan Provincial Institute of Family Planning, mirrors the conception of individual self-indulgence that was perceived to lead to more serious problems.

> The media's considerable and idealized portrayal of youthful love has caused public concern that young people will be too easily influenced to become involved in a love relationship before they are ready. The consequences of this emphasis on young love in terms of increased sexual intercourse, pregnancy, and early marriage are obvious. (H. Lin 1990: 277)

Because Lin considers the results of love and overromanticization to be "obvious," he does not explain what they might be. Fortunately, this statement is an extension of an earlier analysis that he and others published, so we can now refer to that.

In a collaborative article, George Cernada,[4] Chang Ming-Cheng, Lin Hui-Sheng, and Sun Te-Hsiung outlined what they saw to be some of the possible consequences of increasing premarital sex in Taiwan:

> These changing sexual mores, of course, have significant social implications (mental health, unwanted pregnancy, premature marriage, higher adolescent fertility, possibly juvenile delinquency) which undoubtedly are affecting the quality of our human resources. Early sex behavior leading to premature marriage may lead to an unstable family structure, and hence, weakens the social structure. [. . .] In addition to these considerations, these changing mores disturb the economic as well as social balance in society because of their demographic effect. (Cernada et al. 1975: 1–2)

This academic work exhibits more or less the same implicit assumptions as the other materials I have cited above. The analysis assumes that sexuality is the pivotal point for a surprisingly wide range of personal and societal ills. While their claims concerning unwanted pregnancy and premature marriage might seem reasonable, their assertion that early sexual behavior leads to problems with "mental health" and possible juvenile delinquency is unfounded. For example, they do not explore the possibility that problems might arise from the cultural stigma against sex rather than being naturally caused by the act itself. Nor do they explore the possibility that Taiwan's urbanization or its economic and/or political changes could be the cause both of the phenomena they list and of the new sexual permissiveness in Taiwan. Nor do they explore the possibility that the youths who break laws might also be more inclined to violate sexual taboos, thereby reversing the cause-and-effect scheme upon which they base their assumptions. Instead, the implication is that an intrinsically harmful causality issues from the sexual act itself. Accordingly, the solution does not reside in safe sex but self-control.

Cernada and his cowriters also assert that mass-media culture is in large part responsible for changing sexual mores (Cernada et al. 1975: 17), and they go on to attack what they see as an overromanticization of the idea of love:

> Given the considerable mass media emphasis on youth in love and its overly idyllic benefits, society in Taiwan has good reason to be concerned that the present youth may be influenced to move too easily, too early and much too uninformed to this idyllic state of being in love. The consequences in terms of increased sexual intercourse, pregnancy, and early marriage are obvious. (Cernada et al. 1975: 19)

The tone of this excerpt might at first seem confusing. The critique of sexuality is understandable, though problematic, but a critique of "love" itself? Yet this makes sense in the context of the other writing on sexuality I have just presented. If we read the warning against Western influence on love as a warning against passion and subsequent loss of control, the underlying logic is essentially the same as that of the Tang dynasty Daoist tracts, the Republican China documents, or Taiwan's current family-planning propaganda, in that all of them use scientific grounds to advocate sexual self-restraint and moderation as well as traditional sexual morality.

There has been an ongoing liberalization of sexual attitudes in Taiwan for quite some time, but the changes have become more dramatic and rapid in recent years. These changes are commented on in the press and in day-to-day conversations, with reactions ranging from a general concern with more prevalent, and more public, high school and college age physical expression and sexual activity to specific public controversies featured in the newspapers.

One such example is a newspaper article entitled "The Problem of Pregnancy for Today's Loose Women," which states that women have become loose (*haofang nü*) because abortion is so readily available and tolerated in Taiwan (S. Lin 1989b: 13). Another article, reminding us of the criticisms of fetus-ghost appeasement that I outlined in Chapter 5, addresses the issue of abortion and sexuality in relation to fetus-ghost appeasement.

> Eighteen-year-old Little Lan had sex when she was a sophomore in high school and within a year she had already had three abortions. She often felt depressed, guilty, and often at night she couldn't sleep. When she did sleep she had one nightmare after another. Gradually she felt that life was not going smoothly and she had bad luck. Her mental state became worse and worse. She even thought a fetus ghost was after her for revenge.
>
> Little Lan's illness was actually a result of teenagers running sexually rampant, which is one of civilized societies' biggest problems. These harmful side effects of abortion have already become common symptoms in hospitals and psychological counseling institutions. (Sheng 1990: 6)

Such anxiety about abortion and sexuality is often voiced in Taiwan. A prominent factor in these fears is the speed with which cultural mores about sexuality have changed. As an example, Ms. Yang, a middle-aged woman from the south of Taiwan, told me a story of her best friend's husband that took place some thirty years before. Ms. Yang told me that it took him six months to muster up the courage to hold his girlfriend's hand, and this was only after they had consumed an entire bottle of wine. When I asked if it was normal to wait so long to hold hands at that time, Ms. Yang responded, "Oh no, usually it would only take two months." People's reluctance to have bodily contact was, and to a lesser degree still is, partly a result of the traditional expectation that one would marry one's first boyfriend or girlfriend. Thus, the terms "boyfriend" or "girlfriend" took on the meaning of what an American would associate with "fiancé," and outward displays of affection were a commitment in that direction.

Today it is far more common to have more than one boyfriend or girlfriend before one is married, yet many of the traditional ideas about sexuality still ring true. For example, I spoke with one woman who told her mother that she had a foreign boyfriend. The mother said she did not object to her daughter dating a foreigner, but assumed that her daughter planned to remain a virgin until marriage and was worried that her boyfriend, being a foreigner, would want to have sex. The woman told her mother, "Don't worry, Mom, he respects me," to indicate that she had not had sex with him.

The contrast between traditional values of chastity and current dating patterns has caused anxiety for many today. A sixty-year-old doorman at an apartment complex told me:

> When I was young if you had a girlfriend that was it, you were going to get married. Today I look at my two daughters and I worry about them. They both have boyfriends but there's no security for them. Who knows if their men will stick around and who knows what they are up to when I'm not around.

This worry about sexual promiscuity and lack of stability in relationships in turn reflects an equally strong concern with a perceived breakdown in the social order in modern times. Many people I spoke with expressed angst concerning sexual excess and abortion in relation to society. On the one hand, most people I interviewed believed that abortion was necessary, both to keep their family size down and to curb national population growth. On the other hand, in the words of one woman in her seventies whom I interviewed, "Abortion has led to young people becoming too casual [*suibian*] in their relations; our families and our society no longer have any meaning [*meiyou yiyi*]." It is in this setting that belief in fetus ghosts has flourished.

Sexual Excess, the Individual, and the Haunting Fetus

In the quotations I have cited one can see a perceived cause and effect between sexuality and deteriorating health. Fetus ghosts influence people's health because their very presence disrupts the *yin/yang* balance of the living.

Ms. Xu told me that the spirit of a fetus ghost is thought to be drawn to an intense light in the spirit world that is caused by mortals engaging in sexual activity. Once the spirit is on the scene it will occupy the newly fertilized egg. The former belief presents a fear of *yin/yang* imbalance through sexuality; the latter integrates this, as ghosts are considered to be excessively *yin*. Thus, the introduction of fetus ghosts adds to the risk of the already spiritually dangerous sexual act.

Daoist Master Bob told me that a person appeasing fetus ghosts or raising fetus demons should not have sex, because the fetus ghosts and fetus demons are just children who do not understand such matters and it would confuse and anger them. Furthermore, he said, if someone wants to get married, she or he should first put the troublesome fetus spirit under his charge so that it will not harm the living during the consummation of the wedding.

One might ask, if the concept of sexual excess extends to both men and women, why it is that it is almost always women who take the brunt of societal criticism for abortion and for invoking the wrath of the haunting fetus, and why it is usually women who concern themselves with the haunting fetus and its appeasement? An obvious answer is that it is the woman who has an abortion; thus the experience is more directly tangible for her, both physically and emotionally. For believers, it also follows that, as it is the woman who walks into a clinic to abort a fetus in her body, the spirit of the fetus would hold her responsible. Yet, as I have shown, men too feel guilt about abortions. Also, fetus ghosts are thought to be all-knowing, and therefore should be aware that the choice to have an abortion is rarely a woman's alone, and in some cases not the woman's at all—patrilines have long made the decisions in such matters. Thus, to attribute the woman's perceived responsibility to her physical connection with the fetus, or to her decision to have an abortion, is an important yet incomplete explanation.

A less obvious component of this question rests in the fact that, although traditional Chinese conceptions depict men as active (*yang*) and women as passive (*yin*), men are in fact perceived to be highly vulnerable to women's or female spirits' almost irresistible power of temptation (Ebrey 1993: 156, 162; Honig and Hershatter 1988: 67; Mann 1987: 48; van Gulik 1961: 48). Some scholars have suggested that this power was linked to a certain invulnerability on the part of women. Ahern suggests that in traditional China it was thought that, although women could not be harmed by the sexual act because of their inexhaustible *yin* essence, men were very much in danger of losing their *yang* essence (Ahern 1975a: 209). Along the same lines, Ruan Fang-fu notes that in traditional China, female masturbation and lesbianism were considered to be harmless because of the belief that women's *yin* was inexhaustible (F. Ruan 1991: 135). In contrast, van Gulik cites Chinese texts that warn of the dangers of improper *yin/yang* balance through sexual activity for women as well as men (van Gulik 1961: 138, 158). In spite of some discrepancies here, this analysis taps into an underlying fear of the supernatural invulnerability and/or spiritually polluting effects of women.[5] Thus, it may be that women, as the objects of sexual desire, are held responsible because men are thought to be unable to resist them.

In Ms. Xu's fetus-ghost morality tract (1995) she asserts that a woman should be at least twenty-two years old and a man at least twenty-five years old before they can safely engage in sexual intercourse, stating that their bodies are not fully mature until that age. She then quotes traditional Chinese texts on sexual activity, suggesting that the reader follow these guidelines:

1. When engaging in sexual activity one should keep one's eyes closed and turn off the lights, otherwise one will go blind. Also, one should not have sex under the sun, moon, or stars,[6] or in front of a large fire.

2. One should not have sex if drunk or else it will be easy to get sore joints.

3. One should not have sex during the summer equinox, winter equinox, the first day of spring, the first day of summer, the first day of fall, the first day of winter, etc.

4. Also, one should not have sex during the sixteenth day of the fifth month of the lunar new year. This is because on this day *yang* and *yin* are at the farthest extremes.

5. One should not have sex when there is a large wind, when there is a big rain, when there is a heavy fog, when it is extremely cold, when it is extremely hot, when one has eaten too much, when one is drunk, when angry, when thunder or lightning are close together, during a solar or lunar eclipse, during an earthquake, on the Buddha's and Bodhisattvas' divine birthdays, on the Daoist immortals' birthdays, on one's parents' birthdays, on the anniversary of one's parents' deaths, on the husband's and wife's astrological days that are prohibited by the almanac. Otherwise, when a husband injures himself, the injury will be one hundred times worse than it would have been, and the wife will get sick easily. A son who is conceived through such behavior is more likely to be insane, retarded, sickly, to be a deaf mute, to have deformed limbs, and he will have a short life and be unfilial and unkind.

6. One should gradually decrease sexual activity as one gets older. When one is forty years old, one should not have sex more than once every four days; when one is fifty years old, once every five days; when sixty years old the most one should have sex is once every six days; at seventy years of age one should just abstain from sexual activity altogether. At the same time, no matter if one is old or young one should not engage in sexual activity more than twice a day.

7. One should not engage in sexual activity for two hours after one has eaten breakfast, lunch, or dinner. If one needs to urinate but still hasn't eliminated, and one holds it in while one is having sex it will be easy to get gonorrhea. If one engages in sexual activity while one has to defecate it is easy to get hemorrhoids. If one engages in sexual activity after drinking alcohol it is easy to get jaundice.

8. If one engages in sexual activity on an empty stomach it can be very harmful to one's vital energy. After engaging in sexual activity one should not fan oneself with a fan and drink cold or ice water or tea. When a woman is having her period, sexual activity can cause blood disease, and both the man and the woman will get sick. (Xu 1995: 110–111)

A strong current of fear of excess runs through this excerpt. Notice the elements of extremity in numbers 1, 2, and the beginning of 5. One should not have sex if one is drunk, angry, or if one has eaten too much. Presumably, cold is acceptable but extreme cold is not. Wind and rain are not mentioned when moderate, but sex is prohibited when they are heavy. Avoiding natural elements such as the sun, storms, or a large fire point to the symbolic aspects of nature and passion as representations of uncontrollable natural forces. Clearly, these prohibitions are less concerned with medicine than signifiers of the contaminative force of sexuality. In avoiding such extremes, Xu's tract adopts the call for moral order that can be found in the other texts I have reviewed in this chapter. Note, for example, the concern with *yin/yang* and extremity in number 4. In number 6 we have essentially the same time regulation as Daoist tracts on sexual avoidance of *yang* exhaustion.

Ms. Xu draws on these traditional Daoist bedchamber prohibitions and applies them to her tract on fetus ghosts, connecting a traditional theme of self-control with this new religious practice. Yet there is an important difference here, for Ms. Xu uses these texts while divesting them of the previous connecting elements of the pleasures and benefits of sexuality. In doing so she takes them out of context and links them with images of the wrathful *yingling* in other parts of her tract. Thus, the meaning of these texts shifts from the original message, in which one was instructed to regulate yet enjoy the benefits of sexuality, to one of regulation and fear.

Sexual Excess, Social Order, and the Haunting Fetus

If belief in fetus ghosts carries with it familiar themes of self-control and excess, it is also a reminder of one's links with others. In Ms. Xu's tract, for example, in addition to the danger to an individual's health, there is the threat (quite literally) that one can pass harm down to future generations. In this context, the fact that Ms. Xu focuses on the ill effects that parents' actions specifically have on their sons (number 5 in the quoted excerpt), rather than on both male and female offspring, exemplifies an anxiety not only about their ability to perform their parental roles but also about the stability of successive generations. Thus, seemingly unrelated risks to the son's physical and emotional well-being end in "unfilial and unkind" personality traits that endanger both the parents' security in old age and the patriline as a whole.

In the spirit world, abortions are not all of equal consequence. In one interview, Ms. Xu told me that a fetus ghost is acutely aware of the variety of reasons for an abortion, and that it would forgive its parents if it knew that they wanted to have it but could not for health reasons. In contrast, she said, the fetus ghost would strike with a furious wrath if it knew that it had been conceived from self-indulgent, pleasure-oriented sex and had been aborted to allow its parents to continue their behavior. Both the ritual avoidance of sexual activity and the fetus ghost's judgmental stance stress a need to maintain order and exert restraint in one's sexual habits. The themes of sexual excess and self-control that we see in beliefs about fetus ghosts are clearly consistent with the views manifest in earlier texts, but the introduction of fetus ghosts and their appeasement provides a new link between these older moralistic themes and one's responsibility for one's children.

In earlier chapters I noted that fetus-ghost appeasement benefits those who feel that they have failed as parents because of their abortions. As evident in the other materials I have cited, individual actions are also thought to influence society. The idea that individual actions affect the health of the nation is evinced in one of Teacher Lin's morality tracts. He begins by outlining some of the effects that fetus ghosts can have on one's children, including harming their health, making them temperamental, and adversely affecting their studies (J. Lin 1996b: 88–89). This is followed by a warning of the impact this can have on society:

> This not only causes problems within a family. A country's future relies on youths taking responsibility. Therefore, with the exception of cases in which there is no alternative, one should not carelessly have abortions. This results in disaster for society. If one has an abortion, one must resolve the problem by providing for [gongyang] the fetus ghost. This eliminates [the ghost's] resentful hatred. Purifying [jinghua] the yingling lets everyone have happy lives and society will be peaceful and stable. (J. Lin 996b: 89)

A fetus-ghost haunting is a reminder that each individual is part of a greater whole. It is also a criticism of those who have had abortions, suggesting that to do so is self-indulgent and does not take into account the responsibility owed to others, thereby asserting the need to curtail one's own desires and actions for the general good. There is a subtle change in emphasis here, in that the traditional Chinese sex tracts I have cited allowed room for a discussion of the individual in a broader setting that emphasized group orientation. The practice of fetus-ghost appeasement, in contrast, discourages the pursuit of individual physical pleasure by emphasizing the negative consequences for an individual's health and for the soul of the aborted fetus, which then lead to social chaos and disruption of the spirit world. Thus we see a shift from a combination of pleasure, fear, and regulation in attitudes concerning sexuality, to one of regulation, reduction, and prohibition. In both cases, however, regulation and avoidance of excess are the underlying themes.

To review, beliefs about fetus ghosts reflect traditional conceptions of sexuality. Such ways of thinking have changed, however, for we no longer see encouragement of the pursuit of pleasure. Instead, the continuity resides in fear of individual excess, because of its effects on both the health of the individual and society as a whole. As I noted in Chapter 5, in addition to continuing concerns with regulation and excess, the growing popularity of fetus-ghost appeasement reflects changes in intergenerational hierarchies through the act of parents praying to children while also evincing parental anxiety over a perceived breakdown of familial hierarchy and moral order. In this respect, it marks a shift from traditional Daoist tracts that focus on the individual in a primarily group-oriented cultural setting to the use of belief in fetus ghosts to reaffirm familial ties, responsibility to others, and social order in an environment that is increasingly allowing space for individualism.

10
Blood-Drinking Fetus Demons
Greed, Loathing, and Vengeance
through Sorcery in Taiwan

> I think these people [who raise fetus demons] are really scary.
> Some of them will grind up part of a fetus' body, like the heart
> or the brain or another organ, and they will keep it in a bottle
> so that they can pray to it and get it to do what they want.
> What? Do I believe it works? Yes, but I don't think it's right, it's
> really disgusting if you ask me. (A thirty-seven-year-old male taxi
> driver)

WHO could argue? This chapter addresses the as yet unstudied
subject of sorcerers who feed "fetus demons" (*xiaogui*) human
blood in order to enslave the spirits. In the following pages I will
describe the new growth of fetus-demon sorcery in Taiwan and discuss
the religious imagery that surrounds the belief in relation to abortion,
capitalism, and the urban environment.

The majority of scholarly work done on sorcery and witchcraft has
focused on accusations directed at people who may or may not have
actually engaged in the practice. In part this must derive from our own
history of witchcraft, in which the most compelling issue at hand was
not the idiosyncratic nature of those who actually practiced witchcraft
but the mass hysteria and persecution that surrounded it. No doubt
this bias also arises from the very real difficulty of interviewing practitioners of sorcery.

Along the same lines, I should confess from the outset that this
chapter is almost completely based on indirect sources such as interviews I conducted with people who do not practice fetus-demon sorcery and Taiwanese newspaper articles and television programs. Because religious masters did not want to openly acknowledge being
involved with this practice, I was able to conduct only one interview

with a Daoist master who admitted to dealing with fetus demons. For this reason, I cannot confidently claim to present "truth," if indeed there is such a thing, but rather I can offer suggestions, possibilities, and provocations. While this limitation of case studies is not ideal, I offer this chapter as a first step toward better understanding the fascinating phenomenon of fetus-demon sorcery in Taiwan, a practice that provides an outlet for the expression of greed, hatred, and a desire for vengeance that cannot normally be expressed in Chinese culture.[1]

First Contact

My only interview with a Daoist master who admitted to dealing with fetus demons was in September 1996. I was in Gaoxiong, the largest city in southern Taiwan, conducting an interview with a Daoist master who, among a wide range of other duties, appeased fetus ghosts (*ying-ling*). That day was an anthropological gold mine. In twelve hours I had conducted my interview about fetus ghosts; I had seen the Daoist master bless a child and perform a two-hour magic trick in which the gods left candy and rice alcohol in a cardboard box; I witnessed him phone-networking to get a young hoodlum (*liumang*) who had just been arrested transferred from prison to a drug rehabilitation program; I had gone on a midnight tour of the local cemeteries to look for ghosts; and, for the first time, I came face to face with a practitioner of fetus-demon sorcery.

Before I arrived in Gaoxiong the woman who was to introduce me to this Daoist master told me that he "raised" (*yang*) fetus demons. I had heard of this practice but at the time thought that this was only the stuff of legend, something akin to ancient stories of magicians who commanded corpses to hop hundreds of miles home so that they could be buried—common mythology but not really practiced. I also thought that fetus demons were merely a folkloric extension of the fetus ghosts that I was already studying. I was wrong on both counts.

The Daoist master, whom I will call "Daoist Master Bob," is a short, well-built man, and nothing if not a bundle of good-natured energy. In truth he reminded me more of a forty-year-old party animal looking for a good time than a Daoist master who deals in all matters of the occult. At the end of our interview about fetus ghosts he casually remarked, "To tell the truth, I've had more experience with fetus demons."

When I asked him about this he explained matter-of-factly, "Sometimes I will have a client who has been wronged by someone. When that happens he comes to me and I bind a fetus demon to do my bidding to seek revenge." He tilted back on his chair and glanced across the street absently.

A bit taken aback, I asked, "How do you get a fetus demon to do your bidding?"

He pointed nonchalantly to a shot-glass-sized cup on the altar, "Oh, I feed them blood in a little cup like that," he said, glancing at me out of the corner of his eye.

"Oh . . ." I was not sure I really wanted to pursue this subject further, feeling as though I was in the middle of a horror story that I didn't much enjoy but couldn't quite put down. After a moment I tentatively asked, "What kind of blood do you feed it, chicken's blood, pig's blood?"

"No, no," he laughed. "What would a fetus demon want with that? Ha ha!"

"So . . . you feed it . . ." My voice trailed off and I found myself fidgeting in my chair, not quite sure how to proceed.

"Human blood of course! Ha ha!"

"And . . . where do you get this blood?"

"Oh, I have a friend who works at a hospital. I get it from him." Laughing amiably, he absentmindedly began to search around his desk. I hadn't slept much the night before, and for a split second I thought he was looking for a knife and I jumped in my seat when he suddenly thrust a pack of imported cigarettes at me.

"Hey! Want one?" he asked, waving the pack of cigarettes back and forth a few inches from my face.

Never one to talk about a subject for more than a few minutes, Daoist Master Bob began to show me his gold Rolex watch, insisting I hold it so that I could assess that it was real gold from the weight. He also showed me his gold rings, saying, "I don't like to wear these things but the client who gave them to me would be hurt if I didn't wear them, what can I do?" He shrugged, smiling amiably, as always.

Daoist Master Bob is wonderfully energetic and adventurous, and I look back on that day and night as one of the most fascinating and —yes—fun experiences in my fieldwork. But between a cardboard-box magic trick and a truly bizarre evening spent wandering through cemeteries, I had judged him to be a bit of an eccentric. And although I had already conducted a fairly wide range of interviews on fetus ghosts, I had not met anyone else who fed fetus demons blood. For these reasons I had placed this experience in a category of "non-standard belief," suspecting that Daoist Master Bob's practices did not so much reflect Taiwanese or Chinese culture as his own individual quirkiness. In retrospect I find that this assessment was both right and wrong. Daoist Bob is a bit of an eccentric, and providing for fetus demons is not standard practice. But after conducting interviews, seeing a handful of news articles and television shows on the subject, and watching the news coverage of an extremely publicized scandal involving raising fetus demons, I have come to realize that this form of sorcery is rarely practiced but widely believed in.

Sorcery and Fetus Demons in Taiwan: An Overview

> I have heard that some spirit mediums will buy *xiaogui* [fetus demons] from their mothers. For example, a fortuneteller [*suanming*] might buy a memorial plaque for the baby. The *xiaogui* can know some things about the future or fate of people and they are too small and clever to be controlled. A spirit medium [*lingmei*] can just feed a fetus demon some blood twice a week and the fetus demon will work hard for him. But they can only do this for two or three years because the fetuses must be reincarnated. I don't know if you have heard this before or not but it's the truth. It happened in Taiwan recently. I believe it, what about you? (A twenty-six-year-old female computer analyst)

In modern Taiwan, folk beliefs about geomancy (*fengshui*) and taboos about certain words[2] and actions[3] create a conceptual framework in which one's statements or actions can have supernatural consequences. These conceptions lend credibility to the belief in sorcery in modern Taiwan (C. Ruan 1985). Indeed, there is a wide spectrum of religious belief in Taiwan which points to the power of the living to control ghosts, ranging from spells to exorcise spirits (Jordan 1972: 58–59, 161–162; Le 1967; Yi 1988: 49–50) to the recalling of wandering spirits (H. Zhong 1980).[4]

Sorcerers (*wushi*) and sorcery (*wushu*) are nothing new in Chinese religious thought. Scholarship on Taiwan has recorded the prevalence of belief in sorcery in modern Taiwan, including documentation of the fear of aboriginal sorcery (Jordan 1972: 161–162) and sorcerers' spells cast to ensure long life (C. Ruan 1985: 141), to end supernaturally caused illnesses and spouses' marital affairs (Gu 1966: 35), and to make money for patrons (Le 1967: 78; C. Ruan 1985: 141). Other magical practices have also been recorded, such as transferring one's own bad luck by leaving a red envelope with a coin and one's own hair in it on the street so that an unwitting person who picks up the envelope will acquire the ill fortune (C. Ruan 1985: 137), and grass or paper dolls or paper amulets that can be used to ward off evil or to harm one's neighbors (C. Ruan 1985: 136, 141–142). Philip Kuhn describes the eighteenth-century use of clay figurines, hair, a piece of underwear, or fingernails for sorcery (Kuhn 1990: 101–104). Though fetus-demon sorcery has become a well-known phenomenon only in recent years, magazines are full of temples' offers to use sorcery for a wide range of purposes, including making money, providing love potions, and curing spouses of their infidelity, as well as producing more general talismans that are used to ward off bad fortune.

Fetus-demon sorcery in Taiwan gained widespread popularity, or rather notoriety, only in the 1980s. This is not to say that it did not exist before that time. Gary Seaman briefly refers to funeral dramas or an ancient use of human fetuses in black-magic potions (Seaman 1981: 392). Dyer Ball tells of a nineteenth-century account of the belief that the bones of dead infants or children could be used by women to magically kill their husbands (Ball 1892: 375–376).[5] A slightly different but related phenomenon can be seen in rituals used to expel fetus demons dating back to at least 217 B.C. (Harper 1996). But Taiwanese news coverage of fetus-demon sorcery has brought it to the forefront of public discussion, and in criticizing the practice so publicly, the press has unwittingly acted as advertiser for its supposed effectiveness.

The meaning of the term *xiaogui* itself has changed. Twenty years ago, it was commonly used as a whimsical word to describe a mischievous child,[6] much in the way that a "liquor devil" (*jiugui*) is playfully used for a perennial drunkard. Although *xiaogui* is still used in this way today, it is quickly becoming dated and is most often used by people sixty years of age or older.

Fetus demons are thought to be particularly powerful because they are in a liminal state in which they are in touch with the secrets of the natural universe in ways that an adult ghost is not. This gives them knowledge of everything from people's darkest secrets to, as the following excerpt from a magazine article shows, quite trivial matters.

> It was getting dark and Li's grandfather was thinking to himself that he still hadn't been able to find pork at the market and his [the grandfather's] wife had asked him to bring some home. He was thinking this to himself when he heard a voice saying, "Where will you go to buy it?" A child's voice suddenly came from his pocket, "You should go to the south market." Li's grandfather felt in his pocket and found a wooden doll, and knew he had accidentally picked up someone else's fetus demon. He went to the southern market and really did find pork there.[7] (Liang 1997: 4)

Another example can be found in a magazine article that quotes an expert as saying that fetus demons can cause problems ranging from family disharmony to bringing mice, cockroaches, and mosquitoes to someone's house (Du 1997: 63).

The trivial nature of the ghost's actions is somewhat surprising. Yet my account of Daoist Master Bob and the story of the pork-buying fetus demon should not lead one to overlook the more serious dimensions of the practice. As I will show, if the issue occasionally evokes a smile, it is more often taken very seriously, causing true terror in some.

> Being involved with this practice includes an element of risk. Some people believe that fetus demons have a strange power to help them. These people pray to fetus demons with blood, but this can be dangerous. One man did this and died. It is said that a fetus demon came back and killed the man. Maybe he forgot to feed the fetus demon blood. (A twenty-year-old female university student, Taibei)

In addition to carelessness, another danger in raising a fetus demon is that of greed on the part of the sorcerer. There is a natural time limit to each spirit's tenure. If it serves a sorcerer for two to four years, it is thought to have the right to go on to be reborn into its next life. Fetus demons are believed to be all-knowing, and they are therefore very aware of this right. If a sorcerer becomes greedy and does not release a fetus demon's spirit when the time comes, the fetus demon will turn on its master, inflicting great harm or possibly even killing him.

Lu Guoxiong also speaks of the benefits and dangers of raising fetus ghosts in a book explaining more generalized conceptions of ghosts and the spirit world (G. Lu 1995).[8] He relates one story of a Taiwanese man who used sorcery to bind six fetus demons to do his bidding and as a result was able to live unmolested in a dangerous area of New York (G. Lu 1995: 101–102). But Lu precedes this with an admonitory story. In this account a woman used sorcery to bind a fetus demon to do her bidding, but her powers were not sufficient and in the end the fetus demon would not let her leave her room, insisting that she stay and play with him (G. Lu 1995: 97–100). In the end she grew physically weak and doctors could not cure her; she took on the appearance of a ghost herself until she went to a Buddhist temple to exorcise the spirit, after which she recovered (G. Lu 1995: 97–100). In short, like any weapon, fetus demons are thought to be dangerous to others if one knows what one is doing but also potentially lethal to oneself if one is careless or untrained.

Sorcery on Trial

In 1997, for the first time on legal record in Taiwan, a government prosecutor formally set out to try a religious master for sorcery, asking the courts to fine the sorcerer, Hong Shihe, NT$500,000,000 (US$14.7 million) and to jail him for ten years (Gao 1997b: 4). Hou Kuanren, a prosecutor from the bureau of investigation, formally accused Hong Shihe, leader of the religious organization *Taijimen*, not only of fraud, extortion, and tax evasion, but also of sorcery. In doing so the prosecutor asked another sorcerer to assist in the investigation (Gao 1997a: 4). The following two news articles quote Hou Kuanren, the prosecutor, on the case: "[Hong Shihe] used talismanic writing to command *xiaogui* to control his students' hearts and minds. He did not use the power of the gods but relied on strong and very horrible black magic" (Gao 1997a: 4). Also, "Hong Shihe really has strong evil magical powers, and uses his spells to control his students. He misleads people and traps them into becoming fanatical religious members of the occult world" (Gao 1997c: 4). When asked how one raised fetus demons, the prosecutor "laughed and said [. . .] he couldn't reveal these aspects for fear that everyone would begin to raise *xiaogui*" (Gao 1997a: 4). As support for his claims the prosecutor referred to "additional documents which contain *Taijimen*'s students' accounts of how they were harmed, and doctors' records certifying *xiaogui* black magic had possessed their bodies and caused real harm" (Gao 1997a: 4). This included inducing his followers to buy bad stocks (Zhan 1997: 4) and making the teenage child of a movie star become schizophrenic (Gao 1997c: 4). The government's evaluation of the matter is unclear, as Hong Shihe is also being accused of fraud and tax evasion. Yet the fact that a government prosecutor would be allowed to file such charges in the first place is worth noting.

I will now turn to the services that sorcerers offer, which can roughly be broken into three categories: protection, greed, and vengeance.

Protection

One time [a spirit medium] met a young woman who was burdened by a ghost. She often fainted and she would often mutter to herself without even knowing what she was saying. The spirit medium then assigned a talented *xiaogui* to stand by her side to negotiate with the ghost that was possessing the young woman, and to offer that ghost certain benefits if it left. The spirit medium also encountered some ghosts that were very hard to communicate with and the ghosts continually pestered and harmed people. Then the spirit medium had no patience and told the *xiaogui* to go investigate the ins and outs of those spirits' situations in order to assess "suitable magical tools" to deal with those spirits. (Du 1997)

The most common motivations for using fetus-demon sorcery are greed and revenge. As the above quotation testifies, however, one can also use such sorcery for protection and to gain information. In some cases fetus demons are used to spy on the living. As in the above example, the spirit can be used as servant, spy, and spiritual bodyguard.

Greed

[A] spirit medium [*lingmei*] agreed to meet the customer's requests to turn his luck around at the gambling table. After one has communicated with a fetus demon, the fetus demon will discuss its own requests until an agreement is reached. On the first day, this customer tied the fetus demon to his body. But he tried to be too crafty. Because he was afraid others would see the fetus demon, he used tape to tightly cover the entire fetus-demon idol and went into the gambling house. The result was that after one night he had tremendous losses. He then went back home and angrily threw the fetus-demon idol to the ground.

The fetus demon felt mistreated because this confused customer had taped over its eyes and the fetus demon couldn't see anything, so losing was hardly strange. After the fetus demon told the spirit medium the problem, the spirit medium helped to mediate between the customer and the fetus demon to help them get along again. The result was that the next time the customer went to gamble, the fetus demon helped him to win for eleven straight days. The ghost and customer had agreed on twelve days, but after the twelfth day the customer wanted to win even more, so he kept going, but the fetus demon was tired. Therefore, the furious fetus demon let him suffer great losses. The customer didn't understand why he lost not only his money but his stores as well and felt like he was going crazy.

Although fetus demons can help you, they have a natural ability to harm you as well. Water can hold up a ship but it can sink it too, it's the same idea. The spirit medium explains that originally this kind of thing only needed the two to continue the "agreement." But because of the client's own actions, the spirit medium had no way to fulfill his client's wishes. (Du 1997)

Fetus demons are also used to gain knowledge that can be used to make money or to spy on others. In contrast to the above account, the relationship between the sorcerer and the fetus demon is usually thought to be one of master and slave.[9] But if it is a slave, it is an unruly and powerful one that carries the potential for fatal danger for anyone dealing with it.

From this account we can see that stories of fetus demons allow for greed but warn against excessive greed. I suspect that this is an unintentional offshoot of the practical need for such sorcerers to have an excuse for failure. Clearly, that a man was promised he would win at gambling for twelve straight days does not even hint at a moral lesson on the part of the sorcerer. Yet, when failures occur, explanations must be offered that do not place either the fetus demon's or the sorcerer's power in question. As a result, a certain kind of morality concerning greed emerges. It is allowable to want to exploit a fetus demon in order to win other people's money by gambling for twelve days in a row. It is not acceptable, however, to do so indefinitely or without gratitude.

Fury, Loathing, and Vengeance

Using the spirit world for one's own advantage is nothing new in Chinese culture. In fact, perhaps the most common form of prayer in Taiwan is a direct request made with a promise of gifts for the god that grants the wish. Using supernatural forces to harm one's enemy has an equally long history, although it is less commonly practiced. Even geomancy (*fengshui*) has been categorized as sorcery in some cases (Le 1967: 78; C. Ruan 1985: 134), because it is a manipulation of supernatural forces that evince antagonisms and rivalry.

Hugh Baker translated a wonderful account of two families using geomancy to harm each other's clans (Baker 1979: 219–225). In it, two rival clans hire *fengshui* masters to help them benefit from the *fengshui* of their ancestors' graves while simultaneously using the geomantic forces to harm each other's lineages. As the *fengshui* war progresses, the two sides take actions ranging from planting large trees and building a cesspit above the rival clan's gravesite, to diverting a stream, secretly digging up their rival's plot to investigate their *fengshui,* and finally relocating their own ancestors' graves and leaving a large quantity of excrement in the old plot to influence the rival clan's grave (Baker 1979: 219–225). While *fengshui* is not exactly sorcery, the use of such supernatural forces to harm others carries a similar psychological weight.

In Chinese culture one bases one's humanity on one's ability to act morally, and morality on one's ability to comply with social norms (Silin 1976: 127). This severely limits the situations in which one can truly express one's emotions, for one fears that expressing egocentric behavior is in direct conflict with one's morality (Silin 1976: 127). Expressions of anger carry connotations of individuality and social breakdown. Fetus-demon sorcery allows for the expression of these tabooed emotions. As Malinowski has emphasized, the essence of black magic lies in metaphorically twisting the knife in one's victim (Malinowski 1925: 71). Fetus-demon sorcery provides a way of expressing forbidden emotions such as fury, loathing, greed, and a desire for vengeance, all in the presence of a Daoist master.

When a client goes to a Daoist master, he has a chance to express these unsanctioned emotions in the form of confession, or a Taiwanese equivalent of a psychology session, if you will. Fetus-demon sorcery is a way of letting one's id scream, "Me," albeit only in the company of one religious master.[10]

Yet, in addition to helping to dissipate such feelings through providing a sense that revenge has been taken, a fetus-demon sorcerer also strengthens such emotions by validating them, and potentially extends them (both in time and scope) in the hope of extending the period of his business dealings. Because this practice fulfills a psychological need, one might be tempted to suggest that it is therefore a benefit to Taiwanese society, a safety valve if you will. But it may also be that, except for some small satisfaction on the part of the client and somewhat more satisfying financial profit on the part of the sorcerer, such practices are both anomalous and a cancer in the system rather than an outlet leading to better health. Is Malinowski correct, one must ask, in stating that in venting passions through magical acts one dissipates one's tension and regains equilibrium, even one's "harmony with life" (Malinowski 1925: 80–81), or do these acts only focus one's hatred and frustration?

Economic Forces and Religious Imagery

In the remaining pages of this chapter I will ask a series of related questions. What changes in religious morality have occurred in relation to the urban capitalist setting of modern Taiwan? Why are dead fetuses such a potent image for black magic? How does fetus-demon sorcery draw on traditional beliefs?

In looking at other regions of the world one sees a number of scholars working on the ramifications of traditional religious beliefs in new economic settings. Gananath Obeyesekere, in his research on Sri Lanka, linked sorcery to the possibility that modern urban capitalist environments can be a breeding ground for religious paranoia (Obeyesekere 1981: 108). Aihwa Ong demonstrates the ways in which Malaysian factory workers use traditional beliefs about possession and the spirit world to protest their industrial working environments in a new capitalist era (Ong 1987). Michael Taussig examines the religious imagery of the Devil as it is used to portray the evils of capitalism, both for plantation workers in Colombia and in the tin mines in Bolivia (Taussig 1980). Jean and John Comaroff have examined the rise of sorcery in the modern era of political and economic uncertainty in South Africa (Comaroff and Comaroff 1999). All of these studies examine the attempts of shifting religious beliefs to adapt to the industrial setting that has introduced new forms of discipline, control, and exploitation. In this context, religious belief provides a means to protest against these newly regimented systems.

This religious protest does not seem to fit the case of Taiwan, however. Though modern Taiwan certainly has exploitative labor conditions, there is less of a sense of a great departure from an idyllic past, for both China and Taiwan have long traditions of a small elite ruling over a multitude of poor people working long hours for bare subsistence. The farmer of traditional China had to pay his landlord exorbitant percentages of his crops, and women were literally bought and sold as prostitutes, servants, and wives. If anything, modern Taiwan is experiencing unprecedented, if relative, equality in either Taiwanese or Chinese history. Working hours have been limited to some extent, and outside income has led to relative freedom from familial demands.[11] This is not to say that industrial exploitation does not take place, but rather that the contrast with the past is less dramatic.

Religious reactions to changing labor and market structures in China date back to at least the eighteenth century. Philip Kuhn notes that accusations of soul stealing inevitably focused on marginalized people, including vagrants, strangers, beggars, and wandering monks who could not be trusted because of their lack of familial connections (Kuhn 1990: 41–44). An equally suspect group were the "traitor-monk or heterodox Taoist," who were "deluding good subjects" (Kuhn 1990: 11, 44). Part of such scares arose from government's attempt to hold onto the power of licensing religions and practitioners, thereby controlling religious legitimacy (Kuhn 1990: 109–112, 212–213). Kuhn suggests that this was a result of the population explosion of the time and the new economic competition that was ushered in by contact with Spanish traders exchanging silver and promoting the sale of land and labor (Kuhn 1996: 31).

At this time textiles and handicraft labor introduced a new "commercialized society" to people who had traditionally lived in farm communities. This in turn created the problem of population density in industrial areas, declining per capita income, and declining social mobility (Kuhn 1990: 229) in contrast to increasing signs of wealth among the bureaucratic, scholarly, and commercial elites (Kuhn 1990: 133).

Sometimes such sorcery was projected onto Catholic missionaries. Paul Cohen points to a late-nineteenth-century painting depicting Catholics removing a woman's fetus and placenta so that they could use it as medicine and for alchemy (Cohen 1997: 166). He cites accusations that Catholics hollowed out pregnant wombs for sorcerers to use to harm their victims (Cohen 1997: 167). Cohen suggests that the telling of such stories was an attempt to control potential agents of chaos by pinpointing specific sources of stress and disorder (Cohen 1997: 167). He also links such mass hysteria in part to highly dense populations of strangers brought together for the trade economy (Cohen 1997: 171). He connects accusations against Catholics to drought, scarcity of food, and lack of employment, in which uncontrollable forces were associated with malevolent sorcerers (Cohen 1997: 156).

Geschiere, in his work on sorcery in Cameroon, points out that while accusations of witchcraft are often used to criticize new economies or, more particularly, those who succeed in new economies, an equally common theme in such stories evinces a strong determination to use magical forces to appropriate the potential wealth or to legitimize the success that such new economic systems offer (Geschiere 1997: 166–167). Accompanying the condemnation of sorcerers, then, is the lure and excitement of dealing with unknown and untamed powers (Geschiere 1997: 1). This brings us to the world that Geschiere terms "the modernity of witchcraft," in which modernization and continuing themes of the occult no longer seem paradoxical but a logical extension of religious function in a constantly changing socioeconomic environment (Geschiere 1997: 3).

Turning our attention to the last few decades in Taiwan, Robert Weller demonstrates that in Chinese religions the advantage of praying to ghosts is that they will do anything if worshiped properly and presented with the proper gifts (Weller 1994: 127, 1996). As he has noted, ghosts are far more amenable to immoral contracts with the living than are bureaucratic gods, who must ultimately adhere to traditional moral principles (Weller 1996: 260). Gods, then, can be perceived as social, for they protect the community and are in return provided for by the community, as opposed to ghosts, who are far more amenable to helping individuals at the expense of community needs, thus providing a service for individualistic and immoral desires (Weller 1994: 129–130, 146–147, 152). Weller relates this approach to capitalism in Taiwan in the 1980s, suggesting that religious individualism in Taiwan arose at the same time that success in the capitalist economy seemed to come as a result of greed and luck rather than hard work or integrity (Weller 1994: 149, 1996: 262). In such a setting, he argues, "capricious deities matched the capricious nature of profit itself" (Weller 1996: 262).

Weller thus forcefully links changing religious perceptions with the new capitalist infrastructure, suggesting that modern-day economics promised greater and faster profit but with far greater risks (Weller 1994: 140). His account of the Eighteen Lords Temple, which "attracts thousands of visitors every day to offer cigarettes to seventeen dead bodies and a dog" (Weller 1996: 251),[12] offers insight into modern religious experience as it relates to capitalist ethics, or the lack thereof, which he sees as more like a contract with mobsters who know no moral boundaries, with the same potential for amoral and great assistance or quick and dire retribution (Weller 1996: 260). Along the same lines, a handful of discontented or greedy patrons in Taiwan ask sorcerers for help with fetus demons, which are thought to be particularly dangerous and effective in making money because the spirits have not yet been taught right from wrong.

Sorcery and the Imagery of Dead Fetuses

As I noted in earlier chapters, Taiwan has a long history of abortion, but its legalization in 1985 brought it into the public sphere as the press discussed a wide range of related issues, ranging from abortion rates to teenage pregnancy, sexuality, family planning, fetus-ghost appeasement, and fetus demons. All of these problems carry unresolved tensions, both for the individual and for society as a whole. Belief in fetus ghosts helps to resolve these tensions. But those who deal with fetus demons do not attempt to resolve these anxieties—to the contrary, such people thrive on them.

There has been very little scholarly mention of the use of fetuses or dead infants in sorcery. Frazer cites ancient Christian mythology concerning evil priests who drank water from a "well into which the body of an unbaptized infant [had] been flung" (Frazer 1922: 54). Seaman (1981) and Ball (1892) briefly document the historical use of dead fetuses for sorcery in Chinese culture.

Mauss also mentions sorcery and fetuses briefly, although his argument is problematic. He states that fetuses used in black magic fall into a broader category of discarded materials, such as excrement, nail clippings, and leftovers from meals (Mauss 1950: 47). He then places them in a category of objects that are used for black magic because they have been discarded or are thought to be of no use (Mauss 1950: 47). In creating such categories Mauss misses the significance of the imagery evoked by each item. Dead fetuses are not used in black magic because they have been thrown away and are considered useless; they are used because they are the ultimate anomaly in social and religious systems. Miscarried or aborted fetuses call into question one's religious faith that there is reason in the universe. Why, one might ask, would the gods or fate allow a woman to become pregnant if that fetus were not intended to have a life? An aborted fetus symbolically points to a child who has been killed by its parents, who is unborn yet human in form; it represents a being as yet completely unsocialized, and thus human yet animal. In short, a dead fetus is seen as something against nature, an incarnation of pure evil.

The more horrific the imagery associated with fetus-demon sorcery, the more it seems to attest to the effectiveness of the magic. The very image of an aborted fetus that has turned into a ghost, black or dark-green from lack of blood, evokes fear and disgust. And the imagery of a breach against nature and society that abortion represents strengthens this view. In part this attests to the morbid nature of the ghost. Daniel Harper traces fetus-demon rituals dating back to 217 B.C. in which violent imagery is repeatedly used as a part of such techniques (Harper 1996: 244–250). The techniques included imprisoning the spirits of dead newborn infants, slashing them with scrub brushes so that they "died," and boiling and eating them (Harper 1996: 248). One could also scatter yellow soil to dispel demon babies (Harper 1996: 249). This is part of a wider array of violent imagery used to dispel demon spirits, including striking them with hammers, throwing shoes at them, striking them with a staff, and shooting them with straw arrows (Harper 1996: 249).

I opened this chapter with an excerpt from an interview that spoke of grinding up part of a fetus and keeping it in a bottle for fetus-demon sorcery. Another example of the gruesome images involved with this belief is cited in a magazine article that lists some equally unappealing alternatives. This includes seeking out pregnant women who have died in car crashes, drowning, or other accidental deaths, and using the brain fluid or blood from the heart of a dead fetus "to catch its soul" (Du 1997). With this fluid or blood, the sorcerer can then write talismanic characters to beckon the spirit (Du 1997). The examples I have just provided are specifically associated with violent deaths that evoke images of pain and struggle. In addition to the vividly grotesque imagery of brain fluids and blood, the violence of the deaths themselves adds to the material's talismanic powers.

Another method used in fetus-demon sorcery is to use the body of an infant that has been buried for a long time.

> The most effective method to capture a fetus demon's spirit is to use the body of an infant that has been buried for a long time. Because the child's bones have been buried for many years, they can absorb the spiritual energy of heaven and earth, the sun, moon, mountains, and rivers. Therefore everyone recognizes that their magical power is the strongest. This experienced spirit medium says that you cannot use just any bone, but must use the bones that have part of the soul in them [*San hun qi po*] to be of any use. Once you have gotten this bone, the spirit medium must use "special stuff" to offer in sacrifice, only then can they get the full effectiveness. (Du 1997)

We see here that sorcerers also draw on traditional animistic beliefs for fetus-demon sorcery. In this way the power of "heaven and earth, the sun, moon, mountains, and rivers" is channeled through the corpse of an infant, which is seen to be closer to nature because it has not yet been socialized.

Like the scholarship I have outlined in the previous section, magic, sorcery, and possession in the modern industrial world all draw on traditional religious concepts, yet they must adapt to meet the new demands of their changing environments. The basic emotions and motivations associated with fetus-demon sorcery have not changed so much from those of traditional black magic. But they draw on the imagery of abortion, which is meaningful precisely because of rising abortion rates connected to a modern urban environment that discourages families from having too many children.

Also, greater literacy and freedom of the press have brought abortion into the public sphere. Newspaper coverage on abortion often includes representations of social chaos and moral decay. Fetus-demon sorcery thrives on the anxieties associated with death, urbanization, and self-fulfillment at others' expense—whether it is abortion or success in a capitalist system that prioritizes profit over morality. Thus, the belief does not signify resistance to modern industrial social inequalities and labor exploitation, as has been suggested by attempts to explain folk-religious beliefs in other areas of the world. Rather, it exemplifies a heightened exaggeration of the capitalist desire to achieve success within the system at any cost. The changes we have witnessed here point to a need to believe in the efficacy of one's own agency while being forced to face with growing certainty our own insignificance in urban environments that include a widely extended range of economic, political, and personal relationships.

11
Conclusion
Fetus Spirits and
the Commodification of Sin

Part of the difficulty, and the interest, of writing on this subject has been the fact that for every rule there is at least one exception. Yet some conceptions of the spirit are prevalent enough that they can, as a general rule, be used to describe the ghost. In Taiwan, Buddhist gods are a larger presence than Daoist gods despite the fact that the number of Daoist temples engaging in fetus-ghost appeasement are equal to and probably greater than Buddhist temples that do so. Fetus ghosts are usually thought to grow older in the spirit world but to stop at the age of three to five years. Sometimes they are believed to be loving, sometimes angry; but for the most part they are considered to be young spirits in need of assistance from their living parents. They are usually thought to cause physical or psychological harm either through intent or from an excess of *yin* energy, which disrupts the *yin/yang* balance of the living. Usually, the proper action to take when dealing with a fetus ghost is to beg forgiveness and, with the help of a religious master, send it on to its next life. On the whole, fetus ghosts are thought to be in their situation because of a lack of fate with their parents, most often their mothers. Yet in spite of this element of fate, aborted fetus ghosts are for the most part thought to exist because of their parents' sins.

Aside from these similarities, there is a sense that anything goes. Fetus ghosts may be vengeful, benevolent, or victimized. The appeasement process may take a few minutes or go on indefinitely. The amount charged may be only a few hundred NT dollars or thousands. The people appeasing the ghost may assume most of the responsibility for the process or may leave it to religious authorities.

An interesting point here is that fetus-demon sorcery is far more standardized than fetus-ghost appeasement, despite the fact that the practice became popular during roughly the same time period. This is not to say that there are no differences, but that the variables seem to be due to how best to bind the spirit to do one's bidding rather than a disparity in the ghost's thought and intent. The best explanation I can offer for this relative uniformity of belief is the fairly narrow focus of the services being offered. Fetus-demon sorcery inevitably boils down to fear, loathing, and greed. In contrast, we have seen a wide spectrum of concerns associated with fetus ghosts, ranging from a desire for financial success and good fortune, to physical and psychological illness, to a more general sense of guilt related to abortion. Reasons for guilt, in turn, branch out to different issues, such as killing life and being a bad parent to being selfish and sexually decadent, even if that decadence is within the framework of a monogamous relationship.

If we look at the different aspects of the beliefs in fetus spirits, certain patterns emerge as to the marketing strategies used by those who make their living from this practice. In examining the various needs that are fulfilled by fetus-ghost appeasement and fetus-demon sorcery, one sees growing demands that enterprising religious practitioners are meeting and, in some cases, helping to create. Fetus-demon sorcery is at one extreme end of this spectrum, for it is completely devoid of emotional attachment to the spirit. Religious masters involved with fetus-demon sorcery seem consciously to exploit their clients' vices, promising fulfillment of their most selfish desires. Such religious practitioners make a sizable income. In this case, one is promised individual success in the capitalist market, safety from the spiritual attacks of one's enemies, and fulfillment of the desire for vengeance against one's enemies.

The use of talismanic objects such as dolls shaped like human beings or parts of dead fetuses' bodies attests to the fact that the sorcerer and his client are willing to do anything to achieve their goals. The price for this service is likely to be large because of the supernatural danger for the sorcerer. This threat is likely to be a marketing tool in and of itself, for if a client is unwilling to pay the sorcerer's price, the sorcerer can accuse that client of lacking the proper commitment for success. If this sounds familiar as modern economic rhetoric, it is because fetus-demon sorcery has grown in, and responded to, the modern industrial-capitalist environment.

In the previous pages I have taken issue with the criticism that practitioners of fetus-ghost appeasement manipulate their patrons for their own ends. Yet in doing so I do not mean to suggest that such manipulation, and in some cases exploitation, does not exist—indeed, I have provided a good deal of evidence to support such accusations of excess. We can see this in the random approaches of people on the street offering strangers spiritual redemption at a price, and in some of the case studies I have presented. In these instances, we see people with no religious training declaring themselves able to aid the forlorn spirits. Daoist Master Bob, for example, has become a millionaire through his religious dealings, and both of the people I met who paid for his services later felt that they had been cheated.

In previous chapters we have seen the different portrayals of fetus ghosts and the ways in which these images can be manipulated for specific purposes. The fact that the perceived sin of abortion is such a resonant experience means that when this is offered as an explanation for one's hardships, it "feels true" to those involved. Thus, anxiety that one has escaped spiritual punishment for a deed that one believes to be morally wrong creates a setting in which a religious master's assertion that problems have been caused by the spirits of aborted fetuses is meaningful to a great many.

Yet critiques of the practice tend to err in reducing a highly complex belief into too narrowly defined roles. If we see religious masters as responding to, or even creating, market demands for this belief, we should also look at the services they choose to provide. For example, we should note the remarkable disparity between the services offered for fetus-demon sorcery and fetus-ghost appeasement. Fetus-demon sorcery both vents and enhances already existing antisocial emotions. In contrast, fetus-ghost appeasement offers spiritual redemption, a sense of security, and curative solutions for one's concrete problems in life. It is a process that relieves guilt, restores familial harmony, and reinforces one's sense of humanity.

As I have pointed out, fetus-ghost appeasement is part of a larger body of religious practice and belief that might be called a commodification of sin, in which one can atone for one's wrongs through financial sacrifice in one form or another. This has traditionally involved large sums of money and conspicuous expenditures for temples and temple goers alike. Fetus-ghost appeasement does not create a significantly more exploitative system but merely extends the services offered in a larger religious tradition. As an example, the woman who paid NT\$20,000 to appease a fetus ghost seemed quite proud that she had spent so much money. She was not at all ashamed that she had paid so much, nor did she say she felt cheated.

As I have also noted, religious masters could not market this belief if there were not a demand. The fact that there is a preexisting need for fetus-ghost appeasement is highlighted by the fact that several of the people I interviewed told me of others who went to temples to burn incense and say prayers of apology for their fetus ghosts without ever talking to a religious master about the matter.

While one should not ignore the existence of greedy or manipulative religious practitioners, nor should one forget those who offer such services for relatively reasonable sums. In the latter cases, it is possible to acknowledge that someone makes a good income while still doing good. As a parallel example, though we might feel that the price of a psychologist's therapy is excessive, we can still acknowledge the degree to which it has given some people hope. Temples that perform fetus-ghost appeasement allow for the expression of both love and regret, and provide a means for worshipers to come to terms with the hard choices they have made and the hard realities that have been forced upon them.

This book demonstrates the rich variety of cultural interpretations and methods for dealing with some of the most emotionally charged issues of the human race. In spite of the very different religious, political, and cultural backgrounds of Taiwan and the United States, for example, their concerns with morality, order, and self-restraint in relation to sexuality and abortion are surprisingly similar. For this reason, I hope that this study will not only help us to better understand Taiwanese and Chinese perceptions of sexuality, abortion, and the spirit world, but also give us a valuable comparison through which we can more rationally examine our own.

Someone once told me that Michelangelo spoke of his sculptures less as figures he had created than as forms that beckoned to be released from their shapeless exteriors. While the creation of this book has fallen to a less able craftsman, the writing process has been quite similar. Especially in the final months of writing I felt less like a master of my chosen project than—dare I say it?—I was possessed by it and forced to do its bidding. Although I can describe the actions involved in fetus-ghost appeasement, it is hard to convey the often contradictory emotions both of the worshipers and the anthropologist studying them. I will conclude by sharing an excerpt from my fieldnotes that I wrote moments after walking through Dragon Lake Temple alone one night.

> The temple has closed for the evening, and as I walk through the main room devoted to fetus ghosts I am faced with the spirits' idols and the toys and food that have been left for them. The smell of incense is ever present, and candles are still burning and will continue to do so throughout the night. Everyone else has gone to sleep and there is a peaceful serenity that sharply contrasts with the busy activities of the day.

> I walk through this temple, past the offerings that have been left for the dead. As I look at the fetus-ghost idols covered in the warm red glow of the candles, I cannot help but remember the day's events—the distraught faces and the silent tears confront me like an all-too-vivid nightmare. But nor can I forget the comforted expressions of those who walked by, or the serenity with which they talked of providing for their "children." While walking past these idols I am struck by the thought that here lie the hearts of so many mourners—their fallen dreams, and their hopes for a better day to come. It is strange that something can be so sad and so beautiful at the same time.

Appendix
Dragon Lake Temple's Red Contract

A Red Contract for Pacifying Resentment and Undoing Entanglements
by Providing Salvation for Fetus Ghosts

I [the person appeasing the spirit] prostrate myself so that the majesty of sagely virtues, whose divine benevolence is vast, may wash away a millennium of hatred. From this point we resolve 100 years of trouble. To investigate good and evil to see who should take responsibility, I [the person appeasing the spirit] present this appeal:

Taiwan, Province _____

City _____ Prefecture _____ District _____

Village _____ Township _____ Alley _____

Lane _____ Number and Floor _____

Person seeking to end dispute [person appeasing the ghost]

Petitioner's date of birth: Year_____ Month_____ Day_____

Hour_____ Age _____

With great awe I kowtow to entreat the great presence of the fetus ghost to grant resolution to the grievance and to untie this knot of conflict. I hope you can understand this humble person's problematic situation. An old sin that I still have not made amends for follows my body so that my life often turns out to be the opposite from my dreams, my fate has been perverted. Alas! Such are the burdens caused by accumulated resentment and wrongdoing! A fetus ghost is haunting me or taking revenge for my previous misdeeds. In the past I did a bad thing and now I have no way to escape. Happily there is a gateway [to deliverance] by saving the fetus ghost by sending him/her on to his/her next life.

Today, I receive the favor of the resplendent miracles of Dragon Lake Temple, as well as the limitless spiritual power and miraculous transformations of its sages and deities. While kowtowing, a revelation via the flying phoenix came from the Supreme Emperor of the Dark Heavens and other assembled sages and deities, and thus I knew that this resentment was caused by you haunting me because I harmed you and dragged you down. With sincere and heartfelt repentance I make my plea to receive the great favor of having this offense resolved. Moreover, having received benevolence [from the temple's gods], I will make offerings [to the fetus ghost] from:

Year _____ Lunar Month _____ Lunar Day _____

until

Year _____ Lunar Month _____ Lunar Day _____ .

I have reverently prepared this red contract and burn this holy incense and recite the Amitabha Sutra and the Mingsheng Jing. I raise my head to the heavens to beseech the Emperor of the Dark Heavens to beg that he show mercy and grant this exceptional request for universal salvation and vast mercy. For this reason I sincerely express my wishes by contributing this money—Amount given[1]_____
—to provide for those in need or to contribute to temple construction or other works of merit in order to gain deliverance from fetus ghosts and to resolve a wrong that would influence me for many lives.

I prostrate myself and hope that the ruler of Dragon Lake Temple, the god Xuantian Shangdi, Supreme Emperor of the Dark Heavens, beloved and respected teacher, and gods from the three religions;[2] the sages, Buddha, the Daoist immortals, deities, and benevolent lords will all decree salvation [for the spirit] and provide limitless release from resentment and entanglement. May the Bodhisattva on the lotus throne, the Bodhisattva Ksitgarbha, as well as his majesty the Supreme Emperor of the Eastern Peak, and the Ten Luminous Kings of the Underworld inspect and receive [this offering]. May they show pity and mercy toward me and be lenient, accepting responsibility on my behalf. I respectfully beseech you to grant special favor to help me escape the fetus ghost's resentful hatred and to eliminate the bad karma that my wrongs have created so that I am freed from past resentful hatred. From this point, make [my] bad karma disappear. The two parties [the appeaser and the ghost] should both have a realization and come to understand clearly. In this way let body and heart be peaceful and without conflict, and no disaster can affect me. With limitless gratitude I thank the gods and reverently pray.

Solemnly presented in worship.

Respectfully received.

Transmitted [to the gods] on

Year [on the Daoist Calendar] _____ Lunar Month _____ Lunar Day _____, kowtowing and pleading to pacify resentment on behalf of this commoner.

With ceremony and worship, [I] present this appeal.

Notes

Chapter 1

1. I use the term "Taiwanese" to refer to anyone living in Taiwan. Current socio-political movements in Taiwan have been (re-)constructing a Taiwanese identity, and for this reason it would be inaccurate to refer to people in Taiwan as Chinese. Nor do I intend the term to exclude the mainland Chinese who came to Taiwan in 1949, Hakka, or other ethnic groups in Taiwan. Though each of these groups is distinctive, I have not found significant differences in relation to this study. Thus, the term "Chinese beliefs" refers to traditional Chinese conceptions that have helped to mold current ways of thinking in Taiwan about family, sexuality, and religious convictions. The term "Taiwanese beliefs" refers to modern opinions held by people living in Taiwan today. While this division of terms is not ideal, it has proven to be the most concise and least distracting way of describing the belief systems that I outline in the following pages.

2. As David Jordan has pointed out, many Daoist and Buddhist temples in Taiwan have adopted practices that are not traditionally associated with these religions, and as such should be considered folk-religious temples (Jordan 1972: 28). In fact, most temples involved with fetus-ghost appeasement and fetus-demon sorcery should be called folk-religious temples. When I refer to a temple or religious master as "Daoist" or "Buddhist," I do so because that is the term used by the religious master being discussed. Although this has the disadvantage of losing the distinction between these claims and the views taken of such practitioners by certified Buddhist and Daoist groups in Taiwan, it preserves the identification with these two religious traditions that the religious masters I interviewed were eager to maintain.

3. This is no doubt partly due to Americans' open mirth toward the concept. It is also partly due to the relative privacy of the issue. In general, people who had experiences with fetus ghosts volunteered their stories to me because they knew of my research. It was not a subject that people discussed with me before I began my study.

4. I have no confirmation as to how widespread the belief may be in these countries.

5. I asked many mainland Chinese, Taiwanese, and Westerners if they had heard of this belief while living in mainland China, but no one had even heard of the belief there. This is perhaps surprising considering the prevalence of abortion in mainland China. It may be the case that the belief was suppressed, if not extinguished, in the communist era. I find it likely that, because of continuing government antagonism toward religious activities, some might practice it in secret.

6. The idea that friends help friends, otherwise translated as "reciprocity."

7. There is also potential for exploitation other than financial. Daoist Master Bob, whom I describe later in this book, is reported to have slept with one of his married clients, who paid him over NT$10 million (US$293,800) for religious services not associated with fetus ghosts. In one of his books the exorcist Zhong Xing, writing of his experiences with fetus ghosts, included several letters from people who had had experiences with fetus ghosts. One of these letters (X. Zhong 1994b: 215) is from a woman who recounted how she was tricked into having sex with a spirit medium who told her it was necessary to replenish her energy field (*cichang*, lit. "magnetic field"). I have no way of verifying the authenticity of the letter, but recent news coverage of a Taiwanese government agent who allegedly used the excuse of performing *qigong* to undress and molest his friend's daughter (B. Huang 1998: 3) suggests that this occurrence may be more common than one might think. Critics have focused on what they see to be the financial and emotional exploitation of women involved in fetus-ghost appeasement, but in fact there are also other possible abuses involved with this practice, and in encounters with immoral religious practitioners in general.

Chapter 2

1. This is not to say that it does not happen, but it is quite rare, and when a woman does give birth out of wedlock it is usually kept secret to the extent that this is possible.

2. Such scenes are typical of the entire genre, at least as distributed in Taiwan. Also, whether or not the actresses really are minors is hard to say, but often the women in such movies wear schoolgirl uniforms, which are presumably intended to represent both their youth and their supposed virginal status.

3. This expectation is slowly changing in Taibei but is still the norm in most other areas of Taiwan. Also, it should not be taken to signify that young women *are* remaining virgins until marriage. Remember, for example, the statistics I have already presented, which indicate that a sizable number of people are engaging in premarital sexual activity.

4. The law was passed in 1984 but not implemented until 1985.

5. I suspect this is because the government tends to prosecute only when a spouse makes the issue public. The two cases of violation of the abortion law that I was able to find in the press, for instance, both reported women who had been arrested because they had had abortions without their husbands' consent (Xie 1991: 5; Zhan 1992: 4). I have not heard of a case of a minor who had an illegal abortion being taken to court. It is likely that, because of the prevalent condemnation of single motherhood in Taiwan, abortions would be approved of in these cases.

6. Again, because clinics perform a good many illegal abortions, there are no accurate statistics on the medical problems resulting from abortion in Taiwan. Even for legal abortions, however, one study of Taiwan states that in the two-month period after a "simple induced abortion," 28.3% of their respondents reported having side effects from the abortion, and 8.5% reported side effects two to four months after their abortions (Hsieh 1990: 96). Symptoms listed for "simple induced abortion" included faintness, headaches, lumbago, excessive bleeding, bleeding for longer periods, lower abdominal pain, unusual amount of discharge, malodorous discharge, fevers, and repeated curettage (Hsieh 1990: 112). There is a troubling point in Hsieh's statistics, however, in that in table 18 (Hsieh 1990: 113), private clinics had substantially fewer reported side effects than military, public, city, and private hospitals; yet private clinics are known to be less sanitary and to have less skilled practitioners. Thus, the percentages of side effects of abortion are likely to be far higher than Hsieh suggests.

7. The divorce rates in Taiwan tripled from 1970 to 1990 (M. L. Lee et al. 1994: 256), and statistics suggest that by 1990 approximately 3% of all women and men between the ages of thirty and fifty were divorcees (M. L. Lee et al. 1994: 258). In 1996 there were 1.7 divorces per 1,000 people in Taiwan (Anonymous 1997: 4).

8. Although there is no legal recourse, occasionally personal relations do come into play. For example, I knew one woman in her early thirties who had reached an agreement with the mother of her ex-husband to spend some days with her children without her ex-husband's knowledge. For a mother-in-law to side with her divorced daughter-in-law rather than her son, however, is almost unheard of.

9. For women who have already given birth to three to five children, the male-to-female birthrate for successive children is approximately 129:100 (Hu 1994: 3; Y. Cai 1992: 1).

10. Van Gulik states that such tablets were popular among both Daoists and Buddhists (van Gulik 1961: 246).

11. The term most often used was "guilt" (*zuiegan*), but people also referred to their "regret" (*houhui*) and "guilty regret" (*kuijiu*).

12. The author's pen name, Si Jiao, is clearly fictitious, for Jiao is a woman's name and *si* means "thinking of." Thus, the name literally means "Thinking of [a woman named] Jiao."

Chapter 3

1. They do not make origami tributes in Taiwan.

2. Many worshipers at the Daoist Dragon Lake Temple also went there of their own volition, although in this case the temple is known to appease fetus ghosts and its patrons could have been responding to its religious tracts or media coverage on the temple.

3. In this chapter I mention a number of religious masters and a movie. I do not explain them fully here but will present them in more detail in the following chapters.

4. This is not to say that Confucian temples or Christian churches engage in this practice; they do not. But on occasion I have met people who consider themselves Confucianists or Christians who were appeasing fetus ghosts in much the

same way that some Buddhists or Christians in Taiwan burn incense for their ancestors.

5. Worshipers also go to this temple to pray to ancestors and other gods and ghosts, but the vast majority of people at these semiannual ceremonies go to appease fetus ghosts.

6. Occasionally people do run into neighbors or friends. Usually this is because many people first hear of the temples from friends who have also gone there. At other times it is a source of embarrassment for both parties.

Chapter 4

1. The majority of people whom I have interviewed believe that fetuses have souls at conception. A handful of people I have talked to, however, believe that the soul does not enter the baby until its birth.

2. Many people have told me of common taboos for pregnant women, including the idea that she should not touch scissors or needles or her child might have a cleft lip, and that she should not hit a nail with a hammer. Yet although the traditional avoidance rules are known by many, most people now call them "superstitions" (*mixin*), and few connect this with the idea that the soul of the fetus wanders outside of its mother.

3. Part of this discrepancy is the result of where one draws one's lines in the terminology used. Wolf and Thompson are no doubt referring to the term *bai bai*, which is used for worship of one's ancestors or gods. None of the masters I spoke with used the term *bai bai*, though some worshipers did. *Yang* is the term most commonly used in reference to dealing with fetus demons. The more reverential form of the term, *gongyang*, is most commonly used with fetus ghosts. Both *yang* and *gongyang* mean "to raise," as in raising one's children, and "to provide," as in providing support for one's parents. Ms. Xu, a Buddhist master, stopped me when I used the word *gongyang* in an interview, however. She told me that I should say *chaodu*, a Buddhist term that means to raise a soul from its suffering in the next world. I have settled for the phrases "to provide for," "to appease," or "to send on to its next life," according to the context. Yet, if these terms have slightly different resonances from "worship," they are equally differentiated from exorcism (*qugui, qumo*), or chastisement of deceased offspring that occurred in earlier times. As with worship, people appease fetus ghosts both out of concern for their own welfare and that of the spirits.

Chapter 5

1. This is a gray area in the belief. Most people do not believe that *yingling* include infants who have died, but I have talked with many who do.

2. In traditional Chinese thought *yin* and *yang*, the two basic forces in the universe, must remain in balance. *Yang* represents maleness, strength, sunlight, and other positive forces. *Yin* represents femaleness, weakness, darkness, and other negative forces. Laying aside an obvious gender analysis for the moment, the relevance of *yin* and *yang* here is that ghosts are excessively *yin*, which disrupts the *yin/yang* balance of the living, thereby causing illness.

3. Many temples in Taiwan are places for the elderly to gather and have puppet shows and other activities that younger people seem less interested in.

4. In fact she had signed a written guarantee for her friend. She was not sure what this signified, but she said that it probably meant she would have to pay for further operations or buy a coffin if anything went wrong. She thought it also meant that in the case of a lawsuit being brought by parents or others she would be held responsible. I went to a public hospital to ask about this. The receptionist told me that it was not so much a liability waiver as a testament that the woman seeking the abortion had thoroughly thought about it. The necessity for single women to have cosigners is not mentioned in the actual abortion law, but it is a common requirement at hospitals. Apparently the fetus ghost also took this contract seriously.

5. "Third eyes" (*di san yan*). Some call this "*yin/yang* eyes" (*yin/yang yan*).

6. Elizabeth Harrison has documented similar critiques in Japan while also pointing out that the issue is more complex than this (Harrison 1999).

7. Interestingly, the owner said that he got the idea from the Japanese practice of having pet cemeteries (Kyne 1998: 8).

8. Literally, "teacher-father" or religious master. The expression is a common title used in addressing monks or nuns.

9. In Taiwan, to be divorced or a single mother is highly stigmatized, and the majority of women who marry there do so before the age of thirty.

10. As a sign of the times, such tracts are slowly being squeezed out by credit card applications. Morality tracts can still be found at most temples, however.

Chapter 6

1. The presence of Christianity in this movie is fairly tangential to the plot. Mrs. Li has two confrontations with her Christian boss who opposes abortion, this being one of them. Also, in the final battle scene with the ghost, which I will discuss below, a Christian priest is present along with a Buddhist and Daoist master. Christians do occasionally engage in fetus-ghost appeasement, using the same religious temples that other Taiwanese use. I do not know of any Christian churches that engage in fetus-ghost appeasement, however.

2. This portion of the movie was filmed at the Daoist Dragon Lake Temple. Ironically, the Buddhist master in the movie specifically states that fetus-ghost appeasement is a Buddhist practice, not a Daoist one, in spite of the fact that this scene was filmed at a Daoist temple.

3. This bridge is traditionally thought to be the gateway from the world of the living to the realm of the dead. All deceased people must go there to pass to the underworld.

4. They do not actually show the fetus, only a glowing plastic bag with a drawing of a fetus flashing in front of the screen. A woman who recently worked at an abortion clinic told me that it is still quite common for aborted fetuses to be thrown away as trash. In general, the dumping of medical waste is fairly common (Anonymous 1998: 18). I also visited a hospital and a clinic whose staff claimed they paid someone to pick up the fetuses to bury them properly. In both cases the staff was unable or unwilling to give me a phone number or an address where I could reach these people. It seems improbable that they would provide proper burial in a country where property is so highly priced.

5. I have not heard of this anywhere else in Taiwan. Helen Hardacre, however,

cites Japanese beliefs about fetus ghosts that are exactly the same (Hardacre 1997: 30). Thus it is probable that this part of the plot was inspired by the Japanese tradition.

6. It is also possible that this was an oversight and that one pile was meant to be for Mrs. Li and the other for Mrs. Li's husband. This argument would be supported by Mingming's speech at the end of the movie, in which she tells the Lis that they have both been forgiven by their ghost.

7. Again, fetus ghosts are usually thought to age in the spirit world until they are three to five years old.

8. Shangping's expression of guilt and sorrow, and her desire to make amends by buying her daughter-ghost clothing, candy, or toys, are also highly resonant with the emotions of women and men I spoke with who were involved in fetus-ghost appeasement. At Dragon Lake Temple, for example, this practice is quite common, although the temple does not request that they do so.

9. In one case the ghost was actually two brothers' aborted younger sister, but the basic outline that I am providing holds true for this chapter as well.

10. Note that in the story "Daughter Butterfly," for example, the ghost was frightened by her mother's tears.

11. In these stories the term *xiaogui* has none of the evil connotations of common usage of the word; they do not drink blood, nor do they do a sorcerer's bidding. Thus, according to popular conceptions of the spirit, he is misusing the term.

12. Though, again, they should be wary of the ghost's harmful excess of *yin*.

13. The Old Man in the Sky is a vaguely defined folk deity, sometimes associated with the moon and said to be in charge of fate (and especially matchmaking). He generally wants for temples, but he figures in many a lighthearted folktale or popular expression, even among unbelievers.

14. This would include above-mentioned examples, such as when he says that some parents give food and clothing to the spirits but that this is not necessary, as well as his portrayal of the spirits as pitiful fetus ghosts rather than as one of the other popular notions of the spirit.

Chapter 7

1. Literally, "god hall."

2. The Chinese believe that on the seventh month of the lunar year the gates of hell open and ghosts enter the world of the living. This is thought to be a particularly dangerous time of the year. Many are afraid to swim during this time, for example, because it is thought that drowned spirits will drag living swimmers under the water. During this period special food offerings are set out for the ghosts to ensure that they will not harm the living, and people will burn money and incense to provide for the ghosts.

3. The first temple was established in 1990. Ms. Xu's temple was established in 1993. When I first went to the first temple in 1996, there were dozens of memorial plaques for fetus ghosts as well as for other ghosts. By the end of 1997 this branch of the temple no longer dealt in fetus ghosts. They explained this as a result of people leaving the plaques at the temple and not coming back for them,

after which workers at the temple were at a loss as to how to deal with them. A more important factor, I suspect, is that Ms. Xu works at the second branch, and because she is the one who publishes a morality tract on fetus ghosts and is more willing to help people send fetus ghosts on to their next lives, those who are interested in appeasing *yingling* are more likely to seek her out. Because the first temple no longer deals with fetus ghosts in any significant fashion, I will limit this discussion to the second temple.

4. Usually appeasers will just write their family name, although I have seen some with full names on them.

5. The master of the founding temple assumed the name Miao Xuanzhuan when he became a Daoist master. Until fairly recently, he continued to participate in Dragon Lake Temple's semiannual ceremonies and to help participants choose names for their fetus ghosts. Teacher Lin paid him for this service. In 1998 Miao Xuanzhuan stopped coming to the ceremonies. I was told this was because of failing health, but when I went by his temple I noticed that he was having a rather grandiose new stone entranceway installed as well as a new building to the left of the temple, which might suggest a growing sense of competitiveness with Dragon Lake Temple.

6. Food given as offerings for gods can be eaten. For this reason, those who come to the temple set out the food offerings before they begin their prayers and take the fruit with them when they leave. In contrast, offerings left for ghosts are thought to become contaminated. Rather than risk the ill effects of this contamination, or the eventuality that the ghosts might follow them home, offerings for the fetus ghosts are left at the temple.

7. It is fairly common for a person to pay for more than one fetus ghost. In one extreme case, a woman was appeasing six fetus ghosts from abortions she had had in one year alone.

8. See the translation of this contract in the Appendix.

9. The idea that gods can control ghosts for the sake of the living is in keeping with traditional conceptions of gods as imperial bureaucrats who command their subjects.

10. Sponsoring such an idol is a means of paying tribute to that god. In return, the god is asked to assist the contributor with her or his request.

11. These were not there when I first arrived, but Teacher Lin is slowly branching out, so that at every semiannual ceremony there is a new statue or set of statues.

12. The gods, as they appear on this altar, from left to right (as one faces them) are: Mulian Pusa, Dizangwang Pusa, Taishangdaozu, Amida Buddha (Emituo Fo), and Dongyuedadi.

13. The gods on this altar are in the following order, from left to right: Santaizi, Baihexiangu, Chifuqiansui, Tianshangshengmu, Guanyin, Wangye, Tangsanzhang, and Xuanzhuang.

14. The temple also provides free food for the biweekly Sunday ceremonies.

15. In part this reflects a sincere desire to contribute to the community at large, and in part it exemplifies a politic aim to be on good terms with the local government. Hill Gates, for example, talks of another temple being told by the city government to spend more of its income in "visible and socially useful ways"

(Gates 1996: 233). Considering the precarious position of the practice of fetus-ghost appeasement in Taiwan, such contributions no doubt also serve to deflect local government or public objections.

16. David Jordan has made a similar point about self-diagnosis in consulting oracles of the Little God in anticipation of arranging a spirit marriage (Jordan 1972: 141).

17. This is *poe* in Taiwanese, *jiao* in mandarin Chinese. Taiwanese has become the most common usage for this term, to the point where most people I have talked to, including those who normally do not speak Taiwanese, do not even know the Chinese word.

18. One way to keep such memorial tablets at home without offending the ancestors or announcing the presence of the anomalous ghost to all visitors is to keep it separately in a back room (Harrell 1986: 108; Jordan 1972: 142).

19. Ms. Xu's Temple does offer some group activities, such as meditation classes, but these gatherings are not associated with fetus-ghost appeasement in any way. Dragon Lake Temple also serves the local community, but the majority of its patronage is from other areas of the country. Neither temple has the community involvement of Cai Wen's temple or the Gaoxiong Buddhist temple, for example.

Chapter 8

1. "Has more *yuan.*" This term is difficult to translate into English. It refers to *yuanfen*, which describes the relationship of two people who have a good destiny together, and is often used for two people who are destined to marry. Thus, any translation of the word should imply that the two people have known each other in other lives, that they have a special relationship as compared to other people they have known in other lives, and that they have a good relationship in this life because of this fact. I have settled on the term "predestined relationship," but it is an unsatisfying translation, and one should keep the full range of nuances in mind.

2. This is the only case I know of in which an urn was set up in a pagoda for a *yingling*. The number of my interviews was limited, however, and I think it likely that others have also used this approach. I suspect that setting up urns in funeral towers is less popular than other forms of appeasement, however, because fetuses are not cremated. Note that in the above cases two of the *yingling* were deceased infants rather than aborted fetuses; as dead infants they were cremated, and the problem remained as to what to do with their ashes.

3. This is a common symptom thought to be caused by fetus ghosts.

4. Fetus ghosts are not usually thought to age beyond the ages of three to five, though they might have come into existence as long as forty or fifty years ago.

5. The Daoist master never stipulated a time limit, so in theory he could have gone on charging her indefinitely had she been willing to pay.

6. In this case, Jeffrey had already begun to appease his fetus ghosts at another temple in Taibei. This is the only instance I know of in which someone was simultaneously appeasing the same fetus ghosts at different temples. A similar example can be found in a short story written by a fetus-ghost exorcist (X. Zhong 1994b: 95), in which someone was being haunted by a fetus ghost that had already

been appeased by another religious master. The fact that the previous appeasement was thought not to have worked, and that Zhong Xing's services as an exorcist were needed for the same ghost, could serve as an additional marketing strat-
egy. These cases suggest that, if potential clients tell a religious master that they
have already appeased their fetus ghosts, the religious practitioner can simply
assert that the first appeasement process did not work and that the spirit needs
to be appeased again.

7. Although Jeffrey did hint that he was also involved in fetus-demon worship, he never said so outright, so I did not include this case in the fetus-demon
chapter.

Chapter 9

1. Although they are apparently devoid of the religious implications of the
texts quoted in this chapter, mainland medical beliefs also seem to mirror these
conceptions. Harriet Evans' study of mainland China shows similar concerns when
she cites medical advice that women's reproductive capacities are not fully developed until the age of twenty-three or twenty-four (Evans 1997: 42). She also cites
modern written materials that advise that young people limit their sexual activity
to once or twice a week, and that this should drop to once every two weeks or less
as one gets older (Evans 1997: 44). And like Ms. Xu's morality tract, which I quote
later in this chapter, Evans cites the belief in mainland China that sexual activity
when drunk can lead to unhealthy fetuses (Evans 1997: 155). Clearly, then, although traditional Chinese tracts tended to focus on male pleasure and health,
they have had a widespread influence on both men and women in modern Chinese culture, both in Taiwan and in mainland China.

2. Surprisingly, neither van Gulik, Furth, nor Wile addresses the possibility
that, in a setting where such scholars did not exercise, a daily regimen of aerobic
sex might have had real positive physical effects.

3. Similarly, Susan Sontag has suggested that in the Untied States fear of AIDS
contamination both strengthens American moralism concerning sexuality and
justifies individualism as "simple medical prudence" (Sontag 1989: 161).

4. George Cernada was directly involved with the family-planning program in
Taiwan beginning a year after its inception in 1964. By 1970 he was the Taiwan
resident adviser for the East Asia Office of the Population Council (Cernada
1970: vii).

5. For more on this, please see Emily Ahern 1975a: 193, 202, 1988: 165; Phyllis
Andors 1983: 50; Hill Gates 1996: 185–187; Steven Harrell 1986: 113–114; Francis
Hsu 1948: 209; Gary Seaman 1981: 395, 1981: 388–389; Arthur Wolf 1974: 151; and
Margery Wolf 1974: 160.

6. In other words, one should not have sex outdoors.

Chapter 10

1. I want to avert any misperception that Chinese or Taiwanese people commonly raise fetus demons. Remember, for example, the quotation at the outset of
this chapter that expressed a common disapproval of and revulsion toward this
practice. The significance of this belief lies not so much in the number of people
who practice such acts as in the prevalence of those who give it credence.

2. One example of this is the avoidance of the number 4 (*si*) because it sounds like the word for death (*si*).

3. This includes prohibited actions for pregnant women, whistling at night during a full moon, and other traditional beliefs that are common superstitions in modern Taiwan.

4. *Shouhun fa:* the practice of casting spells to recall deceased relatives' wandering spirits.

5. As I mentioned earlier, sorcerers feed fetus demons human blood. Human blood has also been used in traditional Chinese sorcery to exorcise demons (Ahern 1975a: 198; Graham 1961: 140), as has menstrual blood (Ahern 1975a: 213).

6. The American movie *Home Alone,* for example, is called Xiaogui *at Home* (*Xiaogui dang jia*).

7. For reasons not outlined in the above account, the grandfather continued to go shopping despite the fact that the doll in his pocket was talking to him.

8. In his book *Explaining the Strange Phenomenon of Spirits* (1995), Lu Guodong states that he is a professor of philosophy and religion in an American University, and sets out to explain the nature of the spirit world.

9. A fetus demon could be categorized as a slave, in the sense that it cannot refuse its master's commands, though because of its two-to-four-year tenure, it might be more accurate to describe this as the relationship of master and indentured servant.

10. The sorcerers themselves do not seem to use such practices for their own vindictiveness, but rather exploit their patrons' emotions to generate income.

11. This is less true for married women, in that most of them are expected to fulfill their traditional domestic duties in addition to working outside of the family.

12. This refers to a cult that began when a boat washed ashore a century or more ago carrying eighteen human corpses and a living dog (Weller 1996: 258). Later, as the bodies were being buried, the dog jumped into the grave with them. The facts that the dog had survived the trip and "decided" to be buried with the dead humans were seen as proof of its divine status (Weller 1994: 126, 1996: 258). Weller is perhaps too polite to suggest that the dog might have been following its food supply.

Appendix

1. At the time of this writing, the standard amount was NT$1,200 (US$35) annually for three years.

2. This refers to Buddhism, Daoism, and Confucianism.

Glossary

baibai	拜拜	*gui yue*	鬼月
Baihexiangu	白鶴仙姑		
ban xin ban yi	半信半疑	*haofang nü*	豪放女
bu yao	不要	*houhui*	後悔
buhaoyisi	不好意思	Huang Juanjuan	黃娟娟
Cai Wen	蔡文	*jiao (poe)*	筊
chaodu	超渡	*jinghua*	淨化
Chifuqiansui	池府千歲	*jiugui*	酒鬼
cichang	磁場	Jiutianxuannü	九天玄女
Ciji	慈濟		
Cimu Tang	慈母堂	*kuijiu*	愧疚
Dimuniangniang	地母娘娘	Laotianye	老天爺
di san yan	第三眼	*lingmei*	靈媒
diulian	丟臉	Lin Jianyi	林健一
Dizangwang Pusa	地藏王菩薩	Lishalaomu	驪山老母
Dongyuedadi	東獄大帝	Li Taitai	李太太
		liumang	流氓
Emituo Fo	阿彌陀佛	*luan*	亂
fengshui	風水	Mazu	媽祖
Foguan Shan	佛光山	*meiyou yiyi*	沒有意義
		Miao Xuanzhuan	妙玄傳
gongyang	供養	Mingming	明明
guandian	觀點	*mixin*	迷信
Guangong	關公	Mulian Pusa	目蓮菩薩
guanxi	關係		
Guanyin	觀音	Naihe Qiao	奈何橋
(Guanshiyin Pusa)	(觀世音菩薩)	*nan geng nü zhi*	男耕女織

nan zhu wai, nü zhu nei	男主外女主內	Wulucaishen	五路財神
		wushi	巫師
peitai	胚胎	*wushu*	巫術
qi	氣	*xiaogui*	小鬼
qigong	氣功	*xiaogui dang jia*	小鬼當家
Qingshuizhushi	清水祖師	*xiaohai*	小孩
Qiulian	秋蓮	*xiaojie*	小姐
qugui	驅鬼	*xiaolaopo*	小老婆
qumo	驅魔	*xiaonanhai*	小男孩
		xiaonühai	小女孩
renao	熱鬧	Xingtian Gong	行天宮
		xiuxing	修行
san hun qi po	三魂七魄	Xuantian Shangdi	玄天上帝
Santaizi	三太子	Xuanzhuang	玄奘
Shangping	尚萍	Xu Qiongyue	許瓊月
shentan	神壇	Xu Xiaojie	許小姐
shifu	師父		
Shijiamouni Fo	釋迦牟尼佛	*yang*	養
(Benshishijiamoni Fo)	本師釋迦牟	*yang (yin/yang)*	陽(陰／陽)
尼佛		Yaochijinmu	瑤池金母
shouhun fa	收魂法	Yaoshi Fo	藥師佛
shushu	叔叔	Yiguandao	一貫道
si	四	*yin (yin/yang)*	陰(陰／陽)
si	死	*yin/yang yan*	陰／陽眼
Si Jiao	思嬌	*yindu*	引渡
songjing	誦經	*yinger*	嬰兒
suanming	算命	*yingling*	嬰靈
suibian	隨便	*yingxiang*	影響
		youdeng	油燈
taier	胎兒	*yousheng baojian fa*	優生保健法
Taijimen	太極門	*you yuan wu fen*	有緣無份
Taishangdaozu	太上道祖	*yuan*	緣
Tangsanzhang	唐三藏	*yuanfen*	緣份
Tianshangshengmu	天上聖母		
		Zhishengxianshi	至聖先師
Wang Kai	王凱	*zhong nan qing nü*	重男輕女
Wangye	王爺	Zhong Xing	鐘星
wenrou	溫柔	*zuiegan*	罪惡感
wo wandanle	我完蛋了	*zuofa*	作法
Wucaishenye	武財神爺		

Bibliography

Ahern (Martin), Emily. 1975a. "The Power and Pollution of Chinese Women." In *Women in Chinese Society*, ed. Margery Wolf and Roxanne Witke, 193–214. Stanford, Calif.: Stanford University Press.

———. 1975b. "Sacred and Secular Medicine in a Taiwan Village: A Study of Cosmological Disorders." In *Medicine in Chinese Cultures: Comparative Studies of Health Care in Chinese and Other Societies*, ed. Arthur Kleinman et al., 91–113. Washington, D.C.: U.S. Department of Health, Education and Welfare, National Institute of Health.

———. 1988. "Gender and Ideological Differences in Representations of Life and Death." In *Death Ritual in Late Imperial and Modern China*, ed. James Watson and Evelyn S. Rawski, 164–179. Berkeley: University of California Press.

Andors, Phyllis. 1983. *The Unfinished Liberation of Chinese Women 1949–1980*. Bloomington: Indiana University Press.

Anonymous. 1989. "Zhuan 'gin a shen' qian!" 賺'死囝仔'錢! (Using 'dead children' to make money!). *Shoudu zaobao* 首都早報 (The Capital's Morning Post), October 30:6.

Anonymous. 1990. "Wei zhongfohui ji ju gongdaohua" 為中佛會説幾句公道話 (In order for the Chinese Buddhist Association to publicly say a few words in someone's defense). *Zhong fohui kan* 中佛會刊 (Chinese Buddhist Association Publication). September 30:3.

Anonymous. 1997. "Population, Divorce on the Rise." *Free China Journal* 3:4.

Anonymous. 1998. "Soong Blasts Irresponsible Dumping of Medical Waste on Island's Beaches." *China Post*, April 21:18.

Baker, Hugh. 1979. *Chinese Family and Kinship*. New York: Columbia University Press.

Ball, Dyer J. [1892] 1982. *Things Chinese*. Hong Kong: Oxford University Press.

Baptandier, Brigitte. 1996. "The Lady Linshui: How a Woman Became a Goddess." In *Unruly Gods: Divinity and Society in China*, ed. Meir Shahar and Robert P. Weller, 105–149. Honolulu: University of Hawai'i Press.

Cai Cuiying 蔡翠英. 1988. "Yingling gongyang guangao fengpo fang yu weiai" 嬰靈供養廣告風波方興未艾 (Advertisements to provide for fetus ghosts cause an endless amount of disturbances). *Zili wanbao* 自立晚報 (The Independence Evening Post), October 27:3.

———. 1990. "Yingling guangci fomen fengpo zai qi" 嬰靈官司佛門風波再起 (*Yingling* lawsuit Buddhist incident comes up again). *Zili wanbao* 自立晚報 (The Independence Evening Post), January 23:1.

Cai Wen 蔡文. N.d. "Yingling hui zuonie ma?" 嬰靈會作祟嗎? (Can *yingling* haunt?). *Daojiao shenghuo changshi xiaobaike.* 道教生活常識小百科 (Daoist common sense life encyclopedia). Taibei: *Qunhui yingshua chang* 春暉印刷廠 (*Qunhui* Printing Company).

Cai Yingying 蔡鸞鶯. 1992. "Zhongnan qingnü: liangxing he xietian bianshu" 重男輕女:兩性和諧添變數 (Male preference: The variable between the balance of the two sexes). *Mingsheng bao* 民生報 (Min Sheng Daily), December 17:1.

Cernada, George P., ed. 1970. *Taiwan Family Planning Reader: How a Program Works.* Taizhong: The Chinese Center for International Training in Family Planning.

Cernada, George P., Chang Ming-Cheng, Lin Hui-Sheng, and Sun Te-Hsiung. [1975] 1985. "Adolescent Sexuality: Implications for National Policy on Secondary School Education in an East Asian Setting." University of Massachusetts at Amherst Asian Studies Committee Occasional Papers Series, no. 11.

Chang Chin-ju. 1996. "Why the Lack of Debate on Abortion?" *Sinorama* 21(2): 17–21.

Chang Ching-sheng. [1927] 1967. *Sex Histories: China's First Modern Treatise on Sex Education,* trans. Howard Levy. New York: Paragon Book Gallery.

Chang Hsun. 張珣 1996. "Daojiao yu mingjian yiliao wenhua—yizhi zhujing zhenghouqun weili" 道教與民間醫療文化—以著驚症侯群為例 (Daoism and folk religious medical culture—the example of fright syndrome). In *Yishi, miao yu shiqu* 儀式,廟與社區 (Ceremonies, temples and communities), ed. Li Fengmao and Zhu Ronggui, 427–457. Taibei: Academia Sinica, The Institute of Culture and Philosophy.

Chen, Chao-nan. 1983. *An Experiment about Family Planning Attitude Change.* Taibei: Institute of Economics, Academia Sinica.

Cohen, Paul A. 1997. *History in Three Keys: The Boxers as Event, Experience, and Myth.* New York: Columbia University Press.

Comaroff, Jean, and John L. Comaroff. 1999. "Occult Economies and the Violence of Abstraction: Notes from the South African Postcolony." *American Ethnologist* 26(2):279–303.

Dikötter, Frank. 1995. *Sex, Culture and Modernity in China: Medical Science and the Construction of Sexual Identities in the Early Republican Period.* Honolulu: University of Hawai'i Press.

Ding Shanxi 丁善璽, Director. N.d. *Yingling* 嬰靈 (Fetus ghosts). Taibei: Xinchuan dianying qiye youxian gongsi 新船電影企業有限公司 (New Ship Film Enterprise Co. Ltd.).

Douglas, Mary. 1966. *Purity and Danger: An Analysis of Concepts of Pollution and Taboo.* London: Routledge & Kegan Paul.

Du Yuxuan 杜毓炫. 1997. "Xiaogui dangjia" 小鬼當家:台灣社會的黑色事件 (Fetus demon at home: The black events in Taiwan's society). *Xin xinwen* 新新聞 (The Journalist) 529:61–68.

Duara, Prasenjit. 1988. "Superscribing Symbols: The Myth of Guandi, Chinese God of War." *The Journal of Asian Studies* 47(4):778–795.

Ebrey, Patricia Buckley. 1993. *The Inner Quarters: Marriage and the Lives of Chinese Women in the Sung Period.* Berkeley: University of California Press.

EL. [1984] 1993. "Yousheng baojian fa" 優生保健法 (The Eugenics and Health Protection Law). In *Xinpian liu fa* 新編六法 (Six new laws), ed. 林紀東 Lin Jidong et al., 1985–1986. Taibei: Wunan tushu chuban gongsi 五南圖書出版公司 (Wunan Library Publication Company).

EL Bylaws. [1984] 1993. "Yousheng baojian fa shixing xizhi" 優生保健法施行細則 (The Eugenics and Health Protection Law bylaws). In *Xinpian liu fa* 新編六法 (Six new laws), ed. 林紀東 Lin Jidong et al., 1986–1987. Taibei: Wunan tushu chuban gongsi 五南圖書出版公司 (Wunan Library Publication Company).

Evans, Harriet. 1997. *Women and Sexuality in China.* Cambridge: Polity Press.

Fischer-Schreiber, Ingrid. 1996. *The Shambhala Dictionary of Taoism.* Trans. Werner Wünsche. Boston: Shambhala Publications.

Foucault, J.-B.-L. [1978] 1990. *The History of Sexuality:* Vol. 1, *An Introduction.* Trans. Robert Hurley. New York: Vintage Books.

———. [1984a] 1990. *The History of Sexuality:* Vol. 2, *The Use of Pleasure.* Trans. Robert Hurley. New York: Vintage Books.

———. [1984b] 1986. *The History of Sexuality:* Vol. 3, *The Care of the Self.* Trans. Robert Hurley. New York: Vintage Books.

Frazer, Sir James George. [1922] 1925. *The Golden Bough: A Study in Magic and Religion.* London: MacMillan and Co.

Freedman, Ronald, and John Y. Takeshita. 1969. *Family Planning in Taiwan: An Experiment in Social Change.* Princeton, N.J.: Princeton University Press.

Freedman, R., M. C. Chang, T. H. Sun, and M. W. Weinstein. 1994. "The Fertility Transition in Taiwan." In *Social Change and the Family in Taiwan,* ed. Arland Thornton and Hui-Sheng Lin, 264–304. Chicago: University of Chicago Press.

Furth, Charlotte. 1994. "Rethinking Van Gulik: Sexuality and Reproduction in Traditional Chinese Medicine." In *Engendering China: Women, Culture, and the State,* ed. Christina K. Gilmarten et al., 125–146. Cambridge, Mass.: Harvard University Press.

Gallin, Bernard. 1975. "Comments on Contemporary Sociocultural Studies of Medicine in Chinese Societies." In *Medicine in Chinese Cultures: Comparative Studies of Health Care in Chinese and Other Societies,* ed. Arthur Kleinman et al., 273–280. Washington, D.C.: U.S. Department of Health, Education and Welfare, National Institute of Health.

Gao Nianyi 高年億. 1997a. "Hou Kuanren: Zhentuo zhi shi xiezhu zhuicha" 侯寬仁:曾託方術之士協助追查 (Hou Kuanren Has Asked for the Help of a Sorcerer to Assist in his Investigation). *Lianhe bao* 聯合報 (The United Daily News), April 4:4.

———. 1997b. "Taijimen changmenren Hong Shihe be qiu xing shi nian" 太極門掌門人洪石和被求刑十年 (Ten-Year Jail Sentence Sought for *Taijimen's* Leader, Hong Shihe). *Lianhe bao* 聯合報 (The United Daily News), April 4:4.

———. 1997c. "Qisu Hong Shihe yang xiaogui chaokong xueyuan" 起訴書指洪石和養小鬼操控學員 (Formal Indictment Accuses Hong Shihe of Raising Fetus Demons to Control Students). *Lianhe bao* 聯合報 (United Daily News), April 4:4.

Gardiner, Beth. 1999. "22% of All Pregnancies Aborted, Study Says." *San Diego Union Tribune,* January 22, A8.

Gates, Hill. 1996. *China's Motor: A Thousand Years of Petty Capitalism.* Ithaca, N.Y.: Cornell University Press.

Geschiere, Peter. 1997. *The Modernity of Witchcraft: Politics and the Occult in Post-colonial Africa.* Charlottesville: University Press of Virginia.

Ginsburg, Faye D. 1989. *Contested Lives: The Abortion Debate in an American Community.* Berkeley: University of California Press.

Graham, David. 1961. *Folk Religion in Southwest China.* Washington, D.C.: The Smithsonian Institute.

van Gulik, R. H. [1961] 1974. *Sexual Life in Ancient China.* Leiden: E. J. Brill.

Gu Qun 顧群. 1966. "Taiwan de wushujie jianjie" 台灣的巫術界簡介 (A synopsis of the world of sorcery in Taiwan). *Taiwan fengwu* 台灣風物 (Taiwan Folkways) 16(3):35–36.

Hardacre, Helen. 1997. *Marketing the Menacing Fetus in Japan.* Berkeley: University of California Press.

Harper, Donald. 1996. "Spellbinding." In *Religions of China in Practice,* ed. Donald S. Lopez, Jr., 241–250. Princeton, N.J.: Princeton University Press.

Harrell, Stevan. 1974. "Belief and Unbelief in a Taiwan Village." Ph.D. diss., Stanford University.

———. 1979. "The Concept of Soul in Chinese Folk Religion." *Journal of Asian Studies* 38(3):519–528.

———. 1986. "Men, Women, and Ghosts in Taiwanese Folk Religion." In *Gender and Religion,* ed. Caroline Walker Bynum, Stevan Harrell, and Paula Richman, 97–116. Boston: Beacon Press.

———. 1991. "Pluralism, Performance and Meaning in Taiwanese Healing: A Case Study." *Culture, Medicine and Psychiatry* 15:45–68.

Harrison, Elizabeth G. 1999. "'I Can Only Move my Feet towards Mizuko Kuyo': Memorial Services for Dead Children in Japan." In *Buddhism and Abortion,* ed. Damien Keown, 93–120. Honolulu: University of Hawai'i Press.

Hermalin, A., P. K. C. Liu, and D. Freeman. 1994. "The Social and Economic Transformation of Taiwan." In *Social Change and the Family in Taiwan,* ed. Arland Thornton and Hui-Sheng Lin, 49–87. Chicago: University of Chicago Press.

Ho, Ping-ti. 1959. *Studies of the Population of China, 1368–1953.* Cambridge, Mass.: Harvard University Press.

Honig, Emily, and Gail Hershatter. 1988. *Personal Voices: Chinese Women in the 1980's.* Stanford, Calif.: Stanford University Press.

Hsieh, Shwu-Ching. 1990. "A Follow-Up Survey of Married Women Receiving Induced Abortion in Taibei." In *Comparative Study of Fertility Control Experiences in the Republic of Korea and the Republic of China,* ed. Sun Te-Hsiung and Dal-Hyun Chi, 91–121. Seoul: Korea Institute for Health and Social Affairs.

Hsu, Francis. 1948. *Under the Ancestor's Shadow.* New York: Columbia University Press.

Hu Youhui 胡幼慧. 1994. "Xinde keji duonutai" 新的科技墮女胎 (New Technology Results in Aborting Female Fetuses). *Taiwan libao* 台灣立報 (Lih Pao Daily), October 3, 11.

Huang Bochuan 黃泊川. 1998. "Zemme an, an nali—Cheng Quan shuoci fanfu"

怎麼按,按哪裡——程泉説詞反覆 (How to Press, Where to Press—Cheng Quan Can't Keep His Story Straight). *Ziyou shibao* 自由時報 (The Liberty Times), July 9, 3.

Huang, Chien-yu Julia, and Robert P. Weller. 1998. "Merit and Mothering: Women and Social Welfare in Taiwanese Buddhism." *The Journal of Asian Studies* 57(2):379–396.

Huang Hanhua 黃漢華. 1994. "Sange xiaonü huaiyun pinjun yi ren duotai" 三個少女懷孕平均一人墮胎 (On Average, for Every Three Teenage Women's Pregnancies, One Ends in Abortion). *Lienhe bao* 聯合報 (United Daily News), January 15, 14.

Huang Hungchun 黃鴻鈞. 1990. "Rengongliuchang yu jiu cheng sirenzhensuo jinxing" 人工流產逾九成私人診所進行 (Over Ninety Percent of Abortions Are Conducted at Private Clinics). *Lienhe bao* 聯合報 (United Daily News), September 9, 4.

Hughes, James. 1999. "Buddhism and Abortion: A Western Approach." In *Buddhism and Abortion*, ed. Damien Keown, 183–198. Honolulu: University of Hawai'i Press.

Johnson, Elizabeth. 1988. "Grieving for the Dead, Grieving for the Living: Funeral Laments of Hakka Women." In *Death Ritual in Late Imperial and Modern China*, ed. James L. Watson and Evelyn S. Rawski, 135–163. Berkeley: University of California Press.

Jordan, David K. [1972] 1985. *Gods, Ghosts, and Ancestors: Folk Religion in a Taiwanese Village*. Berkeley: University of California Press.

Jordan, David K., and Daniel J. Overmyer. 1986. *The Flying Phoenix: Aspects of Chinese Sectarianism in Taiwan*. Princeton, N.J.: Princeton University Press.

Kleinman, Arthur. 1975. "Social, Cultural and Historical Themes in the Study of Medicine in Chinese Societies: Problems and Prospects for the Comparative Study of Medicine and Psychiatry." In *Medicine in Chinese Cultures: Comparative Studies of Health Care in Chinese and Other Societies*, ed. Arthur Kleinman et al., 589–643. Washington, D.C.: U.S. Department of Health, Education and Welfare, National Institute of Health.

———. 1982. "Patients Treated by Physicians and Folk Healers: A Comparative Outcome Study in Taiwan." *Culture, Medicine, and Psychiatry* 6(4):405–423.

Kuhn, Philip A. 1990. *Soulstealers: The Chinese Sorcery Scare of 1768*. Cambridge, Mass.: Harvard University Press.

Kyne, Phelim. 1998. "Taipei's Pet Cemetery." *China News*, June 28, 8.

LaFleur, William R. 1993. *Liquid Life: Abortion and Buddhism in Japan*. Princeton, N.J.: Princeton University Press.

Lagerwey, John. 1987. *Taoist Ritual in Chinese Society and History*. New York: MacMillan Publishing Company.

Lai Shuqi 賴淑姬. 1990. "Duotairen you duoshao yongyuan shi yi ge mi" 墮胎人有多少永遠是一個謎 (The Number of People Having Abortions Will Forever Be a Mystery). *Lienhe bao* 聯合報 (United Daily News), April 17, 5.

Le Longlong 樂融融. 1967. "Taiwan mingjian zongjiao xinyang ji wushu" 台灣民間宗教信仰及巫術 (Taiwan's folk religious beliefs and sorcery). *Taiwan fengwu* 台灣風物 (Taiwan Folkways) 17(4):74–79.

Lee, Bernice J. 1981. "Female Infanticide in China." In *Women in China: Current*

Directions in Historical Scholarship, ed. Richard W. Guisso and Stanley Johannesen, 163–178. New York: The Edwin Mellon Press.

Lee, M. L., A. Thornton, and H. S. Lin. 1994. "Trends in Marital Dissolution." In *Social Change and the Family in Taiwan,* ed. Arland Thornton and Hui-Sheng Lin, 245–263. Chicago: University of Chicago Press.

Li Keqi 李克齊. 1997. "Shaonian nannu quizhi zhizhi xingwei dadan." 少年男女 缺之知識行為大膽 (Young Men and Women Lack Knowledge Which Leads to Reckless Behavior). *Zhongguo shibao* 中國時報 (China Times), December 29, 3.

Li Xiu 李修. 1996a. "Xiaonanhai de yuanhun" 小男孩的怨魂 (A small boy's resentful spirit). In *Nuzi danshen sushe guihua* 女子單身宿舍鬼話 (Ghost stories about single women's dormitories), 87–95. Zhiqing Pindao chuban youxian gongsi 知青頻道出版有限公司 (Zhiqing Pindao Publishing Company Limited).

———. 1996b. "Nishui xiaomeimei guihu" 溺水的小娃娃鬼魂 (A drowned little girl's ghost). In *Nuzi danshen sushi guihua* 女子單身宿舍鬼話 (Ghost stories about single women's dormitories), 105–113. Zhiqing pingdao chuban youxian gongsi 知青頻道出版有限公司 (Zhiqing Pindao Publishing Company Limited).

Li Yih-yuan. 1985. "On Conflicting Interpretations of Chinese Family Rituals." In *The Chinese Family and Its Ritual Behavior,* ed. Hsieh Jih-Chang and Chuang Ying-Chang, 263–281. Taibei: Institute of Ethnology, Academia Sinica.

Liang Yufang. 1997. "Yang xiaogui: Neng bu neng ban shang fating?" 養小鬼:能 不能搬上法庭? (Raising Fetus Demons: Can They Be Taken to Court?). *Lienhe bao* 聯合報 (United Daily News), April 4, 4.

Lin Fangmei 林芳玫. 1996. "Duotai zhenyi zhong de muzhi lunxshu: Jiangou huyi yu ren de muzi guanxi" 墮胎爭議中的母職論述:建構互異與認的母子關係 (A discussion of the mother's responsibility for her infant as the heart of the abortion controversy: The construction and agreement of mother and child relations). In *Tuobian/koubian shihuishui yan tanhui* 拓邊／扣邊：社會學研討會 (Contested frontier: A sociological symposium), Donghai University, November 9–10.

Lin Hui-Sheng. 1990. "Implications for Students' Sex Education in Taiwan." In *Comparative Study of Fertility Control Experiences in the Republic of Korea and the Republic of China,* ed. Sun Te-Hsiung and Dal-Hyun Chi, 255–280. Seoul: Korea Institute for Health and Social Affairs.

Lin, H. S., M. L. Lee, and A. Thornton. 1994. "Trends in the Timing and Prevalence of Marriage." In *Social Change and the Family in Taiwan,* ed. Arland Thornton and Hui-Sheng Lin, 202–224. Chicago: University of Chicago Press.

Lin Jianyi 林健一. 1996a. *Lingyilingjie shixiang* 靈異靈界實相 (The truth about the mysterious spirit world). Taibei: Mingsheng chuban 明生出版 (Mingsheng Publishers).

———. 1996b. *Zinü kaiyun yu zuxian* 子女開運與祖先 (Sons, daughters, improving one's luck, and ancestors). Taibei: Mingsheng chuban 明出生版 (Mingsheng Publishers).

———. 1996c. *Yingling yu jiayun* 嬰靈與家運 (*Yingling* and a family's luck). Taibei: Mingsheng chuban 明生出版 (Mingsheng Publishers).

Lin Shuling 林淑玲. 1989a. "Huanle jixi aiqing duo: duotai xinli shanghai nan pingfu" 歡樂極兮哀情多：墮胎心理傷害難平復 (Little Happiness, Much Sorrow: The Psychological Harm of Abortion Is Hard to Recover From). *Zhongguo shibao* 中國時報 (China Times), July 9, 13.

———. 1989b. "Xiandai haofangnü huaiyun you wenti" 現代豪放女懷孕有問題 (The Problem of Pregnancy for Today's Loose Women). *Zhongguo shibao* 中國時報 (China Times), July 9, 13.

Lin Wanyi 林萬億. 1997. "Biyun weihun huaixuesheng zue xuyao zhengque xing zhizhi" 避免未婚懷學生最要要正確性知識 (To Avoid Unmarried Pregnancies Students Need Accurate Knowledge about Sex). *Zhongguo shibao* 中國時報 (China Times), December 29, 3.

Lin Wenchun 林奴純. 1993. "Meinian rengongliuchang yue 12 wan ci" 每年人工流產約12萬次 (There Are Approximately 120,000 Abortions Every Year). *Zhongshi wanbao* 中時晚報 (China Times Express), September 10, 4.

———. 1994. Lanyong xingbie jianding 120:100 nannüying cha tai duo" 濫用性別鑑定 120:100 男女嬰差太多 (The Misuse of Medical Techniques to Determine the Sex of Fetuses Has Resulted in an Excessive Discrepancy in the Birthrate of 120 Males for Every 100 Females). *Zhongshi wanbao* 中時晚報 (China Times Express), August 11, 1.

Lu Guoxiong 黎國雄. 1995. *Jiedu linghun yixiang* 解讀靈魂異象 (Explaining the strange phenomenon of spirits). Taibei: Xidai Chuban 希代出版 (Xidai Publications).

Lu Junping 陸君萍. 1992. "Shuyu nüren de xinqing gushi" 屬於女人的心情故事 (A Story of Women's Thoughts and Feelings). *Taiwan libao* 台灣立報 (Lih Pao Daily), June 9, 15.

Luo Xiaohe 羅曉荷. 1997. "Xuezhi pingji xingjiaoyu kecheng 'dengyu ling' " 學者抨擊性教育課程 "等於零" (Scholar Lashes Out against Sex Education Curriculum as "As Bad as Not Being Taught at All"). *Lianhe bao* 聯合報 (United Daily News), December 29, 5.

Malinowski, Bronislaw. [1925] 1948. "Magic, Science and Religion." In *Magic, Science and Religion and Other Essays,* 17–92. New York: Doubleday Anchor Books.

Mann, Susan. 1987. "Widows in the Kinship, Class, and Community Structures of Qing Dynasty China." *Journal of Asian Studies* 43(61):37–56.

Martin, Katherine Gould. 1975. "Medical Systems in a Taiwan Village: Ong-Ia-Kong, the Plague God as Modern Physician." In *Medicine in Chinese Cultures: Comparative Studies of Health Care in Chinese and Other Societies,* ed. Arthur Kleinman et al., 115–218. Washington, D.C.: U.S. Department of Health, Education and Welfare, National Institute of Health.

Mauss, Marcel. [1950] 1972. *A General Theory of Magic.* Trans. Robert Brain. Boston: Routledge & Kegan Paul.

McCreary, John L. 1979. "Potential and Effective Meaning in Therapeutic Ritual." *Culture, Medicine and Psychiatry* 3:53–72.

Moskowitz, Marc L. 1988. "The Haunting Fetus: Greed, Healing, and Religious

Adaptation in Modern Taiwan." *Bulletin of the Institute of Ethnology, Academia Sinica.* Taipei: 86:157–196.

———. 1999. "Fetus-Spirits: New Ghosts in Modern Taiwan." Ph.D. diss., University of California, San Diego.

Oaks, Laury. 1994. "Fetal Spirithood and Fetal Personhood: The Cultural Construction of Abortion in Japan." *Women's Studies International Forum* 17(5): 511–523.

Obeyesekere, Gananath. 1975. "Some Comments on the Nature of Traditional Medical Systems." In *Medicine in Chinese Cultures: Comparative Studies of Health Care in Chinese and Other Societies,* ed. Arthur Kleinman et al., 419–425. Washington, D.C.: U.S. Department of Health, Education and Welfare, National Institute of Health.

———. 1981. *Medusa's Hair: An Essay on Personal Symbols and Religious Experience.* Chicago: University of Chicago Press.

Ohnuki-Tierney, Emiko. 1984. *Illness and Culture in Contemporary Japan.* Cambridge: Cambridge University Press.

Ong, Aihwa. 1987. *Spirits of Resistance and Capitalist Discipline: Factory Women in Malaysia.* New York: State University of New York Press.

Ping Lu 平路. 1994. "Wo jian wo si: Tianlun foding? Munü beige?" 我見我思：天倫否定？母女悲歌？(Opinion Page: Happy Family Life Denied? Mother's/Daughter's Lament?). *Zhongguo shibao* 中國時報 (China Times), August 17, 11.

Qi Zhige 祁止戈. 1997. "Xueshao xingjiaoyu bu jige" 學校性教育不及格 (School Sex Education Doesn't Pass the Test). *Zhongguo shibao* 中國時報 (China Times), December 29, 3.

Rosaldo, Michelle Zimbalist. 1974. "Woman, Culture, and Society: A Theoretical Overview." In *Women, Culture and Society,* ed. Michelle Zimbalist Rosaldo and Louise Lamphere, 17–42. Stanford, Calif.: Stanford University Press.

———. 1980. "The Use and Abuse of Anthropology." *Signs: Journal of Women in Culture and Society* 5(3):389–417.

Ruan Changrui 阮昌銳. 1985. "Taiwan mingjian de wushu xinyang" 台灣民間的巫術信仰 (Taiwan's folk beliefs about sorcery). *Taiwan fengwu* 台灣風物 (Taiwan Folkways) 35(2):129–149.

Ruan, Fang-fu. 1991. *Sex in China: Studies in Sexology in Chinese Culture.* New York: Plenum Press.

Sangren, Steven P. 1993. Female Gender in Chinese Religious Symbols: Kuan Yin, Ma Tsu, and the "Eternal Mother." *Signs* 9(1):4–25.

———. 1996. "Myths, Gods, and Family Relations." In *Unruly Gods: Divinity and Society in China,* ed. Meir Shahar and Robert P. Weller, 105–149. Honolulu: University of Hawai'i Press.

Seaman, Gary. 1981. The Sexual Politics of Karmic Retribution. In *The Anthropology of Taiwanese Society,* ed. Emily Martin Ahern and Hill Gates, 381–396. Stanford, Calif.: Stanford University Press.

Shahar, Meir, and Robert P. Weller. 1996. *Unruly Gods: Divinity and Society in China.* Honolulu: University of Hawai'i Press.

Shaw, Thomas S. 1994. " 'We Like to Have Fun': Leisure and the Discovery of the Self in Taiwan's 'New' Middle Class." *Modern China* 20(4):416–445.

Sheng Zhuling 盛竹玲. 1990. "Duotai: Shaonü mengyan zhong de zujishou" 墮胎: 少女夢魘中的狙擊手 (Abortion: Young Woman Has Nightmares about Snipers). *Ziyou shibao* 自由時報 (The Liberty Times), September 10, 6.

———. 1993. "Taiwan meinian yue you 12 wan ren ci duotai" 台灣每年約有12 萬人次墮胎 (There Are Approximately 120,000 Cases of Abortion Every Year in Taiwan). *Ziyou shibao* 自由時報 (The Liberty Times), September 11, 11.

———. 1994. "Duotai Taiwan yi nian shisiwan renci" 墮胎台灣一年十四萬人次 (Abortion: In One Year in Taiwan There Are 140,000 Abortions). *Ziyou shibao* 自由時報 (The Liberty Times), September 1, 8.

Si Jiao 思嬌. 1996. "Daoqian bishi—yanshui li de mimi" 道歉啟事—淚水裡的秘密 (Apology Announcement—The Secret in the Tears). *Lianhe bao* 聯合報 (United Daily News), February 16, 32.

Silin, Robert. 1976. *Leadership and Values: The Organization of Large-Scale Taiwanese Enterprises.* Cambridge, Mass.: Harvard University Press.

Sontag, Susan. [1978] 1989. *Illness as Metaphor and AIDS and Its Metaphors.* New York: Doubleday Dell Publishing Group.

Stacey, Judith. 1983. *Patriarchy and Socialist Revolution in China.* Berkeley: University of California Press.

Sun, Te-Hsiung, and Min-Cheng Chang. 1990. "Current Status and Future Directions of Family Planning Program in Taiwan Area, Republic of China." In *Comparative Study of Fertility Control Experiences in the Republic of Korea and the Republic of China,* ed. Sun Te-Hsiung and Dal-Hyun Chi, 9–40. Seoul: Korea Institute for Health and Social Affairs.

Sung Jin-shiu 宋錦秀. 1997. "Gudian renchen lunshuzhong de 'Yangtai' yu bisha" 古典妊娠論述中的'養胎'與'辟殺' (The fetal sedative, nurturing, and exorcism in the Medical Gestation Texts of Middle China). *Si yu yan* 思與言 (Thought and Words) 35(2):133–186.

Tadesco, Frank. 1999. "Abortion in Korea." In *Buddhism and Abortion,* ed. Damien Keown, 121–155. Honolulu: University of Hawai'i Press.

Tao Fuyuan 陶福媛. 1992. "Qishi ta haishige heizi! Shaonü duotai: Mengyan hui bu qu" 其實她還是個孩子!少女墮胎:夢魘揮不去 (Although She Is Just a Child Herself! Young Woman Has an Abortion: The Nightmares Won't Go Away). *Mingsheng bao* 民生報 (Min Sheng Daily), July 3, 22.

Taussig, Michael T. 1980. *The Devil and Commodity Fetishism in South America.* Chapel Hill: University of North Carolina Press.

Thompson, Stuart E. 1988. "Death, Food, and Fertility." In *Death Ritual in Late Imperial and Modern China,* ed. James L. Watson and Evelyn S. Rawski, 71–108. Berkeley: University of California Press.

Thornton, A., J. S. Chang, and L. S. Yang. 1994. "Determinants of Historical Changes in Marital Arrangements, Dating, and Premarital Sexual Intimacy and Pregnancy." In *Social Change and the Family in Taiwan,* ed. Arland Thornton and Hui-Sheng Lin, 178–201. Chicago: University of Chicago Press.

Tietze, Christopher, and Stanley K. Henshaw. 1986. *Induced Abortion: A World Review 1986.* New York: The Alan Guttmacher Institute.

Topley, Marjorie. 1974. Cosmic Antagonisms: A Mother–Child Syndrome. In *Reli-

gion and Ritual in Chinese Society, ed. Arthur Wolf, 233–259. Stanford, Calif.: Stanford University Press.

———. 1975. "Marriage Resistance in Rural Kwangtung." In *Women in Chinese Society,* ed. Margery Wolf and Roxanne Witke, 67–88. Stanford, Calif.: Stanford University Press.

Turner, Victor. 1967. *The Forest of Symbols.* Ithaca, N.Y.: Cornell University Press.

Unschuld, Paul U. 1976. "The Social Organization and Ecology of Medical Practice in Taiwan." In *Asian Medical Systems: A Comparative Study,* ed. C. Leslie, 300–316. Berkeley: University of California Press.

Waley, Arthur, trans. and ed. [1938] 1989. *The Analects of Confucius.* New York: Vintage Books.

Wang, Janet F. 1981. "Attitude toward and Use of Induced Abortion among Taiwanese Women." *Issues in Health Care of Women* 3(3):179–202.

———. 1985. "Induced Abortion: Reported and Observed Practice in Taiwan." *Health Care for Women International* 6(6):383–404.

Wang Tong, Director. 1997. *Hong shizi* 紅柿子 (Red persimmons). Taibei: Zhongyang dianying shiye gufen youxian gongsi 中央電影事業股份有限公司 (Central Movie Business Stocks Limited Co.).

Weeks, Jeffrey. [1981] 1989. *Sex, Politics and Society.* New York: Longman.

Wei Xinxin 魏忻忻. 1998. "Duotai shenti xinli liangbei jushang" 墮胎身體心理兩敗俱傷 (The Physical and Psychological Harm of Abortion). *Lianhe bao* 聯合報 (United Daily News), 18, 43.

Wu Jingmei 吳靜美. 1993. "Taiwan meinian you jiangjin sancheng yunfu duotai" 台灣每年有將近三成孕婦墮胎 (Every Year in Taiwan Almost Thirty Percent of All Pregnant Women Have Abortions). *Zili wanbao* 自立晚報 (The Independence Evening Post), September 10, 9.

Weller, Robert P. 1987. *Unities and Diversities in Chinese Religion.* Seattle: University of Washington Press.

———. 1994. *Resistance, Chaos and Control in China.* Seattle: University of Washington Press.

———. 1996. "Matricidal Magistrates and Gambling Gods: Weak States and Strong Spirits in China." In *Unruly Gods: Divinity and Society in China,* ed. Meir Shahar and Robert P. Weller, 250–268. Honolulu: University of Hawai'i Press.

Wile, Douglas. 1992. *Art of the Bedchamber: The Chinese Sexual Yoga Classics Including Women's Solo Meditation Texts.* Albany: State University of New York Press.

Will, Pierre-Etienne. 1990. *Bureaucracy and Famine in Eighteenth-Century China.* Stanford, Calif.: Stanford University Press.

Wolf, Arthur P. 1974. "Gods, Ghosts, and Ancestors." In *Religion and Ritual in Chinese Society,* ed. Arthur Wolf, 131–182. Stanford, Calif.: Stanford University Press.

Wolf, Margery. 1968. *The House of Lim.* New York: Meridith Corporation.

———. 1972. *Women and the Family in Rural Taiwan.* Stanford, Calif.: Stanford University Press.

———. 1974. "Chinese Women: Old Skills in a New Context." In *Women, Culture and Society,* ed. Michelle Zimbalist Rosaldo and Louise Lamphere, 157–172. Stanford, Calif.: Stanford University Press.

———. 1975. "Women and Suicide in China." In *Women in Chinese Society*, ed. Margery Wolf and Roxanne Witke, 111–142. Stanford, Calif.: Stanford University Press.

———. [1990] 1992. "The Woman Who Didn't Become a Shaman." In *A Thrice Told Tale: Feminism, Postmodernism, and Ethnographic Responsibility*, 93–126. Stanford, Calif.: Stanford University Press.

Xie Mingjun 謝思俊. 1991. "Zhangfu bian jiu ai qizi qu duotai" 丈夫戀舊愛妻子去墮胎 (Husband Changes Old Love, Wife Gets Abortion). *Ziyou shibao* 自由時報 (The Liberty Times), April 3, 5.

Xu Qiongyue 許瓊月. 1995. *Duotai yingling yu taijiao* 墮胎嬰靈與胎教 (Abortion, fetus ghosts, and educating your fetus). Taibei: 禪門出版社 (Chanmen Publishers).

Yan Yunxiang. 1996. *The Flow of Gifts: Reciprocity and Social Networks in a Chinese Village*. Stanford, Calif.: Stanford University Press.

Yang, C. K. [1961] 1994. *Religion in Chinese Society: A Study of Contemporary Social Functions of Religion and Some of Their Historical Factors*. Taibei: SMC Publishing Inc.

Yi Zhen 毅振. 1988. "Taiwan mingjian quxie zao xishu" 台灣民間驅邪招習俗 (Taiwan's folk-exorcising customs). *Taiwan bowu* 台灣博物 (Taiwan Museum) 7(1):47–51.

Yu Shenglun 俞聖倫. 1992. "Zigong suoyou quan—duotai" 予宮所有權—墮胎 (Uterus Ownership Rights—Abortion). *Taiwan libao* 台灣立報 (Lih Pao Daily), April 25, 13.

Zhan Sanyuan 詹三源. 1992. "Duotai keyi gaizhang xiaoxin" 墮胎可以蓋章小心 (You Can Get an Abortion But be Careful with the Chop). *Lianhe bao* 聯合報 (United Daily News), April 11, 5.

———. 1997. "Yang xiaogui pian huiyuan rengou gupiao" 養小鬼騙會員認購股票 (Raising Fetus Demons to Trick Members into Buying Stock Shares). *Lianhe bao* 聯合報 (The United Daily News), April 4, 4.

Zhong Huncao 鍾華操. 1980. "Taiwan mingjian xinyangzhong de shouhunfa" 台灣民間信仰中的收魂法 (The Practice of Retrieving Spirits in Taiwan's Folk Beliefs). *Taiwan wenxian* 台灣文獻 (Taiwan Wen Hsien) 31(4):141–153.

Zhong Xing 鐘星. 1994a. *Yu yingling shuohua de nanren* 與嬰靈說話的男人 (Stories from a man who has spoken with fetus ghosts). Taibei. Xidai chuban youxian gongsi 希代出版有限公司 (Xidai Publishing Co.)

———. 1994b. *Yingling beige: Baobei duibuqi* 嬰靈哀歌:寶貝對不起 (Elegies for fetus ghosts: I'm sorry, my little treasure). Taibei: Hema wenhua chuban 禾馬文化出版 (Hema Cultural Publications).

———. 1994c. *Hudie nüer* 蝴蝶女兒 (Daughter Butterfly). In Zhong Xing, *Yu yingling shuohua de nanren* 與嬰靈說話的男人 (Stories from a man who has spoken with fetus ghosts), 175–206. Taibei: Xidai shuban youxian gongsi 希代書版有限公司 (Xidai Publishing Co.)

Zhou Meihui 周美蕙. 1989. "Weihun funü duotai bili piangao" 未婚婦女墮胎比例偏高 (The Abortion Rate for Unmarried Women Is Rising). *Zhongshi wanbao* 中時晚報 (China Times Express), December 14, 5.

Index

aboriginal art, 106

abortion: aborting female fetuses, 24–25; Buddhism, 26; disposal of aborted fetuses, 81, 179n. 4; eugenics, 21, 140; guilt, 28–33; health risks, 18, 22, 117, 177n. 6; illegal abortions, 21, 176n. 5, 177n. 6; law, 8, 21, 140, 176nn. 4, 5, 179n. 4; legalization of, 6, 20; preference for boys, 24–25; *qi* energy, 22; rates, 8, 20–22, 28, 46, 49; reasons for, 11; religious demerits, 26; United States, 25. *See also* reincarnation

Ahern (Martin), Emily, 11–13, 44, 116, 144, 183n. 5, 184n. 5

AIDS, 20, 183n. 3

ancestor worship, 12, 25, 50, 69, 101, 107, 112, 178n. 5, 182n. 18

Andors, Phyllis, 183n. 5

Baker, Hugh, 159

Ball, Dyer, 154, 163

Baptandier, Brigitte, 11

belief and disbelief, 2–3, 8–10; *ban xin ban yi,* 8–9; belief in other areas of the world, 3

birth control. *See* contraceptives

birth rates, 22, 177n. 9

Buddhism, 107, 166, 175n. 2, 177n. 4; Daoist views of, 98; fetus ghosts, 81; nunnery, 107; presence in Daoist temples, 106–107, 179n. 1, 184n. 2; prohibition against killing life, 11, 26, 36; reciting scriptures, 96, 105; temples, 94–95. *See also* fetus ghosts; folk religion; Gaoxiong temple; gods; Xu, Ms.

Cai Cuiying, 53–56

Cai Wen, 65–66, 68, 100. *See also* temples

Cai Yingying, 177n. 9

cemeteries, 153

Cernada, George, 140–141, 183n. 4

Chang, Min-Cheng, 14–17, 21

Chang Ching-sheng, 137

Chang Chin-ju, 27, 54, 56

change: education, 8; familial hierarchy, 44–46, 57, 66, 83, 120–121, 149; family size, 8; fetus demons, 184n. 6; filial piety, 25; individualism, 16, 149; industrialism, 161; marriage patterns, 7, 15–16; news coverage of abortion, 36; parental control, 8, 45–46 (*see also* filial piety); politics, 8; public/private division, 27; religious, 1, 34–39, 44–46, 178n. 3, 179n. 10, 180n. 3; sexual mores, 15, 142–143, 147–149; transformation of Jizō, 34–35; urbanization, 15, 94; women's roles, 184n. 11. *See also* population; women

Chang Hsun, 44

chaos, 135, 137, 148

chastity. *See* sex, chastity

Chen, Chao-nan, 138

Chen, Mr., 23

Child rearing, 119–121

About the Author

MARC L. MOSKOWITZ received a Ph.D. in cultural anthropology in 1999 from the University of California, San Diego. Between 1988 and 1999 he spent one year in mainland China and six years in Taiwan. Currently, he is an assistant professor in the Department of Sociology/Anthropology at Lake Forest College, Lake Forest, Illinois. *The Haunting Fetus* is his first book.